The Historian and the Diplomat

THE
HISTORIAN
AND THE
DIPLOMAT

*The Role of History and Historians
in American Foreign Policy*

EDITED BY FRANCIS L. LOEWENHEIM

WITH CONTRIBUTIONS BY

HERBERT FEIS, FRANCIS L. LOEWENHEIM,
ARNO J. MAYER, AND LOUIS MORTON

HARPER & ROW, PUBLISHERS
NEW YORK, EVANSTON, AND LONDON

Acknowledgments

This volume includes—in somewhat expanded and revised form—a series of public lectures first delivered in the spring of 1964 at Rice University under the sponsorship of the Sperry and Hutchinson Foundation, as well as an essay by the editor.

The editor wishes to take this opportunity to express his warm thanks to the Sperry and Hutchinson Foundation for the generous grant that made these lectures possible; to Rice University for additional material assistance; and, above all, to Professors Feis, Mayer, and Morton for their distinguished contributions.

Contents

Preface

There are few discussions of modern diplomatic history that do not, sooner or later, get around to quoting the late George Santayana's famous maxim that "those who do not remember the past are condemned to repeat its mistakes," and then proceed to ignore this wise injunction. There are, of course, some people who appear to believe that in an age increasingly dominated by science and technology we need no longer concern ourselves with the past, who believe that ours is indeed a new and different age and that we can best solve the problems of our time by casting off the heavy burden of the past.

This book is not for them. This is a book for those who believe in the relevance of past to present, who believe that there is something to be learned from historical experience, and above all for those who insist that we must first know what really happened in the past before we can make useful judgments about it, before we can hope to apply the experience of yesterday to the problems of today and tomorrow.

This is a book primarily, then, about the role of history and historians in twentieth-century American foreign policy. But this is not a narrowly specialized book for experts. On the contrary, the aim throughout has been to examine the nature of America's experience in world affairs in the broad context of American history, so as to show as clearly and directly as possible what role history—what people knew and thought about the past—has played in the development of American foreign policy since the era of the First World War; for there can no longer be any doubt that our knowledge and understanding of the past have exerted a powerful influence on the shaping of American foreign policy over those years. Whether it was Woodrow Wilson's idea of the nature of the European political system and what in the light of historical experience—as he saw it—America could contribute to the establishment of a just and lasting peace settlement; whether it was President Roosevelt looking back to the diplomacy of the First World War, seeking to avoid what seemed to be Wilson's most serious mistakes; or whether it was President Truman's awareness that for the United States to return to its prewar policy of isolation might well endanger not only the cause of democracy in Europe but also, eventually, American security as well—it seems clear that, time after time, our image of the past has been a determining factor in the making of American foreign policy. That was true in 1917. It was true in 1940. And it remains true today.

Nor, indeed, has this historical influence been limited to the most fateful presidential decisions. It has made itself felt in some of our most passionate national debates in the last half century. Who has forgotten the great debates in this country in the twenties and thirties over the questions of "war guilt" and American intervention in the First World War—debates that left American opinion more inflamed and isolationist than ever? Who has forgotten the bitter debates of the forties and fifties—over Pearl Harbor, the wartime conferences, and the Communist triumph in China? Who is not aware of the fact that much of what we say and do these days about the urgent problems of American foreign policy—about our relations with the Soviet Union and Communist China, about Cuba and Vietnam—is based to a considerable extent on our idea of recent history, the extent to which we think our time resembles the years before 1914 or before 1939. Who can possibly ignore the explosive effect that the words "Munich" and "Yalta" still exert on American politics and the image that "appeasement" conjures up in the public mind? Who can ignore the fact that many of our current differences of opinion regarding foreign policy are based largely on profound differences of opinion about the meaning of America's historical experience and its place and role in world affairs? It is one of the principal purposes of this volume to make these connections as explicit and widely understood as they deserve to be.

But this book has still another general theme. In an age increasingly aware not only of the powerful impact of science on politics but also of the great influence of politics on science *and* scientists, there has been a concern throughout to show something of the influence that foreign policy has often exerted on American historical scholarship and on writing about American diplomacy generally. History is—and doubtless will remain—a highly political art and science. This was so in the age of Turner and Beard, and it remains true in the days of Kennan, Lippmann, and Morgenthau. To ignore the political background and implications of such writing is to overlook one of its most significant facets. This interplay of diplomacy and history, then, also deserves to be made much more explicit than it usually is, and that is what the book has set out to do.

Although this volume is mainly concerned with the interaction of history and diplomacy in this century, there can be no question that neither the course of modern American foreign policy nor most of the historical writing about it can really be understood without reference to the character and main currents of American foreign policy and historical writing before the First World War. This is the task I have set out to perform in the opening essay—first, to provide a broad survey of the relation of diplomacy and historical thought from the eighteenth century to the present, and second, to furnish the essential background and continuity for the essays that follow.

The essays by Professors Feis, Mayer, and Morton were originally delivered as a series of public lectures at Rice University and have been revised and expanded for publication here. Finally, because the subject of this volume is—and doubtless will continue to be—such a controversial one, and also because it is the work of a number of historians writing and thinking independently, it should be noted that the contributors assume full responsibility only for their own essays and do not necessarily agree—or disagree—with the other viewpoints expressed.

F. L. L.

Houston, Texas
June 1966

A Legacy of Hope and a Legacy of Doubt:
Reflections on the Role of History and
Historians in American Foreign Policy
Since the Eighteenth Century
by Francis L. Loewenheim

IN HIS delightful memoirs of nearly forty years in the Foreign Service, Ellis Briggs, one of America's most respected career diplomats, recounts an incident that occurred in the latter 1950's that sheds considerable light on the style, and some of the problems, of recent American diplomacy.

It was the year after "Sputnik," and much of the government in Washington was preoccupied with devising ways and means of persuading our friends and adversaries throughout the world that the United States had not lost its scientific and technological pre-eminence, that it was not—as it was frequently suggested in those anxious days—becoming a second-rate power. Then someone hit on a clever idea. Why not dispatch a leading scientist to each American embassy around the globe? That should do the trick. The President and the Secretary of State seem to have readily approved the suggestion. What most American diplomats thought of it is not known, but from one post the response came strong and clear: "The American Embassy in Rio de Janeiro needs a science attaché like a cigar-store Indian needs a brassiere." [1]

Much has recently been written about the trials and tragedy of American foreign policy, and it is not the purpose of this essay to add to this long, and largely undistinguished, list of works. The purpose here is not to dissect, once more, the operation of current American foreign policy—adding some ingenious suggestions for instant improvement in the bargain—but to try to explain some of

---

[1] Ellis Briggs, *Farewell to Foggy Bottom* (New York, 1964), p. 163. The science-attaché program was not, in fact, a new one. It had been inaugurated by President Truman in 1947, but was suspended by the Eisenhower administration in 1955, largely for economy reasons.

the reasons for our being where we are at the present juncture and to examine some of the intellectual foundations of current American thinking about world affairs. For there can no longer be any doubt that a deep intellectual crisis surrounds the conduct and direction of American foreign policy.

However firm and flexible the President's own policies may be, however careful and deliberate the explanation of these policies by the Vice-President, Secretary of State and other leading officials may be, it seems clear that there exists throughout the country profound concern about the whole course and meaning of American foreign policy, past, present, and future. This concern is not, of course, an entirely recent development, nor is it unique in American history. But it has now assumed—as shown by the recent "teach-ins" and by some of the demonstrations that accompanied them—formidable proportions. We must, therefore, face the unpleasant fact that both the tradition and purpose of American foreign policy, the capacity of the United States to deal effectively with the momentous problems confronting it throughout the world, are being increasingly called into question. The very foundations of American foreign policy are under attack.

The United States, it is argued by some, has not had a settled and generally accepted foreign policy since 1898.[2] American foreign policy, it is said by others, has long been—and continues to be—both too moralistic and legalistic in style.[3] The American people have no real understanding of the nature of political power, and furthermore, the great tradition of statecraft that the United States possessed in its early years died out with the passing of the Founding Fathers.[4]

The United States, it is contended, lacks the necessary social revolutionary experience to be able either to understand or to lead the world revolutionary movements of the twentieth century;[5] besides, the emerging peoples of the world are, in their current neutralist policies, following much the same course of action that the United States itself pursued in its formative years.[6] One influential critic of American foreign policy has gone so far as to say that "America is showing some of that fatal presumption, that overextension of

2 Walter Lippmann, *U. S. Foreign Policy* (Boston, 1943).

3 George F. Kennan, *American Diplomacy 1900–1950* (Chicago, 1951).

4 Hans J. Morgenthau, "The Mainsprings of American Foreign Policy—The National Interest vs. Moral Abstractions," *The American Political Science Review*, XLIV (December 1950).

5 Louis Hartz, *The Liberal Tradition in America* (New York, 1955), and Louis Hartz *et al.*, *The Founding of New Societies* (New York, 1964).

6 Seymour M. Lipset, *The First New Nation* (New York, 1963). See also Chester Bowles, "The Oldest New Nation," *Yale Review*, LIV (Spring 1965).

power and mission, which brought ruin to ancient Athens, to Napoleon's France, and to Nazi Germany."[7]

This is by no means, of course, a complete catalogue of some of the weighty criticisms being hurled at American diplomacy. Still other critics explain the problems of contemporary American foreign policy in different terms: the awful burdens, and disasters, of recent American foreign policy—whether in Europe, or in Africa, or in the Far East—can only be understood on the basis of ideological utopianism, of near-criminal shortsightedness, if not, in the end, subversion and treason.[8]

These attacks, too, have a considerable history of their own, dating back to the conservative isolationism of the 1930's.[9] They began with charges that President Roosevelt was trying to drag the United States into another world war—charges that were followed, after December 1941, with claims that he had not only provoked the Japanese attack on Pearl Harbor,[10] but he had then wantonly given away large parts of Europe and the Far East to the Communists.[11] After the Second World War these charges were resurrected, amplified, and given broad circulation by the McCarthyites and their supporters, and they have been revived, with even greater venom, by the Birchites and their followers in the 1960's.[12]

The general public, no doubt, has good reason to feel confused and concerned amidst these charges and countercharges; and it is not too much to say that what Richard Hofstadter has called the "paranoid style" in American politics has never—at least in the realm of attitudes toward foreign policy—flourished more vigorously than it does at the present time.[13]

---

[7] Senator J. William Fulbright, *The New York Times,* April 29, 1966. Senator Fulbright has elaborated his views in *The Arrogance of Power* (New York, 1966).

[8] This school of thought is best represented, perhaps, in the pages of *The National Review* and, in a more extreme form, in *American Opinion,* the monthly publication of the John Birch Society.

[9] See Wayne S. Cole, *America First—The Battle Against Intervention, 1940–1941* (Madison, 1953).

[10] See George Morgenstern, *Pearl Harbor* (New York, 1947); Charles A. Beard, *President Roosevelt and the Coming of War, 1941* (New Haven, 1948); Charles C. Tansill, *Back Door to War* (Chicago, 1952); Harry Elmer Barnes (ed.); *Perpetual War for Perpetual Peace* (Caldwell, Idaho, 1953); and Robert A. Theobald, *The Final Secret of Pearl Harbor* (New York, 1954).

[11] See William Henry Chamberlin, *America's Second Crusade* (Chicago, 1950); George N. Crocker, *Roosevelt's Road to Russia* (Chicago, 1959); and, for an uncritical discussion of this literature, Louis Martin Sears, "Historical Revisionism Following the Two World Wars," in George L. Anderson (ed.), *Issues and Conflicts* (Lawrence, Kansas, 1959).

[12] See below, p. 52.

[13] One of the troubling shortcomings of Richard Hofstadter's *The Paranoid Style in American Politics* (New York, 1965) is that it is devoted largely to domestic politics and, like his earlier *Anti-Intellectualism in American Life* (New York, 1963), says virtually nothing about the circumstances that gave rise—and a certain plausibility—to extremist views of the Right and Left about recent American foreign policy.

The task of the historian, under these circumstances, is clear and unmistakable. It is, first, to sort out fact from fiction, to separate the new myths from the old realities. But his task does not end there. Perhaps as never before in our history we need to know, and to understand, what America's historical role is in world affairs; what the values and ideas are for which the United States has traditionally stood in international politics; and how these are to be given effective expression in the present revolutionary world.

It is sometimes said that so new and revolutionary is the world in which we live that there is little of interest and value that the historian can say to it. Nothing could be further from the truth. On the contrary, unless we know and understand precisely whence we have come in world affairs, unless we recognize the sources of our great intellectual—as well as material—strength, above all, unless we come to understand how we have been distracted from these ideals and values, we are not likely to be able to cope effectively either with our adversaries abroad or with the sources of division and discord here at home. This is the ground upon which the historian and the diplomat meet.

I

It is a favorite generalization of many contemporary American historians that one of the most striking and important characteristics of the American past is the remarkable degree of political consensus that—with the notable and tragic exception of the slavery issue—has prevailed throughout the nation's history.[14] In short, we have fortunately been spared the deep and dangerous divisions that have beset most of the other Great Powers in the modern world.

There is much to be said for this generalization, although it does require one other important qualification. While we may rightly speak of such consensus prevailing on most domestic issues, it seems clear that there has been increasing dissent over foreign policy since the time of the Spanish-American War, and this difference of opinion has grown markedly since the era of the First World War.

It is quite true, of course, as every student of American history is well aware, that there were profound differences over foreign policy even in the era of the Founding Fathers; indeed, Thomas

14 See Daniel J. Boorstin, *The Genius of American Politics* (Chicago, 1953), and William H. Nelson with Francis L. Loewenheim (eds.), *Theory and Practice in American Politics* (Chicago, 1964).

Jefferson and Alexander Hamilton, and their followers, divided over questions of foreign policy as they did over nearly everything else.[15] Yet it is important to remember that these differences, however strongly put on some occasions, were not nearly so much differences over general goals and objectives as they were disagreements over specific ways and means necessary to achieve them. In other words, while the Jeffersonians and Hamiltonians might, for instance, differ over the desirability of continuing the Franco-American alliance in the 1790's, and while they might disagree over what American policy toward Great Britain ought to be in those years, they did not disagree fundamentally about the proper role and place of the new United States in world affairs.

The reason for this basic consensus is not far to seek. Many of the Founding Fathers, and their contemporaries, were avid students of history and international relations, ancient and modern.[16] They had read and knew a great deal about the origins of wars and the history of the "old diplomacy." They had seen it at work in the New World for many years. They had no illusions about senseless "cabinet wars," fought largely by brutalized mercenary armies and terminated, almost invariably, by short-lived treaties of "perpetual peace." [17] The Founding Fathers wanted none of these things. They were determined to strike out on a wholly new and different course in foreign affairs, believing—as Professor Felix Gilbert was the first to show—that it was part of America's mission in world history to adopt and carry out a new and more civilized foreign policy.[18]

Nor, it should at once be added, was this the view only of a small colonial elite. "All Americans [of this period]," as Paul Varg has written,

regardless of section, believed that they stood for a new kind of society, one in which men were free to pursue their individual interests and where government was the servant rather than the master. From this conviction flowed their view of the existing system of international

15 See Dumas Malone, *Thomas Jefferson and the Rights of Man* (Boston, 1951), 307ff, 420ff.

16 H. Trevor Colbourn, *The Lamp of Experience* (Chapel Hill, 1965).

17 Max Savelle, "Colonial Origins of American Diplomatic Principles," *Pacific Historical Review*, III (1934); "The American Balance of Power and European Diplomacy, 1713–78," in Richard B. Morris (ed.), *The Era of the American Revolution* (New York, 1939); "The Appearance of an American Attitude Toward External Affairs 1750–1775," *American Historical Review*, LII (1947); and John A. Schutz, "Imperialism in Massachusetts During the Governorship of William Shirley," *The Huntington Library Quarterly*, XXIII (1960).

18 Felix Gilbert, *To the Farewell Address* (Princeton, 1961). See also his important earlier studies, "The English Background of American Isolationism in the Eighteenth Century," *The William and Mary Quarterly*, Third Series, I (1944), and "The New Diplomacy of the Eighteenth Century," *World Politics*, IV (1951).

relations as inherently evil. Princes and masters subordinated the welfare of their subjects to considerations of glory; foreign policy did not serve the people. The rivalries of the European courts explained the long history of wars. The people did not have anything at stake in these contests. Only if governments were free to pursue public interests, would rivalry and war give way to peace and cooperation.[19]

This is not to say that the Founding Fathers and their contemporaries had any illusions about the immediate impact of their new approach to international affairs. They knew too much about the history of European politics and diplomacy to believe that any series of declarations by the new United States, however elevated and well intentioned they might be, would get the Old World to mend its evil ways. It was this dual conviction—that the United States could not, for the time being at least, alter or expect a change in the prevailing nature of international politics, and that its comparatively weak military position did not permit any involvement in European politics—that was largely responsible for the oft-quoted "isolationist" phrases of President Washington's Farewell Address of October 1796.[20]

Yet President Washington had seen too much revolutionary change in his own lifetime to enjoin his countrymen once and for all. His injunction that the United States should avoid foreign entanglements for a quarter century proved far more prophetic than is generally recognized: A little more than twenty-five years later, in December 1823, President James Monroe, in his annual message to Congress, extended the fundamental American ideas of self-government and self-determination to the rest of the Western hemisphere.[21]

President Monroe's action was only the first step toward the universal application of these ideas. The ultimate—and entirely logical—extension came about less than a century later when vast technological changes had brought about the geographic unification of the world. This extension came in President Wilson's historic address to the League to Enforce Peace, in May 1916, an address in which Wilson consciously and specifically referred to what he called the establishment of a global Monroe Doctrine.[22] Like Presi-

---

19 Paul A. Varg, *Foreign Policies of the Founding Fathers* (Lansing, 1963), p. 3.

20 This general point is brought out well in Gilbert's *To the Farewell Address;* see also the discerning article of Samuel Flagg Bemis, "Washington's Farewell Address—A Foreign Policy of Independence," *American Historical Review*, XXXIX (1934).

21 For the pertinent sections of Monroe's message, see Henry Steele Commager (ed.), *Documents of American History* (7th ed., New York, 1963), I, no. 127.

22 See Harley Notter, *The Origins of the Foreign Policy of Woodrow Wilson* (Baltimore, 1937), pp. 521ff; Arthur S. Link, *Wilson,* V (Princeton, 1965), 25ff and 265ff; Arthur C. Walworth, *Woodrow Wilson* (2nd ed., Boston, 1965), pp. 36–37, 79.

dent Washington's Farewell Address and President Monroe's dec-claration, Wilson's statement came at a time of profound inter-national crisis, but it mirrored the belief, strongly held in the early days of the Republic, that regardless of the evil state of international politics at the time, one aspect of America's mission in world history was to discover and promote a better way of conducting international affairs.

It was part of the genius of American politics—indeed, one might say that it was the genius of American foreign policy—that the Founding Fathers believed, from the beginning of the Republic, that foreign policy ought to and must be based on much the same spirit and general principles as those governing domestic politics.[23] There was, then, from the beginning of American history, a close and integral relationship between the idea of self-government, upon which the American Revolution was based, and the idea of national self-determination, with which it soon became closely connected, and which, it may be suggested, has been the greatest contribution of the United States to the progress of international relations in modern times.[24]

It was fitting that Thomas Jefferson, as Secretary of State under President Washington, first set forth the relationship between self-government and self-determination, a position that demanded, in the first place, a strong and unmistakable insistence that one state not interfere in the internal affairs of another; for without an end to this long-standing, yet generally accepted practice—of which the progressive dismemberment of Poland was a contemporary example—there was no hope for lasting peace or for progress throughout the world.

This was the point to which Jefferson addressed himself in his famous letter to Thomas Pinckney, the American minister in London, in December 1792. "We certainly cannot deny to other nations," Jefferson wrote on that occasion, "that principle whereon our govern-

---

23 This point is further substantiated by Theodore Sedgwick's original plan for the organization of the State Department, drawn up in 1789. Sedgwick believed that the department should be concerned with not only foreign but also certain domestic affairs, that it should become, in effect, a liaison between the two areas of government. See the interesting study of Richard S. Patterson and Harold D. Langley, "How the Department of State Got Its Name," *The Department of State Bulletin*, Sept. 1964, pp. 370ff.

24 It is one of the anomalies of recent writing on early American history that even some of the best and most interesting works on the period—for instance, Caroline Robbins, *The Eighteenth Century Commonwealthman* (Cambridge, Mass., 1959), Bernard Bailyn (ed.), *Pamphlets of the American Revolution*, Vol. I (Cambridge, Mass., 1965), and Colbourn, *The Lamp of Experience*—largely overlook this striking aspect of the American Revolution. For if the men who made the revolution were truly revolutionary, they were never more so than in their attitude toward foreign policy.

ment is founded, that every nation has a right to govern itself internally under whatever forms it pleases, and to change these forms at its own will; and externally to transact business with other nations throughout whatever organ it chooses, whether that be a King, Committee, Assembly, Convention, President, or whatever it be. *The only thing essential is the will of the people.*"[25]

Here, as Dumas Malone has rightly said, was a statement of truly "genuine historic importance."[26] It is, indeed, one of the cornerstones of American foreign policy. Yet it was not without some ambiguity; for the statement clearly committed the United States to the principles of self-government, self-determination, and nonintervention. But would it consider the pledge valid under any and all circumstances? As might be expected from the author of the Declaration of Independence, Jefferson attached the greatest importance to the exercise of the "will of the people." That requirement having been fulfilled, Jefferson presumably would have favored unqualified adherence to the general policy of nonintervention. But what if a particular government carried on foreign policy without the expressed consent of the people or perhaps—as far as one could tell—against their wishes? And what was to be done in the event that a particular government became, in time, a menace to the peace and security of its neighbors or even to the United States? This dilemma confronted Jefferson at the end of the eighteenth century; it is deeply troubling the United States in the twentieth.

It is quite true, of course, that the United States did not, even in the first century of its existence, invariably adhere to the principle of nonintervention; its most serious violation of that principle—which occurred in the Mexican War—not only produced one of the most bitter political quarrels in its entire history[27] but also led indirectly to the Civil War since the country found itself unable to agree on the political and social constitution of the newly acquired territories.

It is interesting to recall in this connection that Abraham Lincoln, after he was elected to the House of Representatives, was among those who joined (albeit for a variety of reasons) in the vociferous

25 Albert Ellery Bergh (ed.), *The Writings of Thomas Jefferson,* IX (Washington, 1907), 7–8. Emphasis added. The same day, Jefferson wrote in almost identical language to Gouverneur Morris, the U.S. minister to France, "The will of the nation is the only thing essential to be regarded." Paul Leicester Ford (ed.), *The Works of Thomas Jefferson,* VII (New York and London, 1904), 198.

26 Dumas Malone, *Jefferson and the Ordeal of Liberty* (Boston, 1962) p. 42.

27 See James Ford Rhodes, *History of the United States from the Compromise of 1850,* I (New York, 1893), 86ff; and John Bach McMaster, *A History of the People of the United States,* VII (New York, 1915), 445ff.

protests against the Mexican War.[28] It was Lincoln who, as President, even in the midst of the Civil War, never forgot or failed to impress upon foreign diplomats and their governments the importance that the United States attached to the principles of self-government and nonintervention.[29]

There can be little doubt that strong popular approval of the principles of self-government and self-determination—which manifested itself in great enthusiasm for the revolutions of 1830 and 1848[30]—was largely responsible for the widespread support the United States enjoyed in nineteenth-century Europe. This ardent support was not significantly reduced by the awkward fact that the United States had not yet put an end to slavery, that it later failed to provide adequately for the bondsmen once slavery had been abolished, or that the United States was unable, if only for logistic reasons, to give any direct or effective backing to the forces of reform and revolutionary change throughout Europe. It is hardly surprising, then, that the great majority of European liberals and radicals prayed in the 1860's for the success of the Union, and that the cause of freedom in America was widely equated with the cause of freedom throughout the world.[31]

Moreover, the United States championed the principles of self-government and nonintervention not only in Europe. It took much the same position in its relations with the peoples and governments of the Far East. When Caleb Cushing journeyed to China in the 1840's, his formal instructions from Secretary of State Daniel Webster left no doubt whatever in that respect. "As your mission has in view," Webster wrote to Cushing,

only friendly and commercial objects (objects, it is supposed, equally useful to both countries,) the natural jealousy of the Chinese, and their repulsive feeling toward foreigners, it is hoped, may be in some degree removed or mitigated by prudence and address on your part. Your constant aim must be, to produce a full conviction on the minds of the government and the people that your mission is entirely pacific; that you come with no purposes of hostility or annoyance; that

28 Contrary to frequent assertion, Lincoln had not always opposed the war. When he ran for Congress in 1846, he supported it, and did not change his position until after he reached Washington. For the development of Lincoln's thinking on the war and some of the political reasons for the change, see Albert J. Beveridge, *Abraham Lincoln 1809–1858*, II (Boston, 1928), 370ff.

29 Jay Monaghan, *Diplomat in Carpet Slippers* (Indianapolis, 1945) p. 50.

30 See Merle E. Curti, *Austria and the United States, 1848–1852* (Northampton, 1926); Arthur J. May, *Contemporary American Opinion of the Mid-Century Revolutions in Europe* (Philadelphia, 1927); and E. N. Curtis, "American Opinion of the French Nineteenth Century Revolutions," *American Historical Review*, XXIX (1924).

31 Henry Pelling, *America and the British Left* (London, 1956), Chap. 2.

you are a messenger of peace, sent from the greatest power in America to the greatest empire in Asia, to offer respect and good-will, and to establish the means of friendly intercourse.[32]

Nor was Webster insensitive to China's attitude toward the intrusion of imperialistic powers. "The remoteness of the United States from China," he continued,

and still more, toward England, the fact that they have no colonial possessions in her neighborhood, will naturally lead to the indulgence of a less suspicious and more friendly feeling than may have been entertained toward England even before the late war between England and China. It cannot be doubted that the immense power of England in India must be regarded by the Chinese government with dissatisfaction, if not with some degree of alarm. You will take care to show strongly how free the Chinese Government may well be from all jealousy arising from such causes toward the United States.[33]

With this straightforward statement of American policy, the Chinese government of those days could hardly have been under any misapprehension concerning the true nature and policies of the United States; and the record of Far Eastern politics, from the 1840's on, shows clearly that the United States never joined in that tragic process of dismemberment and despoliation that characterized the policies of the other Great Powers from that period until the era of the Second World War.[34]

II

It cannot be said that this quite remarkable record of early American foreign policy—remarkable both in its ideas and execution —has ever received anything like the recognition it deserves. This is especially unfortunate since much of recent American foreign policy, from the beginning of the twentieth century to the present, is so closely connected with the origins and early history of American diplomacy.

In dealing with the first century of U.S. diplomacy, critics of recent American foreign policy have generally followed one of two approaches. One approach has been, quite simply, to ignore the origins of American diplomacy altogether, a practice facilitated

32 *The Writings and Speeches of Daniel Webster*, XII (Boston, 1903), 143.
33 *Ibid.*, p. 146.
34 For a more ambivalent view of American policy toward China, see John K. Fairbank, "New Thinking About China," *The Atlantic Monthly* (June 1966).

by the long-standing neglect of this period by most American historians—a neglect that has begun to be corrected only recently.[35] Other critics have taken a more ingenious tack. Knowing that the age of Washington, Jefferson, and the Adamses could not be ignored entirely, they depreciated the importance of these formative years by pointing to the geographic isolation of the United States in this period and suggesting that this territorial remoteness made American ideas and policies largely irrelevant in world affairs.[36]

Such approaches, it might be suggested, have little to commend them. In the first place, as already noted, not only were the Founding Fathers and their successors well acquainted with the realities of eighteenth-century international politics—an awareness that had much to do with their support of the idea of a "new diplomacy" —but they also made it clear, from the time of the American Revolution on, that they knew how to deal with the best and most experienced diplomats and foreign offices of the Old World. This was shown, quite conclusively, many years ago by Edward S. Corwin[37] and Samuel Flagg Bemis;[38] and Professor Richard B. Morris' detailed study of the Paris Peace Treaty of 1783 leaves no doubt whatever that for all their devotion to the principles of the "new diplomacy," such men as John Adams, Benjamin Franklin, and John Jay had brilliant success in playing the diplomatic game according to the older set of rules they so disliked.[39]

Nor is it correct to say, as Professor Hans J. Morgenthau, for one, has said, that American foreign policy lost most of its acuity after the Founding Fathers had begun to leave the scene.[40] It would be uncharitable, perhaps, to recall that both Jefferson and Madison had failed to resolve the long-standing disputes with Great Britain that led finally to the War of 1812.[41] But it is certainly true that their successors—from James Monroe to James

---

35 Cf. Kennan, *American Diplomacy 1900–1950*, p. 5. The plausibility and widespread acceptance of this position has no doubt been considerably enhanced by the fact that at many leading American universities U.S. diplomatic history before 1898 is all but ignored, and that some of the most important and widely used books on American foreign policy likewise compress the first century of American diplomacy into a few pages.

36 For an important contrary view, see Thomas A. Bailey, "America's Emergence as a World Power: The Myth and the Verity," *Pacific Historical Review*, XX (1961).

37 Edward S. Corwin, *French Policy and the American Alliance of 1778* (Princeton, 1916).

38 Samuel Flagg Bemis, *The Diplomacy of the American Revolution* (2nd ed., Bloomington, 1957).

39 Richard B. Morris, *The Peacemakers* (New York, 1965).

40 See above, p. 2, note 4, and p. 833 of the Morgenthau essay.

41 This much is evident even from Irving Brant's highly laudatory biography of Madison.

K. Polk—were remarkably successful in coping with the dangers of European intervention in the New World, all the while, as in the Monroe Doctrine, seeking to expand the principles of self-government, self-determination, and nonintervention.[42]

It must not be forgotten either that the great saga of nineteenth-century American history—the westward movement—was not only a story of great personal courage and sacrifice. It was also a story of remarkable diplomatic sagacity;[43] for when the United States began this westward movement, it found itself surrounded on all sides by hostile or potentially hostile powers. None of them—Britain, France, or Spain—had any love for the United States, and the slightest diplomatic miscalculation on this country's part might well have had most serious political consequences. Yet, with the exception of the War of 1812, the United States managed not to miscalculate; and when the final Oregon treaty was at last signed in 1846, it made the West safe for American expansion and secured the North American continent at a time when the United States was headed for the greatest internal crisis in its history.[44]

This is not to imply that American foreign policy in the nineteenth century was without its strong and outspoken critics. There was, as every student of the period knows, a great and bitter debate over foreign policy at the time of the War of 1812,[45] a debate that was repeated with even greater ferocity during the Mexican War.[46] Much of what was said in those debates, by opponents of American policy, was not unjustified. Yet perhaps the most striking aspect of these debates—something worth remembering today—is that few of the debaters genuinely believed that the policy they attacked seriously reduced the stature of the United States in international affairs. They did not believe, for instance, that because the United States pursued certain poli-

---

42 Samuel Flagg Bemis, *John Quincy Adams and the Foundations of American Foreign Policy* (New York, 1949); Dexter Perkins, *A History of the Monroe Doctrine* (Boston, 1955); and Frederick Merk, *Manifest Destiny and Mission in American History* (New York, 1963).

43 Most historians of the westward movement, including Frederick Jackson Turner, were largely indifferent to this important aspect. See, however, Joseph Schafer, "Oregon Pioneers and American Diplomacy," Guy Stanton Ford (ed.), *Essays in American History Dedicated to Frederick Jackson Turner* (New York, 1910); Ray Allen Billington, *Westward Expansion* (2nd ed., New York, 1960); and Frederick Merk's impressive studies of the Oregon question.

44 For a memorable account of the post-Mexican War era, see Allan Nevins, *The Ordeal of the Union*, I (New York, 1947).

45 McMaster, *A History of the People of the United States*, IV, 210ff; Bradford Perkins, *Prologue to War* (Berkeley and Los Angeles, 1961), pp. 392ff; and Roger H. Brown, *The Republic in Danger–1812* (New York, 1964), esp. pp. 131ff.

46 See above, p. 8, note 27.

cies toward Great Britain or Mexico, it was therefore disqualified from interjecting itself in the discussion about European politics and diplomacy in those years. In other words, criticism of American foreign policy began at home and it ended at home.

One issue, however, began to cloud the conduct of American foreign policy after the War of 1812—the rise of sectionalism. It is sometimes thought that conservatism in foreign affairs is a comparatively recent phenomenon in the South.[47] But the fact of the matter is that sectional differences on foreign policy began to make themselves felt as early as the European revolutions of 1830, and that such differences of opinion became even more marked at the time of the revolutions of 1848.[48] When Louis Kossuth, the hero of the suppressed Hungarian revolt, came to this country a short time later, the southern members of Congress did not join in supporting his welcome, and it was only in the South that Kossuth experienced an almost consistently disappointing reception—a reaction directly related to the widespread belief that American support of revolutionary change in Europe might well lead, as in fact it probably did, to greater demands for drastic social change in the United States, especially demands for the territorial limitation, even abolition, of slavery.[49]

Such dissent over foreign policy must not, however, be exaggerated. The political passions aroused by the opposition to the War of 1812 soon spent themselves, and there were probably few antislavery men, of any persuasion, who believed that the war with Mexico could have been permanently avoided. The Hartford Convention, with its strong overtones of northern nullification, found no honorable place in the American political tradition; nor were the opponents of war in 1846 the exponents of a new approach to foreign policy. It is important to remember that what these critics of American foreign policy challenged (with the exception of the southern and other conservative opponents of the antebellum period) was not the idea of American foreign policy as it had been established in the era of the American Revolution. They had no quarrel with the notion that the United States was destined to bring forth not only a new way of life and politics but an entirely new approach to the conduct of diplomacy as well. What these critics attacked were not the fundamental ideals of

[47] Charles O. Lerche, *The Uncertain South* (Chicago, 1964).
[48] See, for instance, Curtis, "American Opinion of the French Nineteenth Century Revolutions," pp. 249ff.
[49] McMaster, *A History of the People of the United States,* Vol. VIII, Chap. 78.

that policy, as they had first been developed in the eighteenth century, but what they regarded as the practical violation of these ideals in the conduct of everyday diplomacy.[50]

The United States, to be sure, could not entirely escape the decline of European liberalism. Although it had welcomed the revolutions of 1848 in France, Germany, Austria-Hungary, and Italy with remarkable enthusiasm, the United States was soon confronted by the unpleasant fact that these revolutions, and the high hopes and expectations that accompanied them on both sides of the Atlantic, had, essentially, all been defeated.[51] It was with sadness and reluctance, then, that Secretary of State Webster instructed William C. Rives, the American minister to France, to recognize Louis Napoleon's *coup d'état* of December 1851,[52] and even so liberal a historian-turned-diplomat as George Bancroft, who served as American minister in Berlin in the 1860's and 1870's, was at last forced to reconcile himself to Bismarck's triumph over the forces of Prussian-German liberalism.[53]

On the other hand, the triumph of conservatism in the Old World and the rise of a new militaristic *Realpolitik* that followed it had only slight intellectual impact on this country. In other words, the defeat of the European revolutions did not give rise to any significant wave of historical pessimism—to any widespread feeling that the long-range prospects of democracy had been permanently impaired or that the time had come to abandon hope for the spread of democratic government to other parts of the world. On the contrary, the triumph of conservative nationalism in Germany, which was mirrored most significantly, perhaps, in the lectures and writings of Heinrich von Treitschke and his followers, was not for a moment accepted by the growing number of young Americans who went to study at the German universities in the last decades of the nineteenth century.[54]

50 This was true also of the critics of American foreign policy in the era of the Spanish-American War.

51 See John G. Gazley, *American Opinion of German Unification 1848–1871* (New York, 1925), and Howard R. Marraro, *American Opinion of Italian Unification 1846–1861* (New York, 1932).

52 *The Writings and Speeches of Daniel Webster*, XIV, 451–452.

53 Russel B. Nye, *George Bancroft—Brahmin Rebel* (New York, 1944), Chap. 8. See also Eric F. Goldman, "Democratic Bifocalism," in George Boas (ed.), *Studies in Romanticism* (Baltimore, 1940). Like Carl Schurz, Bancroft developed considerable fondness for the ways of imperial Germany, as though the historic battles of the 1840's and 1860's had never been fought, and generally overlooked the fact that Bismarck's Germany bore only a surface resemblance to the kind of liberal united Germany most Americans, including Bancroft himself, had fervently hoped to see come into existence.

54 See Jurgen Herbst, *The German Historical School in American Scholarship* (Ithaca, 1964), Chap. 5, and the interesting letters in W. Stull Holt (ed.), *Historical Scholarship in the United States 1876–1901* (Baltimore, 1938).

From George Ticknor, Edward Everett, and George Bancroft—who had traveled to Germany after the close of the Napoleonic wars—to Herbert Baxter Adams, James Harvey Robinson, and William E. Dodd—who journeyed there in the latter years of the century—it is striking how little ideological impact the German historical school exerted on these American students. There were, of course, some exceptions; John W. Burgess, the founder of Columbia University's Faculty of Political Science, was the most prominent example.[55] For the rest, however, it seems correct to say that they adopted the "scientific" historical method of Leopold von Ranke and his successors, without at the same time accepting any of its conservative political ideology.[56] There can be little doubt either that some of the most important aspects of Rankean methodology—for instance, his great emphasis on "the primacy of foreign policy"—left its disciples unconvinced. Similarly rejected was the relativistic "historicism" that was to blight German historical scholarship increasingly after the turn of the century.[57]

Indeed, while German historical methodology continued to exert considerable influence in the United States until the time of the First World War, it seems evident that even before 1914 there was a growing reaction in leading intellectual circles in this country against the growing nationalism and imperialism in German historical writing; and whereas the overwhelming majority of German historians no doubt strongly supported the dangerously ambitious *Weltpolitik* of William II, the beginning of the twentieth century saw in the United States the rise of an increasingly self-critical school of historical scholarship—additional evidence that the patriotic spirit of 1898 had not swept everything before it.[58] Most

55 John W. Burgess, *Reminiscences of an American Scholar* (2 vols., New York, 1934). Although Burgess is frequently cited as a typical example of the new, late-nineteenth-century American nationalism and imperialism, he opposed the war with Spain and, even more vigorously, the annexation of the Philippines.

56 On the political character of German historical writing in the age of Ranke and the generation that followed him, see Ludwig Dehio's famous essay "Ranke and German Imperialism," *Germany and World Politics in the Twentieth Century* (New York, 1959); for the intellectual influence of Ranke and his school, see the illuminating study of Georg G. Iggers, "The Image of Ranke in American and German Historical Thought," *History and Theory*, II (1962).

57 Not until the 1920's and 1930's—after the shattering experiences of the First World War and the coming of the Great Depression—did the German "historicist" movement begin to exert significant influence in the United States; and no one reflected this influence more strongly than did Charles A. Beard. See Lloyd R. Sorenson, "Charles A. Beard and German Historiographical Thought," *Mississippi Valley Historical Review*, XLII (Sept. 1955).

58 In this period American historians first began to deal systematically with the history of American foreign policy, and from the beginning their work reflected the spirit of increasing self-criticism so characteristic of American thought after the 1890's. See esp. Albert Bushnell Hart, *The Foundations of American Foreign Policy* (New York, 1901); John Bassett Moore, *American Diplomacy* (New York, 1905); John H. Latané, *America as a World Power, 1897–1907* (New York, 1907); and Archibald Cary Coolidge, *The United States as a World Power* (New York, 1908).

American historians, probably, opposed and criticized the war with Spain, as they had attacked the war with Mexico.[59] Their opinion was not decisive at the time, but one should not discount its ultimate impact on the national conscience and on the subsequent course of American foreign policy.

The great debate over foreign policy in the nineteenth century came, of course, at the time of the Spanish-American War, and much has been written about this critical period in recent years.[60] But the essential questions posed by the events of that period still remain: Did the Spanish-American War and some of the events that followed it signify a fundamental departure in American thinking about world affairs, a lasting change in America's conception of what its historic role in world affairs ought to be; above all, did it precipitate a basic change in American diplomacy itself?

The answer to these questions must, on the whole, be in the negative. It is true, of course, that American economic interests in Latin America and the Far East grew appreciably in the latter years of the nineteenth century, and it is also true that there was increasing talk in the United States about its trading rights in the Far East, and mounting—perhaps justified—concern that the United States not be frozen out of what was expected to be a lucrative Chinese market.[61] Finally, there was also a considerable amount of loose and vacuous talk, most of it emanating from Alfred Thayer Mahan and his circle, about the desirability of building a large navy and the positive advantages to which such a force might eventually be put.[62]

It would be a serious misjudgment, however, to equate such economic interest with the kind of frankly imperialistic policies then clearly dominant in France, Germany, Italy, Japan, Russia, and—over Gladstone's vehement objections—also in Great Britain;

59 See, for instance, Robert Cruden, *James Ford Rhodes* (Cleveland, 1961), p. 110–112.
60 See esp. Ernest R. May, *Imperial Democracy* (New York, 1961), but also Walter LaFeber, *The New Empire* (Ithaca, 1963), and William A. Williams, *The Tragedy of American Diplomacy* (2nd ed., New York, 1965). The lack of widespread imperialist sentiment in the United States before the outbreak of war in 1898 is made clear, among others, by Julius W. Pratt, in *The Expansionists of 1898* (Baltimore, 1936) and his earlier study, "The 'Large Policy' of 1898," *Mississippi Valley Historical Review*, XIX (1932).
61 This concern with America's economic stake in the Far East (and elsewhere) is discussed at some length, and considerably exaggerated, by Williams, *The Tragedy of American Diplomacy*, Chaps. 1–3.
62 Mahan's political importance is often exaggerated these days, and so is his impact as a historian. See Leonard Krieger's comments in John Higham, with Leonard Krieger and Felix Gilbert, *History* (Englewood Cliffs, 1965), pp. 252–253, which should be compared with the balanced assessment of W. Stull Holt, in Merle Curti (ed.), *American Scholarship in the Twentieth Century* (New York, 1953), p. 107.

and it would be equally mistaken to assume that the ebullient outpourings of such men as Mahan, Albert Beveridge, Henry Cabot Lodge, and others represented the real direction of American foreign policy. No American President from Andrew Johnson to William McKinley had any serious imperialistic leanings, as that word is generally understood, nor did any American Secretary of State from Hamilton Fish to John Hay.[63]

It was hardly an accident, then, that the U.S. Declaration of War against Spain in April 1898 was accompanied by the Teller Amendment, overwhelmingly passed in both houses of Congress, which stipulated that the United States had no intention whatever of annexing Cuba at the end of the war—a statement of self-denial unprecedented in the annals of modern war;[64] or that the peace treaty with Spain, providing for the cession of the Philippine Islands, was ratified by the United States Senate with only one vote to spare;[65] or that an amendment providing for the independence of the Philippines upon the establishment of a stable government there was defeated only by the tie-breaking vote of the Vice President.[66]

It is correct to say, however, that some of the unlovely features of American foreign policy in the next decade or so, especially in Central America, seemed to bear out the more pessimistic forecasts made at the time of the war with Spain.[67] The most unfortunate of all such actions—an unmistakable violation of historic American policy, an action that has been almost unanimously condemned by American historians and that has much troubled the American conscience over the years—was, of course, the covert intervention in Colombian affairs, in 1903, to secure the establishment of an Isthmian canal.[68] But this action was never repeated, and even such highly, and in many ways rightly, criticized acts as intervention in the Dominican Republic, Haiti, and Nicaragua

---

[63] The prevailing strength of anti-imperialism in the post-Civil War period, about which, unfortunately, little is usually said, is discussed in Donald M. Dozer, "Anti-Imperialism in the United States, 1865–1895" (Unpubl. diss., Harvard Univ., 1936); see also Merle Curti, *Peace or War* (New York, 1936), which traces the continuing strength of the (anti-imperialistic) peace movement in the last half of the nineteenth century.

[64] Elmer Ellis, *Henry Moore Teller* (Caldwell, 1941), 311ff, 341ff.

[65] It seems generally agreed that the acquisition of the Philippines would not have been approved by the Senate without Bryan's support. See Paola E. Coletta, "Bryan, McKinley, and the Treaty of Paris," *Pacific Historical Review*, XXVI (1957), and J. Rogers Hollingsworth, *The Whirligig of Politics* (Chicago, 1963), pp. 150ff.

[66] Pratt, *The Expansionists of 1898*, p. 359.

[67] For a good account of anti-imperialist opinion at the time of the Spanish-American War, see Fred Harvey Harrington, "The Anti-Imperialist Movement in the United States 1898–1900," *Mississippi Valley Historical Review*, XXII (1935); and "Literary Aspects of Anti-Imperialism," *New England Quarterly*, X (1937); and the recent account of Barbara W. Tuchman, *The Proud Tower* (New York, 1966), pp. 130ff.

[68] On the debate over the Panama Canal crisis, see Dwight C. Miner, *The Fight for the Panama Route* (New York, 1940), *passim*.

were not based on any conventional imperialistic desire to annex these areas or to control them indefinitely for national advantage.[69]

Even Theodore Roosevelt, whose outspoken remarks and dramatic policies sometimes ran counter to established American tradition in foreign policy, was much concerned to emphasize the continuity of his actions and those of his predecessors and to stress that his policies were not, in fact, a departure from such time-honored principles. The so-called Roosevelt Corollary to the Monroe Doctrine has been strongly criticized. Yet a close look at Roosevelt's exact language shows this criticism to be quite unfounded.[70]

"It is not true," Roosevelt declared with considerable emphasis in his annual message to Congress in December 1904,

that the United States feels any land hunger or entertains any projects as regards the other nations of the Western hemisphere. . . . All that this country desires is to see the neighboring countries stable, orderly, and prosperous. . . . Our interests and those of our southern neighbors are in reality identical. They have great natural riches, and if within their borders the reign of law and justice obtains prosperity is sure to come to them. While they thus obey the primary laws of civilized society they may rest assured that they will be treated by us in a spirit of cordial and helpful sympathy. We would interfere with them only in the last resort, and then only if it became evident that their inability or unwillingness to do justice at home and abroad had violated the rights of the United States or had invited foreign aggression to the detriment of the entire body of American nations.[71]

If despite such hopeful pronouncements U.S. policy toward Latin America remained the weakest aspect of American diplomacy in the years following the Spanish-American War, there was in this period also substantial evidence to indicate that the essential spirit and continuity of American foreign policy had not been adulterated by the martial atmosphere of the time.[72] There were indeed

69 See the recent, judiciously critical volume of Dana G. Munro, *Dollar Diplomacy and Intervention in the Caribbean, 1900–1921* (Princeton, 1964).

70 But see also Frank Tannenbaum, *The American Tradition in Foreign Policy* (Norman, 1955), p. 64.

71 For the text of Roosevelt's message, see Commager (ed.), *Documents of American History*, II, No. 362. Such emphasis on the independence of the Latin American states was not incidental. Roosevelt had spoken in much the same terms in his annual message of December 1901. See James D. Richardson (ed.), *Messages and Papers of the Presidents*, X, 441.

72 "We deem the independence and equal rights of the smallest and weakest member of the family of nations entitled to as much respect as those of the greatest empire," declared Secretary of State Root at the Third International Conference of Latin American States, held at Rio de Janeiro in July 1906. "We neither claim nor desire any rights or privileges or powers that we do not freely concede to every

important signs, of an official and unofficial nature, that the gloomy forecasts of many distinguished "anti-imperialists," such as Carl Schurz, and President Charles Eliot of Harvard, were far from coming true. In the first place, it was clear that the powerful militarists and navalist movements that were making about this time such pronounced headway in France and Britain, would make very little progress in this country.[73] Furthermore, the peace movement flourished in this country as it had never done before, enjoying wide and substantial support from important political, religious, and industrial circles; and the United States gave strong, if not invariably consistent, support to the conferences on international peace held at The Hague in 1899 and 1907.[74] Second, there can be little doubt that President Roosevelt performed an important international service by his well-timed mediation of the Russo-Japanese War—for which he received the Nobel Peace Prize in 1906, the only American President save Woodrow Wilson to be so honored—and an equally vital service by accepting William II's request that he help to resolve the dangerous Franco-German dispute over Morocco in 1905–1906.[75]

Moreover, it was about this time—in 1899 and 1900—that Secretary of State Hay set forth the policy of the Open Door in China.[76] Like many American policies in this period, this one has been and continues to be much criticized.[77] Perhaps it would be more accurate to say that it has been widely misunderstood.[78] It

---

American Republic" (Robert Bacon and James Brown Scott [eds.], *Latin America and the United States* [Cambridge, Mass., 1917], p. 7, quoted in Tannenbaum, *The American Tradition in Foreign Policy*, p. 65).

[73] See also Harold and Margaret Sprout, *The Rise of American Naval Power, 1776–1918* (Princeton, 1939), Chaps 15–17.

[74] For a critical account of American policy at The Hague conferences, see Tuchman, *The Proud Tower*, Chap. 5; and for a more balanced recent account, Calvin D'A. Davis, *The United States and the First Hague Conference* (Ithaca, 1962).

[75] For a good account of Roosevelt's diplomacy at Portsmouth and Algeciras see George E. Mowry, *The Era of Theodore Roosevelt* (New York, 1958), pp. 193–196, on Portsmouth esp. Tyler Dennett, *Roosevelt and the Russo-Japanese War* (New York, 1925), and on Algeciras, Allan Nevins, *Henry White* (New York, 1930), Chap. 16. White, whom Roosevelt sent to represent him at Algeciras, was appointed in 1918 a member of the American Commission to Negotiate the Peace by President Wilson.

[76] For the text of Hay's notes, see *Foreign Relations of the United States, 1899* (Washington, D.C., 1901), pp. 128–143.

[77] See A. Whitney Griswold, *The Far Eastern Policy of the United States* (New York, 1938), Chap. 2, and Kennan, *American Diplomacy 1900–1950*, Chaps. 2, 3, which makes too much of the alleged British influence on the formulation of the Open Door Policy. For a careful study of that policy's development, see Paul A. Varg, *Open Door Diplomat* (Urbana, 1952), and also the closely argued account in Tannenbaum, *The American Tradition in Foreign Policy*, pp. 97ff. The continuity of American Far Eastern policy is shown in the impressive work of Tyler Dennett, *Americans in East Asia* (New York, 1922).

[78] "These principles," Henry Stimson wrote about the Open Door Policy in his memoirs nearly a half century later, "were not new in the foreign policy of America. They had been the principles upon which it rested for many years" (Henry L. Stimson and McGeorge Bundy, *On Active Service in Peace and War* [New York, 1947], pp. 249–250). See also Carl Russell Fish, *The Path of Empire* (New Haven, 1919), Chap. XIV.

is frequently asserted that Hay's principal purpose in proclaiming the Open Door Policy was to assure the United States equal access to the Chinese market; and, indeed, such was doubtless part of his intention. Yet to understand properly the full meaning of the policy, it is essential to consider not only the first of Hay's notes, which centered on economic equality (and *ipso facto* assumed the continued existence of an independent Chinese state), but also the last, dated July 1900.

When these notes are considered together, it becomes clear that the United States was concerned not merely with narrowly economic considerations, but with the crucial issue of the territorial integrity of China, which then appeared to be threatened with imminent dismemberment. This concern with the territorial integrity of that unfortunate country was not, moreover, peculiar to Secretary Hay. On the contrary, as we have seen, it had been a fundamental American policy for more than half a century, dating back to the days of Caleb Cushing and Daniel Webster.[79]

This policy of nonintervention in Chinese affairs had been affirmed by the United States on numerous occasions. "This country, you will constantly bear in mind," Secretary of State Lewis Cass had written in May 1857 to William B. Reed, the American minister at Tientsin,

is not at war with the government of China, nor does it seek to enter that empire for any other purposes than those of lawful commerce, and for the protection of the lives and property of its citizens. . . . You will therefore not fail to let it be known to the Chinese authorities that we are no party to the existing hostilities, and have no intention to interfere in their political concerns. . . . With the domestic institutions of China we have no political concern, and to attempt a forcible interference with them would not only be unjust in itself, but might defeat the very object desired.[80]

This was the policy, then, that Secretary Hay restated in July 1900, when in a circular note to the other Great Powers he made it clear that it was "the policy of the United States to seek a solution which may bring about permanent safety and peace to China, [and] preserve Chinese territorial and administrative integrity."

79 See above, pp. 9–10.
80 Ruhl J. Bartlett (ed.), *The Record of American Diplomacy* (4th ed., New York, 1964), p. 263, citing Senate Executive Document (1032), 36th Congress, 1st session, no. 30, pp. 6–11. This statement was an unmistakable effort by the United States to disassociate itself from the demands then being made on China by Britain and France, which, taking advantage of the bloody Taiping Rebellion of 1857, sought forcibly to extract substantial commercial and political concessions from the distracted Chinese government.

This policy was soon put to a crucial test. When the Boxer Rebellion broke out in August 1900, the Great Powers sought to take full advantage of that abortive nationalist uprising, which reached its dramatic climax with the siege of Peking, to impose upon China a crushing indemnity which would furnish them with a convenient pretext for continued interference in China's internal affairs. The United States did everything within its power to prevent such action.[81] It fought and ultimately succeeded in keeping the indemnity far below that originally desired by the other Great Powers. It accepted a share of that indemnity only because it feared that its failure to do so might serve as an excuse for the others to increase their own demands; and in a nearly unprecedented gesture,[82] the United States then returned to China more than half of its share, with the understanding that the funds be used to educate Chinese students in this country.[83] The latter agreement, moreover, was bound to have important advantages for China in the long run; for it would help to meet the country's urgent need for well-trained technical experts and professional men, whose American education would prove invaluable in China's future progress and in its relations with the Western world.

It is well to recall such actions of the United States at a time when relations between this country and Communist China are so badly strained. More important, however, these actions confirm the fact that American foreign policy had not been significantly affected by the outpourings of Admiral Mahan and other adventurous nationalists, and that even in the age of imperialism the United States continued to support the fundamental principle it had set forth and supported since the eighteenth century—that every country had the right to govern itself as it pleased and that no state had the right to interfere in the internal affairs of another.

But how were such principles to be put into effect? Having made clear how it believed the Great Powers should deal with

81 For the efforts of the United States in this matter, see *Foreign Relations of the United States, 1901. Affairs in China: Report of William W. Rockhill, Late Commissioner to China, with Accompanying Documents* (Washington, 1902).

82 It is widely believed that the (partial) remission of the Boxer indemnity was the first such action on the part of the United States. This was not the case. In 1883 the United States had agreed to remit to Japan the indemnity levied upon her following the unprovoked attack on foreign vessels in the straits of Shimonoseki in 1864, and two years later, in 1885, the United States agreed to return its share of a similar indemnity levied on China in 1858. For a revealing account of the Shimonoseki indemnity, which throws much light on American policy toward the weaker states of the Far East in the nineteenth century, see Payson J. Treat, *Diplomatic Relations Between the United States and Japan 1853–1905* (Stanford, 1932), I, 241ff; II, 545ff.

83 For an assessment of the return of the Boxer indemnity, see *American Journal of International Law*, II, III (1908, 1909). The indemnity was returned in two parts, the first in 1908, the second in 1924.

the weaker countries of the world, how did the United States believe the Great Powers could settle most propitiously their own outstanding differences? In this realm, too, the United States had a clear-cut position of long standing, namely that the way to avoid international war was through mediation and arbitration of outstanding disputes.

Although sometimes derided as "moralistic-legalistic," this approach to international peace also had deep roots in the American past and held considerable promise in what were far more law-abiding times than our own. American experience with international arbitration dated back to Jay's Treaty of 1794, which ultimately resolved, if not entirely to this country's satisfaction, some of the vexing issues left unsettled by the Peace of Paris of 1783. The policy of arbitration was invoked again in 1848 when the United States and Mexico agreed, in the treaty of Guadalupe Hidalgo, that in the future all disputes between the two countries should, whenever possible, be resolved by arbitration;[84] and successful arbitration in the 1870's at last put an end to the bitter and protracted controversy between Great Britain and the United States over the hotly disputed *Alabama* claims.[85]

Nor did American interest in arbitration begin to slacken in the last decades of the nineteenth century, when, it is often said, American foreign policy was increasingly dominated by a spirit of expansive, aggressive imperialism. For example, at the First International American Conference, held in Washington in 1889–1890, the United States and the Latin American countries signed a convention providing for the arbitration of all disputes between them, save only questions of national independence—a treaty that for unexplained reasons never reached the Senate.[86] And having come close to hostilities with Great Britain over Venezuela in 1895, President Cleveland in the following year approved the signing of a comprehensive arbitration treaty with the former country—the Olney-Pauncefote Convention which, although strongly supported by President McKinley, was narrowly defeated in the Senate in May 1897.[87]

---

84 See Article XXI of the treaty, reprinted in Commager (ed.), *Documents of American History*, I, no. 34.

85 Goldwin A. Smith, *The Treaty of Washington* (Ithaca, 1941), describes the final settlement and the process by which it was achieved; Allan Nevins, *Hamilton Fish* (New York, 1936), Chap. XX.

86 Davis, *The United States and the First Hague Conference*, pp. 20–21; Richard W. Leopold, *The Growth of American Foreign Policy* (New York, 1962), p. 155.

87 Nelson M. Blake, "The Olney-Pauncefote Treaty of 1897," *American Historical Review*, L (1945). President McKinley, in his first inaugural address, described arbitration as "the leading feature of our foreign policy throughout our entire national history" (W. Stull Holt, *Treaties Defeated by the Senate* [Baltimore, 1933], p. 156).

Such failures, undoubtedly disappointing, did not bring about a change in the basic American approach to the conduct of international relations. On the contrary, in regard to international as well as domestic affairs, there was a growing feeling in the United States that strongly felt differences, whether over territorial or economic problems, could and should be resolved by judicial means.[88] Even so nationalistic a Chief Executive as Theodore Roosevelt sought to crown his achievements in the realm of foreign affairs by establishing general arbitration treaties between the United States and other leading powers. Yet Roosevelt found himself confronted with the Senate's unwillingness to assent to such arrangements. After Secretary Hay had negotiated a number of comprehensive arbitration treaties in 1905, the Senate insisted upon attaching to them a series of crippling reservations—which, in effect, gave the Senate the power to determine which disputes should be arbitrated and which should not[89]—whereupon President Roosevelt fired off a bitterly critical letter to Senator Henry Cabot Lodge and refused to ratify the treaties.[90] Toward the end of the Roosevelt administration Secretary of State Elihu Root negotiated a new series of arbitration treaties, but the Senate again insisted upon attaching a series of restrictive amendments. This time Roosevelt accepted them, although it was widely agreed that the reservations severely limited the usefulness of the new treaties.[91]

President Taft, whose intellectual outlook was highly juridical, was undaunted by Roosevelt's unhappy experience. His Secretary of State, Philander C. Knox, negotiated still another series of arbitration treaties, the scope of which went considerably beyond those signed by Roosevelt in that they now included as negotiable even issues involving "vital interests" and "national honor." Once more, however, the Senate insisted upon mutilating the agreements.[92] Taft was incensed by the Senate's action. Regarding it as a

---

[88] Cf. William D. P. Bliss (ed.), *The New Encyclopedia of Social Reform* (4th ed., New York and London, 1908), pp. 58ff, and Merle Curti, *Peace or War*, Chaps. V-VII.

[89] The Senate's action was probably less an expression of opposition to international arbitration than an example of its growing suspicion that—as in his recent Santo Domingo policies—Roosevelt was trying to invade its constitutional prerogatives. As Hay wrote in his diary, "The President's majority [in the Senate] was too big—they wanted to teach him that he wasn't *it*." William R. Thayer, *The Life and Letters of John Hay*, II (Boston and New York, 1915), 393.

[90] Mowry, *The Era of Theodore Roosevelt*, p. 191–192.

[91] For the text of the Root treaties, see William M. Malloy (ed.), *Treaties, Conventions, International Acts, Protocols, and Agreements between the United States and Other Powers 1776–1909* (Washington, D.C., 1910), pp. 814–815, 549, 992–993; and Philip C. Jessup, *Elihu Root*, II (New York, 1938), 270ff.

[92] For the original and amended texts, see Garfield Charles (comp.), *Treaties, Conventions . . . between the United States of America and Other Powers*, III (Washington, D.C., 1913), 380ff; and for a discussion of the Senate's role in amending the Hay, Root, and Knox treaties, see Holt, *Treaties Defeated by the Senate*, pp. 204ff, 211ff, and 230ff.

gross breach of national good faith, he refused either to promulgate the amended treaties or to ask the other signatories to accept the Senate's amendments. Indeed, like Wilson in 1919, he embarked upon a national speaking tour in behalf of the treaties, denouncing the Senate's action in vigorous terms; and, again like Wilson, he failed to change the Senate's position.[93]

Unfortunate though it was, the Senate's action was, on balance, probably not based on narrowly nationalist considerations. Its attitude toward foreign policy in those years was—not for the last time—highly quixotic. The Senate was neither arrogantly chauvinist nor blindly indifferent to foreign affairs. It proved that conclusively by the passage of the Teller Amendment, by its searching debates on the peace treaty with Spain, and by the remarkable frankness with which it continued to discuss American policies in the Caribbean.[94] Its unwillingness to accept these treaties as originally signed, then, was probably due to a combination of personal resentments and institutional jealousies. Still, it constituted a most disagreeable precedent.

Not surprisingly, considering their backgrounds, it was Wilson and Secretary of State William Jennings Bryan who together brought the policy of peace through international law to a climax in the years 1913–1915. Wilson's intellectual background was as much in jurisprudence as it was in history and government, and it was Bryan who had first directed Theodore Roosevelt's attention to the arbitration movement.[95] Bryan, not discouraged by the experiences of his predecessors, negotiated still another, and in some ways more far-reaching, series of international agreements. Like those of Root, Bryan's treaties also dealt with questions of "national honor." They also provided for a one-year cooling-off period before any power could commence hostilities against another.[96]

Wilson and Bryan considered this last requirement especially

93 Henry F. Pringle, *The Life and Times of William Howard Taft,* II (New York, 1939), 746ff. Robert E. Osgood, *Ideals and Self-Interest in American Foreign Relations* (Chicago, 1953), p. 97. "I think," said Taft at Marquette, Michigan, in September, 1911, the War of 1812 "might have been settled without a fight and ought to have been. So with the Mexican War. So, I think, with the Spanish War." Taft said that given an effective arbitration treaty, the war with Spain might have been avoided. Roosevelt, who by this time had changed his mind and opposed the arbitration treaties, said that was precisely the trouble with them—they would have made both the war and the intervention in Colombia impossible.

94 See, for instance, Holt, *Treaties Defeated by the Senate,* 212ff. "Much of the hostile feeling caused by our interventions in the Caribbean," writes Professor Dana G. Munro, "arose from misconceptions of what we were trying to do. This is especially true in the case of the Taft administration's 'Dollar Diplomacy.'" "Dollar Diplomacy in Nicaragua, 1909–1913," *The Hispanic American Historical Review,* XXXVIII (May 1958), 209.

95 Paul W. Glad, *The Trumpet Soundeth* (Lincoln, 1960), p. 101.

96 For the text of the Bryan "model treaties," see Bartlett (ed.), *The Record of American Diplomacy,* pp. 339–340.

important, believing that the passage of time, combined with the machinery of fact-finding and mediation provided for in the new treaties, made ultimate recourse to arms most unlikely. Moreover, like many contemporary social scientists, Secretary Bryan was convinced that the free reign of social intelligence would be sufficient to avert the use of force. The most important prerequisite for the settlement of international disputes, as he saw it, was therefore to establish the facts at issue. Once this had been accomplished, Bryan was convinced that "we would generally find that there was no real question of honor"—hence no real justification for war.[97]

Because of President Wilson's considerable political influence during his early years in the White House, the Senate agreed, for the first time, to a series of important international treaties without insisting upon substantive changes.[98] As the other Great Powers drifted headlong toward Armageddon, the United States seemed to have taken a significant step toward the establishment of lasting world peace. Indeed, it has been contended that if imperial Germany had been willing to conclude an arbitration (or mediation) treaty with the United States at that time, the two countries could not have gone to war in April 1917.[99]

Yet admirable though these policies were in many respects, can it be maintained that the American approach to foreign policy in the early years of the twentieth century—Roosevelt's mediation of the Russo-Japanese War and the first Moroccan crisis, Hay's statement of the Open Door Policy, and the negotiation of a whole series of arbitration or mediation treaties—was really adequate to meet the needs of contemporary international politics?

American diplomacy in this period has recently been much criticized. On the one hand, Professor William Appleman Williams and his students have contended that toward the end of the nineteenth century the United States was driven, largely by economic considerations, to embark upon a course of aggressive expansion, or imperialism, much like that of the older European states, with the result that the fundamental liberal principles for which the United States claimed to have stood in the eighteenth century largely went down the drain. "In the realm of foreign affairs, at least," Williams has written recently, "the United States has not proved

97 Glad, *The Trumpet Soundeth*, pp. 101–102.
98 Arthur S. Link, *Woodrow Wilson and the Progressive Era, 1910–1917* (New York, 1954), p. 8, and *Wilson*, II (Princeton, 1965), 280ff.
99 Charles Callan Tansill, *America Goes to War* (Boston, 1938), p. 442.

that Marx was wrong. America has been a colonial power. America has practiced administrative colonialism on a significant scale. America has built an informal empire of massive proportions. And America is now face to face with the proof of Marx's thesis that such empires create their own effective opposition both from without and from within. It would appear to be the greater part of wisdom, to say nothing of safety, to admit that Marx was right."[100]

On the other hand, George F. Kennan has maintained that the illness of American foreign policy in this period was not a lack of "morality" but a misplaced surfeit of it. He considers the Open Door Policy, for instance, to be essentially a non-American concern and judges it as a policy at once too forward, too superficially idealistic, and ultimately completely unrealistic. The same was true, as he sees it, of the policy of seeking peace through international treaties—a policy he regards as visionary and entirely unsuccessful, and nothing less than a waste of everyone's time.[1a] Reading Williams and his students, one gets the impression that America, at least after the Civil War, forgot all its moral principles; reading Kennan, one gets the distinct impression that America was smitten with a bad case of moral megalomania and that its policies in Europe as well as in the Far East were largely the result of this dangerous disease.

That there is a kernel of truth in each argument no student of this period would deny. As Williams and his students point out, there was in this period a growing concern with foreign markets and with the question of how American commodities and manufactured goods might find an outlet overseas. It is also true, as already noted, that there was in those years a renewed interest in finding new ways and means of putting an end to international conflict—the kind of interest one would have thought was powerful evidence against the argument that American foreign policy in the era of the Spanish-American War became more and more bellicose, and suffused with the heady spirit of imperialism, navalism, and the like.

Yet a closer look at this period would tend to suggest that America's outlook on world affairs changed really very little. Far from being too forward, too meddlesome, too adventurous, it would probably be more accurate to say that American diplomacy remained, essentially, conventional and conservative. There can be little doubt

100 William A. Williams, *The Great Evasion* (Chicago, 1964), p. 51.
1a George F. Kennan, *Realities of American Foreign Policy* (2nd ed., New York, 1966), pp. 18ff.

that the informed public in the United States was well aware of the realities of international politics. Indeed, there was growing concern that the increasingly troubled domestic situation, to say nothing of the ever more conflicting foreign policies, of the Great Powers would soon lead to an enormous international explosion;[2a] and there was mounting concern over the steadily growing colonial, economic, and military rivalry of the Great Powers, over the dangers and uncertainties posed by the rapidly decaying Ottoman and Hapsburg empires, and over the repulsive treatment being meted out to racial and religious minorities all over Europe.[3a]

This public concern with Europe's problems took many forms. From the 1880's on, for instance, Congress was inundated with a steady stream of petitions and appeals asking that the United States do something to alleviate the plight of the oppressed Russian Jews, and every new pogrom touched off a fresh wave of demands for American action. Yet it was not until 1911 that President Taft finally agreed, and then rather reluctantly, to abrogate the Russian-American Commercial Treaty of 1832.[4a] It was not that the U.S. government was insensitive to such developments. Perhaps the main reason it was so slow to respond was that it knew that there was little that it could do to implement the worldwide humanitarian interests of the American people.

American diplomacy in those days was caught on the horns of a profound historical dilemma. It is true that the Founding Fathers had been convinced not only of the correctness of their political philosophy but also of its universal validity and its ultimate triumph throughout the world. Yet, hard-headed considerations of political realism had led them to reflect that the time was not yet at hand when the United States could hope to do much to advance the cause of freedom outside the North American continent. The most important formulation of this awareness was, of course, to be found in President Washington's Farewell Address. On the other hand, as time went on and American strength increased materially, so did America's moral responsibility to assist other peoples to free themselves from the bonds of tyranny and to protect, as best it could, those who had managed to establish their independence. This was the philosophy that underlay the Monroe Doctrine.

There was also, however, a significant ambiguity in the Founding

2a William C. Askew and J. Fred Rippy, "The United States and Europe's Strife, 1908–1913," *The Journal of Politics*, IV (1942).
3a See, for instance, Tyler Dennett, *John Hay* (New York, 1933), pp. 395ff.
4a Thomas A. Bailey, *America Faces Russia* (Ithaca, 1950), p. 220.

Fathers' attitude toward foreign policy. Just as they felt confident of their own principles, so they also felt a strong distaste for the character of most European governments and their way of conducting international relations. It was almost as if the Founding Fathers and their successors believed—as indeed some did—that by close and intimate association with the European political system, the purity of their own principles would be despoiled. This distaste was in large part responsible for the "isolationist" spirit of early American foreign policy[5a] and for the distaste that many Americans still had for the European state system at the beginning of the twentieth century.

Thomas Jefferson had enjoined his countrymen—and their diplomats—that every country had the right to govern itself as it pleased and that no government had the right to interfere in the internal affairs of another—to which he added the important, perhaps all-important, qualification, "The only thing essential is the will of the people." In practice, from the eighteenth century to the beginning of the twentieth, the United States had developed a compromise formula based on this historic injunction. It had, on the one hand, never ceased to support reform and revolutionary movements in other parts of the world—movements that had as their objective the extension of liberty—while, on the other hand, it had accepted, albeit rather reluctantly, the necessity of working with the existing international state system for an indefinite period. In this sense, such seemingly unrelated developments as the Open Door doctrine and the policy of achieving international peace through international law were in fact parts of the same policy.[6a] They represented, that is to say, the continued application of certain historic American ideals to the conduct of foreign policy, and though perhaps viewed by some Americans at the beginning of the twentieth century as an inadequate realization of these ideals, these policies represented about as much as could be expected at that time.

Finally, it should be recalled that on several occasions in the

5a See, for instance, John Quincy Adams' endorsement of an "isolationist" foreign policy in 1821—a statement quoted with evident approval by George Kennan before the hearings on American Far Eastern policy held by the Senate Committee on Foreign Relations in February 1966. Adams' general position, which has long been well known, represented only one side of the American outlook on foreign policy in the nineteenth century. For accounts of American "interventionist" thought in that period, over which Kennan found it convenient to pass in silence, see the works of Curti, Curtis, and May, cited above, note 30, to which may be added Merle Curti's important essay "Young America," *American Historical Review*, XXXII (Oct. 1926), reprinted in *Probing Our Past* (New York, 1951).

6a Thayer, *The Life and Letters of John Hay*, II, 249.

nineteenth century—first at the time of the Louisiana Purchase, then at the time of the Mexican War, and finally at the time of the Spanish-American War—there was a profound and bitter debate in the United States over whether it was America's historic role in world affairs to expand its frontiers and to bring the benefits of its civilization to other parts of the continent and the world. On each occasion the ultimate decision was to expand, but on each occasion the decision was taken uneasily and it caused great intellectual anguish. The liberal consciousness of the eighteenth century had not died, but it did not believe in paying the price of world political responsibility. The debates of 1898 and after showed that clearly. They also indicated, beyond any doubt, that the American democracy had not yet resolved the question of how its historic role in world affairs was to be fulfilled or, perhaps, even what that role was.

Events abroad, however, would not wait upon an intellectual decision here at home. By the early 1900's it was clear that the United States had done and would do nothing to disturb the essential nature of the international state system. The only question was whether, if the proper opportunity ever presented itself, the United States should seek to fulfill the historic role it had seemed to play since the era of the American Revolution. "We have no choice, we the people of the United States," Theodore Roosevelt remarked not long before he became President, "as to whether or not we shall play a great part in the world. That has been decided for us by fate, by the march of events. We have to play that part. All that we can decide is whether we shall play it well or ill."[7a]

For America the time of decision began in the summer of 1914.

III

When the Great War that had long been in the making in Europe broke out at last in August 1914, President Wilson quickly issued a proclamation calling upon his countrymen to remain "impartial in thought as well as in action."[8a] There was nothing surprising about this declaration, which indeed reflected the President's innermost feelings; for he was a deeply pacific man, and he had come to Washington hoping to devote himself largely to the task of domestic reform. "It would be the irony of fate," he had told a

[7a] Quoted in Archibald Cary Coolidge, *America as a World Power* (New York, 1908), p. 373.

[8a] Arthur S. Link, *Wilson*, III (Princeton, 1960), p. 66.

friend just before leaving Princeton for his inauguration in March 1913, "if my administration had to deal chiefly with foreign affairs.[9a]

The President was not, however, granted his wish, and he had hardly settled in the White House when he was confronted, in the Far East and in Latin America, with a series of troublesome and embarrassing situations. The history of these events—from his withdrawal of official support for the international Chinese railway consortium, to his demand for the repeal of the Panama Canal tolls, his support of an indemnity for the damages done to Colombia in 1903, and, finally, the troublesome border controversy with Mexico—is well known.[10a] But more important here is what Wilson's handling of these problems tells of his reading of the great tradition of American foreign policy and how that tradition should be applied to the even more dangerous problems he was soon to be confronted with in Europe.

Woodrow Wilson was the first professional scholar ever elected President of the United States. As Professor Mayer points out elsewhere in this volume,[11a] there was in the Wilsonian era a close connection between historical consciousness and foreign policy. Wilson, as Professor Mayer reminds us, was one of the "New Historians," who came to the forefront in this country in the early years of the twentieth century.[12a] Unlike the European romantic historians of a hundred years before, who sought to use the past as an intellectual and cultural weapon against the advocates of political and social change, the New Historians believed that much positive good might be derived from the proper study of the past—a past that they tended, for the most part, to see in highly critical terms.[13a]

The New History was not, of course, so completely new as is sometimes believed. From Jared Sparks to Hermann von Holst, most leading American historians had doubtless believed that the past could be made socially useful to the present—at any rate, that it had something of significance to say to the present—but it was no doubt the "New Historians," representing an important part of the growing instrumentalist movement in American scholar-

9a Ray Stannard Baker, *Woodrow Wilson, Life and Letters*, IV, 55, quoted in Link, *Wilson*, II, 276.

10a For contrasting accounts of Wilson's early diplomacy, see Notter, *The Origins of the Foreign Policy of Woodrow Wilson, passim;* Baker, *Woodrow Wilson*, Vol. IV, Chap. 2.

11a See below, pp. 75ff.

12a Higham, Krieger, and Gilbert, *History*, pp. 104–116.

13a Cf. Crane Brinton, "James Harvey Robinson," *Dictionary of American Biography*, Supp. II (New York, 1958), pp. 563ff.

ship, who brought this particular viewpoint to the forefront as it had
never been before. This was the springtime of the social sciences in
America, and there was widespread belief not only in the rationality
of men and events but also in the ability of scholars and experts to
make public policy more enlightened, rational, and generally
effective.[14a]

The New Historians, moreover, were not parochial national historians by any means. James Harvey Robinson and Charles A.
Beard, for example, knew a great deal about European history
and politics, and so—if only because of its close connection with
his major interest—did Frederick Jackson Turner, who had come to
know Wilson when the latter taught at Johns Hopkins in the late
1880's.

Still, the New Historians were scholars, not political philosophers.
They generally accepted the prevailing traditions of American
domestic and foreign policy, and were, for the most part, concerned with making that tradition a more effective instrument
of public policy. Wilson, it soon became apparent, was different.
He was both a scholar and—as he clearly showed in his writings
on the history of American politics and government—a political
philosopher. He knew well what the American tradition was in
the realm of foreign policy, but he was also aware that the changing nature of technology and world politics made it necessary
to bring that tradition and these new circumstances into harmony.[15a]

The historical origins of Wilson's approach to foreign policy
are not, however, to be found in the presidential campaign of
1912, during which little was said by Roosevelt, Taft, or Wilson[16a]
on international affairs—making it appear as if a national consensus had, for the moment, been reached on that subject. Nor
is it to be found in Wilson's first inaugural address—one of his
truly great speeches—which said nothing whatever about international
affairs. Yet his inaugural address did contain a phrase that, before
long, began to serve as an important indication of his approach
to foreign policy. "Our duty," Wilson had said discussing the direction of American domestic policy, "is to cleanse, to reconsider,
to restore. . . . We have made up our minds to square every

14a Morton G. White, *Social Thought in America* (2d ed., Boston, 1957), Chaps. 3–4.
15a "We have come to full maturity . . . and the day of our isolation is past," Wilson
said in December, 1901; and in his inaugural address as President of Princeton University,
in October, 1902, he declared, "A new age is before us, in which, it would seem, we must
lead the world." (Quoted in Baker, *Wilson,* IV, 57; II, 129.)
16a Cf. John Wells Davidson (ed.), *A Crossroads of Freedom* (New Haven, 1956).

process of our national life . . . with the standards we so proudly
set at the beginning and have always carried at our hearts."[17a]

Wilson's early foreign policy—although not entirely successful
in realizing his objectives—soon revealed a strikingly similar affinity
for a policy of restoration, a policy of returning to the diplomatic
principles of the revolutionary generation and its successors. There
was no single occasion and no one speech that revealed conclusively the coming of a new—Wilsonian—revolution in American foreign policy. Yet despite his earlier strong desire to avoid
active involvement in international relations, Wilson soon indicated
what he meant by a policy of restoration in the realm of diplomacy.

Wilson, after being in office for less than a week, began to
show his firm belief in the indissoluble connection between domestic
and foreign policy, between free government and international
peace. "Just government," declared a statement that Wilson himself had drawn up with great care, which was issued by the
White House and circulated to all Latin American missions on
March 11, 1913,

rests always upon the consent of the governed . . . and there can be no
freedom without order based upon law and upon the public conscience
and approval. We shall look to make these principles the basis of mutual
intercourse, respect, and helpfulness between our sister republics and
ourselves. We shall lend our influence of every kind to the realization
of these principles in fact and practice. . . . We can have no sympathy
with those who seek to seize the power of government to advance their
own personal interests or ambition. . . . We are the friends of peace, but
we know that there can be no lasting or stable peace in such circumstances.[18a]

Nor was President Wilson inclined to view the conditions of
peace and international stability largely in political terms. On the
contrary, as one of the New Historians, he had long been concerned with the interaction of economics and politics, and it was
to this theme—as it related to foreign policy—that he turned in
his address at Mobile, Alabama, in October 1913. "There is," he
told the assembled Southern Commercial Congress,

one peculiarity about the history of the Latin American States. . . . You
hear of "concessions" to foreign capitalists in Latin America. You do

17a For the text of Wilson's first inaugural address, see Ray Stannard Baker and
William E. Dodd (eds.), *The Public Papers of Woodrow Wilson*, I (New York, 1927),
1–6.
18a *Foreign Relations of the United States, 1913* (Washington, D.C., 1914), p. 7,
quoted in Notter, *Origins*, p. 223. For the background and significance of this statement,
see Baker, *Woodrow Wilson*, IV, 61ff.

not hear of concessions to foreign capitalists in the United States. They are not granted concessions. They are invited to make investments. . . . It is an invitation, not a privilege; and States that are obliged, because their territory does not lie within the main field of modern enterprise and action, to grant concessions are in this condition, that foreign interests are apt to dominate their domestic affairs, a condition of affairs always dangerous and apt to become intolerable. . . .

The dignity, the courage, the self-possession, the self-respect of the Latin American States, their achievements in the face of all these adverse circumstances, deserve nothing but the admiration and applause of the world. They have had harder bargains driven with them in the matter of loans than any other peoples in the world. Interest has been exacted of them that was not exacted of anybody else, because the risk was said to be greater; and then securities were taken that destroyed the risk—an admirable arrangement for those who were forcing the terms! I rejoice in nothing so much as in the prospect that they will now be emancipated from these conditions, and we ought to be the first to take part in assisting in that emancipation.

Wilson concluded by tieing together the problems of Latin America and of the United States. "What," he asked, "is at the heart of all our national problems? It is that we have seen the hand of material interest sometimes about to close upon our dearest rights and possessions. We have seen material interests threaten constitutional freedom in the United States. Therefore we will now know how to sympathize with those in the rest of America who have to contend with such powers, not only within their borders but from outside their borders also."[19a] It was a noble promise, and if that promise was still in the process of being fulfilled a half century later, it was some indication that the United States was now beginning to move from a purely political and constitutional approach to national and international problems to one that took increased cognizance of economic and social realities, an approach that was increasingly concerned, not with the interests of a limited privileged class but with the needs and wants of the slowly emerging masses. With this address, Wilson was beginning to move from the policy of a New Freedom for America to the policy of a New Freedom for the world.

It was doubtless fitting that Wilson should have aimed his first important statement on foreign policy toward the countries of Latin America, for that was the area where, in the 1820's, Presi-

---

[19a] Baker and Dodd (eds.), *The New Democracy*, I, 66–68. For its background and significance, see Notter, *Origins*, pp. 266ff, and Baker, *Woodrow Wilson*, IV, 281ff.

dent Monroe had sought the first significant extension of the principles of self-government, self-determination, and nonintervention. But Wilson's speech at Mobile was only a beginning, and, little more than a year later, he was forced to stand by as the Great Powers of Europe plunged that continent, and soon the rest of the world, into mortal conflict.[20a]

Wilson's reaction to the outbreak of war seems, on the face of it, conventional enough, and it consisted not only of a neutrality proclamation issued in September 1914 but also of several missions to Europe by his most trusted aide, Colonel Edward M. House, whose instructions called for him to sound out the leading European statesmen concerning the prospects of a negotiated settlement.[21a] These missions, however, proved completely unsuccessful, and before long Wilson began to move toward a dramatic reformulation and extension of some of the most fundamental American principles of foreign policy.

As a New Historian, Wilson was concerned with political and social realities rather than with constitutional appearances.[22a] He doubtless knew, for instance, that ever since the era of the American Revolution, the growth of liberty in Europe had been a constant theme of American foreign policy. But it had also remained largely theoretical because the prevailing state of technology (including transportation) and the comparative economic, political, and military position of the United States—as well as a persistent isolationism—made any other course impracticable. Now, in the last twenty years, these factors had undergone a dramatic change. The United States had become one of the leading industrial powers of the world, and was continuing its amazing growth in human and economic terms. Its economic growth, moreover, had naturally projected it more intimately than ever into Far Eastern and European affairs, a process further intensified by the events and the aftermath of 1898.[23a]

Isolation as a national policy was now a technological, not

20a Baker, *Woodrow Wilson*, Vol. V (Garden City, 1935), Chap. 1, and Link, *Wilson*, Vol. III, Chap. 1.
21a For what House was expected to do, and what he actually did, see Ernest R. May, *The World War and American Isolation, 1914–1917* (Cambridge, Mass., 1959), *passim*, and Link, *Wilson*, Vol. IV (Princeton, 1964), esp. Chap. 4, both of which reveal the serious inadequacy of Charles Seymour's authorized *The Intimate Papers of Colonel House* (4 vols., Boston, 1926–1928), for many years, and for some people still, the standard source on Wilson and House, their work and relationship.
22a Cf. Holt (ed.), *American Historical Scholarship 1876–1901*, pp. 92, 93.
23a "It was a very big world into which this nation came when it was born," Wilson said in May 1916, "but it is a very little world now. It used to take as many days to go from Washington to Charlotte in those days as it now takes hours. I

merely a historical, absurdity. On the other hand, Wilson was too close a student of those great British political philosophers of the last two centuries—notably Edmund Burke, John Bright, John Stuart Mill, and William Ewart Gladstone[24a]—not to realize that the proper alternative to the abandonment of noninterventionism was not just a mindless plunge into the maelstrom of world politics. The United States, as he came to see it, had a historic role to play in the world, but it could play that role only by remaining true to its own principles of political and international conduct.

This was the historic consciousness out of which grew Wilson's most famous and important pronouncements on foreign policy from the spring of 1916 on. In the annals of American diplomacy there exist no more remarkable statements of the United States' role in world affairs than Wilson's address to the League to Enforce Peace, of May 1916—of which Harley Notter has rightly said that it was the most important American pronouncement on foreign policy since President Monroe's message to Congress in December 1823[25a]—and the address Wilson delivered to the Senate on this subject eight months later, in January 1917.

"We are participants," Wilson said in his address to the League to Enforce Peace, "whether we would or not, in the life of the world. The interests of all nations are our own also. We are partners with the rest. What affects mankind is inevitably our affair as well as the affair of the nations of Europe and of Asia." It was obvious, said the President, that the war was the result of "secret counsels and bitter rivalries," and that the future peace of the world depended on "a new and more wholesome diplomacy."

We believe these fundamental things: First, that every people has a right to choose the sovereignty under which they shall live. Like other nations, we have ourselves no doubt once and again offended against that principle when for a little while controlled by selfish passion as our franker historians have been honorable enough to admit; but it has become more and more our rule of life and action. Second, that the small states of the world have a right to enjoy the same respect for their sovereignty and for their territorial integrity that great and powerful nations expect and insist upon. And, third, that the world

---

heard an Irishman say, if the power of steam continued to increase in the next fifty years as it has in the last, we would get to Charlotte two hours before we left Washington." Baker and Dodd (eds.), *The New Democracy*, II (New York, 1926), 181.
   24a Cf. Notter, *Origins*, chaps. 1, 2, *passim*.
   25a Baker and Dodd, *The New Democracy*, II, 185–186, 187. For its background and significance, see Baker, *Woodrow Wilson*, VI (Garden City, 1937), 217ff; Notter, *Origins*, pp. 521ff; and Link, *Wilson*, V, 23ff.

has a right to be free from every disturbance of its peace that has its origin in aggression and disregard of the rights of peoples and nations.

In this speech the foreign policy of Jefferson and Monroe was brought to its penultimate conclusion; and what Wilson said in his address to Congress in January 1917—an address more often remembered for his use of the phrase "peace without victory"— spelled out his developing position even more unmistakably:

No peace can last, or ought to last, which does not recognize and accept the principle that governments derive all their just powers from the consent of the governed, and that no right anywhere exists to hand peoples about from sovereignty to sovereignty as if they were property. I take it for granted, for instance, if I may venture upon a single example, that statesmen everywhere are agreed that there should be a united, independent, and autonomous Poland, and that henceforth inviolable security of life, of worship, and of industrial and social development should be guaranteed to all peoples who have lived hitherto under the power of governments devoted to a faith and purpose hostile to their own.

Then the President came to the heart of his message:

In holding out the expectation that the people and Government of the United States will join the other civilized nations of the world in guaranteeing the permanence of peace upon such terms ... I speak with the greater boldness and confidence because it is clear to every man who can think that there is in this promise no breach in either our traditions or our policy as a nation, but a fulfilment, rather, of all that we have professed or striven for. I am proposing, as it were, that the nations should with one accord adopt the doctrine of President Monroe as the doctrine of the world: that no nation should seek to extend its polity over any other nation or people, but that every people should be left free to determine its own polity, its own way of development, unhindered, unthreatened, unafraid, the little along with the great and powerful.[26a]

Here, then, nearly a year before Wilson's philosophy of international diplomacy reached its final stage in the formulation of the Fourteen Points, we can seek a remarkable fusion of historical consciousness and foreign policy, a striking emphasis on the continuity of American diplomacy from its origins to the present; and whether the new Wilsonian diplomacy would ultimately become political reality or remain largely a noble vision of a better world,

26a Baker and Dodd, *The New Democracy*, II, 411, 413–414. For its background and significance, see Baker, *Wilson*, VI, 412ff, and Link, *Wilson*, V, 264ff.

America's position in international affairs could never be the same again.

Before long, however, Wilson spoke no longer as the head of the leading neutral government, but as the head of the most powerful combatant on either side of the conflict, and he soon recognized that transforming his vision of a new and better world order into concrete political reality would require the kind of specific and detailed research and planning that no government had ever carried on before. Much has been written concerning the circumstances under which the United States become involved in the Great War of 1914[27a] But more important perhaps—and certainly more instructive from our standpoint—is the question of how the United States prepared for the peace to come and why, in the end, the Wilsonian vision was not only politically and diplomatically defeated but also historically discredited.

"I am beginning to think," President Wilson wrote to Colonel House in September 1917, "that we ought to go systematically to work to ascertain as fully and precisely as possible just what the several parties to this war on our side of it will be inclined to insist upon as part of the final peace arrangements, in order that we may formulate our own position either for or against them and begin to gather the influences we can use."[28a] The result of Wilson's proposal—which had first been suggested to him by Felix Frankfurter, then a special assistant to the Secretary of War[29a]— was the establishment of an outstanding group of scholars, most of them historians, whose principal task was to help the President prepare for the crucial peace negotiations that lay ahead.[30a] Though headed by the ineffectual Sidney E. Mezes, House's brother-in-law and president of the College of the City of New York, but with the hard-driving Isaiah Bowman, then head of the American Geographical Society, as its guiding force, the Inquiry (or House Inquiry, as it was often called) symbolized a genuine fusion of historical scholarship and foreign-policy planning, an unprecedented liaison of historians and diplomats, for whose attention and use their researches were largely intended.

Numbering over a hundred, the Inquiry included some of the

27a See esp. the important and well-balanced account of May, *World War and American Isolation, 1914–1917.*
28a Lawrence E. Gelfand, *The Inquiry* (New Haven, 1963), pp. 26–27, quoting Baker, *Wilson,* VII, 254.
29a Gelfand, *The Inquiry,* pp. 23–24.
30a Cf. Gelfand, *The Inquiry, passim,* and James T. Shotwell, *At the Paris Peace Conference* (New York, 1937), Chap. 1.

country's most distinguished scholars—George Louis Beer, Archibald Cary Coolidge, Clive Day, William A. Dunning, William Scott Ferguson, Frank A. Golder, C. H. McIlwain, James T. Shotwell, and William L. Westermann—and some of its most promising younger ones—Austin P. Evans, Sidney B. Fay, Hetty Goldman, Robert J. Kerner, Robert H. Lord, William E. Lunt, Albert H. Lybyer, Frederick Merk, Samuel Eliot Morison, Parker T. Moon, Dana G. Munro, Wallace Notestein, Charles Seymour, Preston W. Slosson, and Lawrence D. Steefel.

Troubled intermittently by administrative uncertainty, the Inquiry nevertheless produced, over the next year, a massive and impressive collection of material.[31a] Its findings, it now seems generally agreed, exerted a considerable influence on President Wilson's Fourteen Points,[32a] and when the President sailed for Europe in December 1918 to attend the Paris Peace Conference, he took with him more than a dozen of the Inquiry's experts and many of its findings and reports.[33a] "Tell me what's right and I'll fight for it," Wilson told the experts on board the *George Washington.* "Give me a guaranteed position."[34a] Yet in the end this remarkable experiment aimed at fusing knowledge, scholarship, and foreign policy proved inadequate for the purpose—a brilliant failure that left many members of the Inquiry (including Walter Lippmann, who acted for a time as its secretary) and many other scholars throughout the country as deeply disillusioned as many of their countrymen.[35a]

What went wrong? The moving story of Wilson's initial triumph and ultimate tragedy, from his repeated efforts to bring about a negotiated settlement in 1915–1916 to the final defeat of the Paris peace treaty in 1920–1921, has often been told, and the debate about these crucial years of American diplomacy has shown little sign of abating. It is sometimes said—it was first argued by John Maynard Keynes, and has more recently been repeated by George F. Kennan, Hans J. Morgenthau, and by Walter Lippmann

31a For contrasting views of the Inquiry, see Arthur S. Link, *Journal of Modern History,* XXXVI (1964), 103–104, and Francis L. Loewenheim, *Journal of Southern History* XXX (1964), 124ff.

32a Gelfand, *The Inquiry,* Chap. 5.

33a One of the experts Wilson took along was Charles Seymour, whose posthumously published *Letters from the Paris Peace Conference* (ed. by Harold B. Whiteman Jr., New Haven, 1965) gave a revealing picture not only of the crossing and some of the Inquiry's later problems but also of how much Seymour left unsaid during his lifetime. See also Shotwell, *At the Peace Conference,* pp. 67ff.

34a Quoted in Gelfand, *The Inquiry,* p. 174.

35a Two historians who were not disillusioned—Charles H. Haskins and Robert H. Lord—recorded their views in *Some Problems of the Peace Conference* (Cambridge, Mass., 1920).

himself—that Wilson was simply too naïve, too idealistic, and also really too ignorant about European and Far Eastern conditions to understand what he was attempting to do or to realize his high-sounding objectives.[36a] That the President no doubt made his share of mistakes—both during the war and at the Peace Conference,[37a] as well as after his return home in July 1919—few historians would now deny, but to understand the bitter reaction not only of many scholars and intellectuals but also of the general public, we must go beyond this simplistic explanation.

To understand something of the enormous public let-down and cynicism that followed the Paris Peace Conference, we must look at another—much less publicized—role played by the historical profession and also by other scholars in the mobilization of national opinion against the Central Powers. There can be little doubt that much of the good work done by the scholars working for the House Inquiry was undone by other scholars working for the Committee of Public Information, known as the Creel Committee, after its director, George Creel.

The work of the Creel Committee was very different from that of the House Inquiry.[38a] Where the latter aimed at precise and, as far as possible, dispassionate studies of highly intricate and controversial political, economic, and social problems, the Creel Committee's task, real or imagined, was to whip up national enthusiasm for the war effort by providing for a steady outpouring of hysterically anti-German propaganda literature. Reading the vast body of material produced by the Creel Committee, it seems clear that only a few of its members—Carl Becker and Guy Stanton Ford notable among them[39a]—were able to withstand the pressure and circumstances of the time. Perhaps the best that can be said for the committee's numerous publications is that probably few reputable scholars would have attached their names to them in less frenetic times.[40a]

[36a] Cf. John Maynard Keynes, *The Economic Consequences of the Peace* (New York, 1920), pp. 43ff; Kennan, *American Diplomacy 1900–1950*, pp. 63ff; Hans J. Morgenthau, *In Defense of the National Interest* (New York, 1951), pp. 25ff; and Walter Lippmann, *U. S. Foreign Policy*, pp. 37ff.

[37a] Wilson's role at the Peace Conference can best be followed in the State Department's important documentary history, *The Paris Peace Conference, 1919* (13 vols., Washington, D.C., 1942–1947), and in Paul Mantoux (ed.), *Les Délibérations du Conseil des Quarte* (2 vols., Paris, 1955).

[38a] Cf. J. R. Mock and Cedric Larson, *Words that Won the War* (Princeton, 1939), Chap. 7. Creel told his story in *How We Advertised America* (New York, 1920) and *Rebel at Large* (New York, 1947).

[39a] Ford discussed his role in *On and Off the Campus* (Minneapolis, 1938), pp. 73–100.

[40a] Cf. Merle Curti, "The American Scholar in Three Wars," *Journal of the History of Ideas*, III (1942), and William T. Hutchinson, "The American Historian in Wartime," *Mississippi Valley Historical Review*, XXIX (1942).

Yet here lay one of the great tragedies of American scholarship. The origins of the war of 1914, like those of American intervention in the war, constitute an enormously complicated subject. By the early 1900's, and certainly by the time of the First World War, the historical profession in this country had achieved full intellectual maturity; it had also gained the justified respect and confidence of the country. It was an achievement not easily attained, one to be treasured, and certainly not to be misused for hyperpatriotism. Yet no one who read the Creel Committee's so-called historical publications—and they poured forth from the government printing presses by the millions—could fail to be more or less misinformed about the essential issues of war and peace. Indeed, the historians (and others associated with them in this work) did their task all too well. For when Wilson returned home, in July 1919, and urged speedy Senate approval of the peace treaty, it was a comparatively simple thing for Senator Henry Cabot Lodge and other opponents of the President, the treaty, and the League to appeal to all the jingoist Germanophobia whipped up only a short time before by some of the country's most distinguished scholars.[41a]

So the treaty failed in the Senate. It failed ultimately not only because of the spiteful antagonism of the Republican Right, desperate for a political issue to use against the President, but also because of the equally intransigent insistence of Wilson and a majority of Democrats, who affected to believe—though they surely knew better—that the treaty was, indeed, what Wilson had promised it would be: a peace without victory, a peace with justice. It cannot be said that the Senate hearings on the treaty, or the protracted debate that followed, or, finally, even some of Wilson's eloquent speeches in defense of the treaty, on his last swing around the country, shed much significant light on the causes of the war and on its ultimate meaning to the United States.[42a] It was the effort of the President and his supporters to defend the treaty item by item that revealed more starkly yet its tragic compromises—compromises about European frontiers, about future economic and colonial arrangements, and about the territorial integrity of China,

41a The dangerous Germanophobia was not stirred up only by the Creel Committee and its propaganda. Much of the damage was done by various highly respected historians working on their own. See, for instance, the highly inflammatory works of Charles D. Hazen, *Alsace Lorraine Under German Rule* (New York, 1917), and William Roscoe Thayer, *Germany Vs. Civilization* (Boston, 1916), and *Volley from a Non-Combatant* (New York, 1919).
42a For a critical account of the Senate debate on the treaty, see Holt, *Treaties Defeated by the Senate*, Chap. 11. Wilson's last speeches in its defense are in Ray Stannard Baker and William E. Dodd (eds.), *War and Peace* (New York, 1927).

whose loss of the Shantung Peninsula to Japan struck many people in the United States as a particularly repulsive violation of its historic friendship toward China, as well as a flagrant violation of Wilson's unqualified pledge that there be no territorial changes without the approval of the peoples concerned.[43a]

But worse was yet to come. No sooner had the Bolsheviks seized power in Russia, and the Hapsburgs and Hohenzollern dynasties been toppled, than there followed from Moscow, Vienna, and Berlin an unprecedented outpouring of diplomatic documents, most of them intended to show the comparative virtue of the issuing country, though the Bolsheviks naturally sought to blame all bourgeois and aristocratic governments, including their own.

The war between the Entente and the Central Powers was followed, then, by a battle of the historians, the Americans prominent among them.[44a] The battle raged for nearly twenty years. In the process a great deal of important documentary material came to light; and in defense of one position or another, there appeared some outstanding works, especially Sidney B. Fay's *The Origins of the World War* (1928), Bernadotte E. Schmitt's *The Coming of War, 1914* (1930)—both in two volumes—and the numerous works of George Peabody Gooch, which appeared throughout the 1920's and 1930's.[45a]

Professor Schmitt's work received the Pulitzer Prize in History in 1931, but it cannot be said that for all their vast learning and impressive argument, his books ultimately proved to be the most influential. That distinction, it now seems clear, belongs to Professor Fay, who had been among the first American historians to challenge publicly the Versailles indictment of Germany,[46a] and whose *Origins of the World War,* itself a massively documented account, closed with a telling and widely shared injunction: "The verdict of the Versailles Treaty that Germany and her allies were responsible for the War, in view of the evidence now available, is historically unsound. It should therefore be revised. However, because of the

[43a] The Far East had caused Wilson endless difficulty from the beginning of his administration. Cf. Notter, *Origins,* pp. 385–386, 402, 410–412; Link, *Wilson,* III, Chap. 9. See also Russell H. Fifield, *Woodrow Wilson and the Far East* (New York, 1952), and the earlier, still important, work of Stanley K. Hornbeck, *Contemporary Politics in the Far East* (New York, 1916).

[44a] The role of American scholarship and its political impact are well discussed by Selig Adler, "The War Guilt Question and American Disillusionment, 1918–1928," *Journal of Modern History,* XXIII (1951), *The Isolationist Impulse* (New York, 1957), and, more briefly, in *The Uncertain Giant, 1921–1941* (New York, 1965).

[45a] See esp. Gooch's *Franco-German Relations, 1871–1914* (London, 1928), *Recent Revelations in European Diplomacy* (4th ed., New York, 1930), and *Before the War* (2 vols., New York, 1936, 1938).

[46a] See his "New Light on the Origins of the World War," *American Historical Review,* XXV (July 1920), XXVI (Oct. 1920, July 1921).

popular feeling widespread in some of the Entente countries, it is doubtful whether a formal and legal revision is yet practicable. There must first come a further revision by historical scholars, and through them of public opinion."[47a]

Much of the best writing on the origins, immediate and more remote, of the Great War was the work of American historians— Eugene N. and Pauline R. Anderson, Ross J. S. Hoffman, Edward Mead Earle, Herbert Feis, Oron J. Hale, Ernst C. Helmreich, William L. Langer, Dwight E. Lee, and Robert H. Lord—and the distinction and balance of their scholarship gained them national and international recognition. Unfortunately, however, the reasoned work of these historians was once more overshadowed by the writings of strident partisans and propagandists. As the years passed there emerged in the United States an increasingly shrill literature of revisionism, which not only sought to place the greatest share of responsibility for the war upon France, Russia, and Great Britain but also saw the schemes of greedy munitions makers and other rapacious economic interests as having fomented the international anarchy that had come to its inevitable end in the summer of 1914.

From John K. Turner's *Shall It Be Again?* (1922), to Harry Elmer Barnes's *The Genesis of the World War—An Introduction to the Problem of War Guilt* (1926), to C. Hartley Grattan's *The Deadly Parallel* (1929), this literature grew steadily.[48a] After the crash of 1929 and the onset of the Great Depression, when national and international economic interests were naturally even more in disrepute, the earlier revisionist literature received powerful support from such equally popular and influential works as H. C. Engelbrecht's and F. C. Hanighen's *Merchants of Death* (1934), and Walter Millis' *Road to War* (1935), the latter having immediately become a Book-of-the-Month Club selection. "The 60,000 men and women who have bought this book," Professor R. J. Sontag wrote a few months later, "have been given enough—a too well disguised pacifist tract, a biased diplomatic history which will probably do no more than correct earlier no less biased views, a good introduction to the study of public opinion, and, above all, a very timely reminder of the hazards

---

47a II, 558.
48a For an incisive discussion of this literature, see Richard W. Leopold, "The Problem of American Intervention, 1917, An Historical Retrospect," *World Politics*, II (1950); Osgood, *Ideals and Self-Interest in American Foreign Relations*, pp. 131ff; and Eric F. Goldman, *Rendezvous with Destiny* (New York, 1952), pp. 235ff, 282, 375ff, which points out well the fateful connection between the New Historians' strong emphasis on economic factors and the postwar stress on the economic origins of the war. One of the progressive New Historians, whose judgments showed the most striking—and simplistic—continuity, was Charles A. Beard. See David W. Noble, *Historians Against History* (Minneapolis, 1965), Chap. 7.

of neutrality."[49a] All of these works emphasized in one form or another either the meaninglessness or the irrationality of the whole struggle, which had cost millions of lives and tens of billions of dollars, and had brought the world to the verge of international civil war.

This "revisionist" history, which went considerably beyond the position of professional scholars like Fay and Gooch, had a certain easy plausibility, and reinforced by the hardships of the depression, it seemed to make a mockery of all the earlier hopes and expectations that the war would, indeed, bring about a new and better world. This literature, moreover, did far more than merely destroy the memory and reputation of President Wilson. It bore bitter fruit in a more direct, immediate, and dangerous way; for this "revisionist" literature was widely accepted by the American Left of the 1930's,[50a] and much, perhaps most, of the agitation for stringent—and, as it turned out, dangerously self-defeating—"neutrality" legislation emanated from that sector of political opinion. Few men could question the sentiment that underlay such moral revulsion against war and military profiteering. But there can be little doubt either that the ultimate impact of such feeling on American foreign policy, from the 1920's up to and even beyond the Munich Crisis of 1938, was highly unfortunate to say the least. No legacy of the war was more embittering and dangerous than the last chapter, which was written by the historians and publicists, many of them in the United States.

Most unfortunately, these books on the origins of the war and on American intervention in the war that continued to roll off the press down to the late 1930's[51a] in large measure obscured the overriding issues of the war—issues that were most important to the United States between the end of the First World War and the beginning of the Second. The fact that Europe was on a long-term

---

[49a] *American Historical Review*, XLI (Jan. 1936), p. 363. "Millis's work," Selig Adler wrote later, "and that of his less able or more penetrating competitors, was picked up hungrily by old Wilson haters, Anglophobes, friends of the Third Reich, victims of the depression, and Marxists consecrated to the theory that capitalism breeds wars. It is almost superfluous to add that these new books made new converts to the isolationist cause" (*The Isolationist Impulse*, p. 258).

[50a] Cf. William E. Leuchtenburg, *Franklin D. Roosevelt and the New Deal, 1932–1940* (New York, 1963), Chap. 9, and Michael Wreszin, *Oswald Garrison Villard, Pacifist at War* (Bloomington, 1965), *passim*. *The Nation* and *The New Republic* both reviewed these "revisionist" works with almost unvarying praise and thus doubtless contributed further to the isolationist temper of the times.

[51a] See, for instance, James D. Squires, *British Propaganda at Home and in the United States from 1914 to 1917* (Cambridge, Mass., 1935); Edwin M. Borchard and William P. Lage, *Neutrality for the United States* (New Haven, 1937, 2nd ed. 1940); Alice M. Morrissey, *American Defense of Neutral Rights 1914–1917* (Cambridge, Mass., 1939); and Horace C. Peterson, *Propaganda for War* (Norman, 1939).

downward economic course (a point which Keynes had first discussed in *The Economic Consequences of the Peace,* a book that did enormous damage to the Wilsonian cause),[52a] that Great Britain and France (even with Russia's aid) could now barely contain the massive power of industrial Germany, that for these reasons alone the United States must henceforth join in a close, continuing transatlantic relationship to preserve the economic, political, and military stability of Europe and the rest of the world—such fundamental considerations were largely lost sight of.[53a]

Nor was there any significant change in such historical writing and political opinion when the Weimar Republic died and was replaced by the brutal Nazi tyranny—about whose ways and objectives, domestic and foreign, the diplomatic cables and the newspapers of the democratic states had a great deal to say. The year of Munich—1938—less than twelve months before the outbreak of hostilities in Europe, saw the appearance of one of the most important and influential works of American "revisionist" history, Charles Callan Tansill's *America Goes to War.*

"Long after the war was over," wrote Edward Mead Earle,

—with full benefit of reflection and documentation—the predominant opinion of American historians and publicists was that our course in 1917 was a mistaken course, that we should have remained out of the war . . . because it made no important difference to us which of the belligerents emerged victorious, provided either did. . . . We learned in the period between two wars that historical interpretation is no mere academic exercise conducted in an ivory tower. . . . Pacifist, isolationist and economic determinist philosophies played ducks and drakes with the truth. . . . As a result, some of our historical writing during the years 1919 to 1939 was not the truth, certainly not the whole truth, withal it was dressed up in the ·impressive regalia of scholarship. A good deal of historical teaching, as well as historical writing, was the direct cause, if not the only cause, of the cynicism and intellectual nihilism which determined the climate of our university campuses for twenty years.[54a]

52a Keynes, *The Economic Consequences of the Peace,* Chap. 2.
53a There is little doubt that Walter Lippmann is quite right in saying that Wilson's failure to discuss such overriding political and strategic questions was a most serious mistake. See *U. S. Foreign Policy,* pp. 33ff. But this failure was not Wilson's alone, and most historians (and political scientists and economists) who should have known better, and in many cases doubtless did, likewise said nothing about such troubling questions either, preferring to devote themselves instead to the wearisome debates about "war guilt" and reparations, and thus contributing their share to the intellectual disintegration of the Atlantic Alliance.
54a Edward Mead Earle, "A Half-Century of American Foreign Policy—Our Stake in Europe, 1898–1948," *Political Science Quarterly,* LXVI (June 1949), 181ff. With characteristic frankness Professor Earle added in a footnote (p. 184): "Lest it be thought that I am a common scold, I sadly plead *mea culpa* to some, although not all, of these crimes and misdemeanors."

It was little wonder that Woodrow Wilson and everything he represented in the great tradition of American foreign policy seemed largely disgraced and discredited. The anti-Wilsonian legend was fed, moreover, by not a few men who had formerly been close to the President. The most prominent of these was Secretary of State Robert Lansing, whose autobiographical writings, widely used against his late chief, revealed openly his frequent disapproval of the President's general goals and objectives, disapproval that led him on several occasions, including at the Paris Peace Conference, to act against the President's explicit wishes.[55a]

The anti-Wilsonian legend was further reinforced by the voluminous writings of Charles Seymour,[56a] a Yale University historian (later its president), to whom Colonel House had entrusted his extensive personal records. Seymour used these as the basis of a remarkable four-volume work, *The Intimate Papers of Colonel House* (1926–1928), which artfully described his career and gained general acceptance as a completely accurate and reliable account. This account, it later turned out, when the House papers at last became available to other scholars, was full of omissions and misconstructions, largely designed to protect House's reputation and, where necessary, to discredit that of Wilson and his cause. But nothing did more damage to the President's reputation than the unfortunate, misguided, and wholly unnecessary refusal of his widow, Edith Bolling Wilson, to permit reasonable access to her husband's records, which made it impossible, until recently, for the President's own version of these crucial years to be fully known.[57a]

Wilson's close friends and associates—Raymond Fosdick, for instance—understood perfectly well that there was an important difference between the nobility of Wilson's goals and objectives and the inadequate means he sometimes used to attain them. "No, I think you are wrong," he wrote, in February, 1924, to Dr. Abraham Flexner, with whom he had corresponded for years about Wilson, the Treaty, and the League.

It seems to me that you are confusing the work of Wilson as a prophet

[55a] See his *The Peace Negotiations* (Boston, 1921), *The Big Four and Others of the Peace Conference* (New York, 1921), and *War Memoirs* (New York, 1935).
[56a] See also his *American Diplomacy During the World War* (Baltimore, 1934) and *American Neutrality, 1914–1917* (New Haven, 1935). What Seymour thought of the origins of the war he made clear at the end of his *The Diplomatic Background of the War 1870–1914* (New York, 1916). "The invasion of Belgium and the participation of Great Britain in the war was thus the inevitable result of Germany's forcing of war upon Russia and France. The aggressive character of her diplomacy all through the crisis of 1914 resulted with almost equal directness from the policy she had followed since 1871" (pp. 285–286).
[57a] The serious difficulties of working from closely held or otherwise severely restricted source materials are indicated, in part, in Link's generous introduction to the second edition of his *Wilson—The Diplomatist* (Baltimore, 1963) and *Wilson*, V, viii–ix.

and teacher on the one hand, and, on the other, the particular technique through which he attempted to put his ideas into effect. His technique was often faulty, but the ideals he stood for represent, to my way of thinking, a new hope for the future. He stood at a cross-road in history and pointed out a new path. What you are objecting to is the method he used in pointing. You say that his tactics in getting the race to follow on the new path were wrong. I grant you that they were not always right, but I come back to this: that he *pointed the way*.[58a]

The Wilsonians, alas, could never change the terms of debate. More and more, as the years went on, the debate tended to be about Wilson the man, not Wilson the philosopher of international peace. More and more, the public and the politicians and—as Edward Mead Earle was to point out later—the historians too were primarily concerned not with what Wilson and the United States had hoped to achieve in the war, but why they had become involved in the war in the first place. It soon turned into bitter, sterile debate—a debate from which, it must be said, the country has never really recovered. For the questions that Wilson posed so movingly in his great speeches remain unresolved: Must the world be made safe for democracy? How can the United States live securely in peace with freedom and unfreedom confronting each other all over the globe?

In any case the U.S. Senate having first repudiated Wilson's peace settlement (which for all its shortcomings was far preferable to its alternative), a good many historians and popular writers now set to work repudiating the general principles and underlying philosophy that had given the United States some of its greatest hours in world history. In the writings on nearly every important period and aspect of American diplomatic history the "isolationist" school was on the ascent; everywhere the spirit of commitment, of international responsibility, was on the defensive.

Probably the best example of the new "isolationist" school of history was Charles A. Beard. A passionate Jeffersonian, he was also very much aware of the close connection between domestic and foreign policy. "War," he quoted Jefferson, "had transformed the kings of Europe into maniacs and the countries of Europe into madhouses while peace had 'saved' to the world the only plant of free and rational government now existing in it." Corruption and tyranny, in his opinion, flowed from armed conflicts, whereas "peace, prosperity, liberty and morals have an intimate connection." Yet Jefferson was

---

58a *Letters on the League of Nations from the Files of Raymond B. Fosdick*, pp. 141–142 (emphasis in original).

forced into war. "The fateful course of events in Europe, beyond the will and purpose of Jefferson, . . . drew him and his immediate followers into domestic policies more autocratic and sweeping than Hamilton's boldest enterprise; hurried them, pacific as they were in intention, into a struggle not of their own deliberate making; compelled them to resort to hated measures of revenue and finance."[59a]

It was not long before Beard thought he saw all the old storm signals rise again. "Confronted by the difficulties of a deepening domestic crisis and by the comparative ease of a foreign war," he wrote in February, 1935, "what will President Roosevelt do? . . . Judging by the past history of American politicians," Beard concluded, "he will choose the latter."[60a] Indeed, Beard's isolationism grew more passionate with every passing year.

"The lines of the Wilsonian creed of world interventionism and adventurism," he wrote scornfully in September, 1939, "are in substance:

Imperialism is bad (well, partly); every nation must have a nice constitutional government, more or less like ours; if any government dislikes the settlement made at Versailles it must put up its guns and sit down with its well-armed neighbors for a "friendly" conference; trade barriers are to be lowered and that will make everybody round the globe prosperous (almost, if not entirely); . . . everything in the world is to be managed as decorously as a Baptist convention presided over by the Honorable Cordell Hull; if not, we propose to fight disturbers everywhere (well, nearly everywhere).[61a]

But Beard was not alone in his growing revulsion against seeing the United States once more deeply involved in international affairs. Many younger historians who came to maturity in the 1930's felt the same way. Not only were Albert K. Weinberg's *Manifest Destiny* (1935) and A. W. Griswold's *Far Eastern Policy of the United States* (1938)[62a] important scholarly works in their own right, but their tone

59a Howard K. Beale, "Charles Beard—Historian," in Beale (ed.), *Charles A. Beard* (Lexington, 1954), p. 137, quoting *The Rise of American Civilization*, I (New York, 1927), 402, 407. For the development of Beard's historical relativism see *A Foreign Policy for America* (New York, 1940). See also Goldman, *Rendezvous with Destiny*, pp. 235–236; George R. Leighton, "Beard and Foreign Policy," in Beale (ed.), *Charles A. Beard*, pp. 161ff; and Bernard C. Borning, *The Political and Social Thought of Charles A. Beard*, pp. 106ff and 236ff.

60a "National Politics and War," *Scribner's Magazine*, XCVII (Feb. 1935), p. 70.

61a Charles A. Beard, "Giddy Minds and Foreign Quarrels," *Harper's*, CLXXIX (Sept. 1939), p. 340.

62a Griswold's book, recently republished in paperback form, had especially great impact. Opposing the earlier standard views of Tyler Dennett, A. L. P. Dennis, and Payson J. Treat, all of whom had argued the essential continuity of American policy in the Far East over the past century, Griswold, in effect, contended that the United States had no genuine interest in the Far East, had become politically involved in that part of the world largely by accident (and a vague proposal—the Open Door note—

and orientation suited the spirit of the times perfectly. It would be difficult to exaggerate the influence of such writings. But when their full impact was ultimately felt—as it was after the fall of France and during the Battle of Britain—the reaction in many informed quarters was bitter indeed.

The postwar generation of hard-boiled "realists," Walter Lippmann wrote in the *New York Herald Tribune* in June 1940, "[has] been duped by a falsification of American history. They have been miseducated by a swarm of innocent but ignorant historians, by reckless demagogues, and by foreign interests, into believing that America entered that other war because of British propaganda, the loans of the bankers, the machination of President Wilson's advisors, and the drummed-up patriotic ecstasy. They have been told to believe that anyone who challenges this explanation of 1917 and insists that America was defending American vital interests is himself a victim or an agent of British propaganda."[63a]

By then it was nearly too late to undo the damage. The historians, among others, had done their work too well and there can be little doubt that the desperate condition of the Atlantic civilization at that time was in large part the tragic result of historical misinterpretation.

IV

It would be pleasant to think that more recent years—the era since the Second World War—have been free of the bitter, divisive, and dangerous historical controversies that so fanned popular discontent and stimulated a new American isolationism between the two world wars. Unfortunately this has not been the case. On the contrary, it is one of the ironies of recent American history that Franklin D. Roosevelt, who in the 1930's was so hemmed in by the contemporary isolationist spirit, was after 1945 the subject of vitriolic charges of hell-bent "interventionism" and near-responsibility for Pearl Harbor, too. Indeed, there can be little doubt that American politics since 1945 has been poisoned by a new wave of historical

---

drawn up by a former British commercial official), and should, presumably, avoid all possible commitments there in the future. Griswold's work continues to be widely read and has evidently had considerable influence on, among others, George F. Kennan.

63a Quoted in Hans Kohn, *American Nationalism* (New York, 1961 ed.), pp. 224–225. Lippmann himself, however, had contributed his share to the intellectual uncertainty he now deplored. Gripped by much the same disillusionment that beset many historians and intellectuals after Versailles, he had written soon after that the only thing he himself was now sure of was that "a war was fought and won by a multitude of efforts, stimulated, no one knows in what proportion, by the motives of Wilson and the motives of [George] Harvey and all kinds of hybrids of the two." (*Public Opinion* [New York, 1922], p. 194.)

"revisionism"—of the Right and (more recently) of the Left—even more vicious and irresponsible than the "revisionism" of the inter-war years, and, like that earlier movement, also set on discovering scapegoats, scandals, and even treason in the highest places.

The great marvel of American diplomacy since the Second World War, as Professor Louis Morton points out elsewhere in this volume, was the remarkably effective response of American foreign policy to the growing challenge of Communist expansion in Europe, the Middle East, and ultimately the Far East. Though the official diplomatic dispatches for this period are not yet available to the historian, there can be little doubt that this policy was carried out in response to full and regular reports on the new international challenge—reports of the kind that had reached President Roosevelt a generation before, without any corresponding action on his part.[64a]

The response of President Truman was markedly different from that of his predecessor. Where President Roosevelt had found no legal basis for coming to the assistance of France during the Rhineland crisis of March 1936;[65a] where he had steadfastly refused to allow the Spanish government to purchase arms in the United States to defend itself against international fascist aggression;[66a] where he had congratulated Neville Chamberlain as he prepared to fly to Munich to seal the doom of Czechoslovakia;[67a] and where he had long shied away from endorsing a national selective-service law during the

[64a] For the remarkable record of American diplomatic reporting in this period, see the volumes in the documentary series *Foreign Relations of the United States* (Washington, D.C., 1949–1956), to which should be added William E. Dodd, Jr., and Martha Dodd (eds.), *Ambassador Dodd's Diary 1933–1938* (New York, 1941), the troubled record of the University of Chicago historian of the Old South, who was Roosevelt's first ambassador in Berlin, and Claude G. Bowers, *My Mission to Spain* (New York, 1954), by the distinguished biographer of Jefferson, who served as American ambassador during the Spanish "civil war."

[65a] *Foreign Relations of the United States, 1936* (Washington, D.C., 1953), I, 217, 218, 228.

[66a] *Foreign Relations of the United States, 1936*, II (Washington, D.C., 1954), 437ff; *1937*, II (Washington, 1954), 215ff; *1938*, I (Washington, 1955), 149ff; and *1939*, II (Washington, 1956), 715ff. When Bowers returned to Washington in March 1939, Roosevelt admitted to him, "We have made a mistake; you have been right all along." (Bowers, *My Mission to Spain*, p. 418). Bowers was only one of Roosevelt's ambassadors who consistently warned him what was afoot in Europe at the time. "My own impression is," he had written in July 1937, "that with every surrender beginning long ago with China, followed by Abyssinia and then Spain, the fascist powers, with vanity inflamed, will turn without delay to some other country—such as Czechoslovakia—and that with every surrender the prospects of a European war grow darker." (Quoted in Leuchtenburg, *Franklin D. Roosevelt and the New Deal, 1932–1940*, p. 224.)

[67a] *Foreign Relations of the United States, 1938*, I, 688. Upon hearing that Chamberlain was flying to Munich the following day to meet there with Hitler, Mussolini, and Daladier, the President sent him a warm congratulatory message: "Good Man. Signed Franklin D. Roosevelt." After the Munich conference, he wrote William Phillips, the American ambassador in Rome, "I want you to know that I am not a bit upset over the final result" (Elliott Roosevelt [ed.], *FDR—His Personal Letters, 1928–1945*, II [New York, 1950], 818).

election campaign of 1940,[68a] President Truman—confronted with the possible disintegration of the Democratic party, a vocal part of which seemed to regard Communist imperialism as a smaller threat than American action to meet that imperialism—recalled the tragic history of the previous decade and acted speedily and, on the whole, with remarkable effectiveness to meet the country's great new responsibilities.[69a]

Indeed, it is not too much to say that Truman's policies—from his initial insistence upon Russian withdrawal from Iran in 1946, to the Greek-Turkish aid program, the Marshall Plan, the North Atlantic Treaty Organization, and the military defense of the Republic of Korea—were, indeed, the ultimate and logical conclusion of traditional American foreign policy.[70a] If that policy had been for more than a century and a half a policy of encouraging, promoting, and supporting the principles of self-government, self-determination, and nonintervention in the affairs of other lands, then it followed that since the United States was now not only the most powerful but also perhaps the only powerful democratic nation in the world, it should embark on the kind of diplomacy that President Truman set forth in his historic address to Congress in March 1947.

"At the present moment in world history," the President said,

nearly every nation must choose between alternative ways of life. The choice is too often not a free one. One way of life is based upon the will of the majority, and is distinguished by free institutions, representative government, free elections, guarantees of individual liberty, freedom of speech and religion, and freedom from political oppression. The second way of life is based upon the will of the minority forcibly imposed upon the majority. It relies upon terror and oppression, a controlled press and radio, fixed elections, and the suppression of personal freedoms.

I believe that it must be the policy of the United States to support free peoples who are resisting attempted subjugation by armed minorities or by outside pressures. I believe that we must assist free peoples to work out their destinies in their own way.... The seeds of totalitarian regimes are nurtured by misery and want. They spread and grow in

68a William L. Langer and S. Everett Gleason, *The Challenge to Isolation 1937–1940* (New York, 1952), pp. 680ff.

69a During most of the postwar period, from 1945 to about 1950, *The Nation* and *The New Republic* strenuously opposed Truman's foreign policy, in Europe as well as in the Far East, and the efforts to supplant him as the Democratic candidate in 1948 were in large part the result of such opposition to his foreign policy. In this respect, then, the general editorial position of these journals has changed little since the 1930's and 1940's.

70a For a perceptive historical appreciation, see Carl N. Degler, "The Great Revolution in American Foreign Policy," *Virginia Quarterly Review*, XXXVIII (Summer 1962).

the evil soil of poverty and strife. They reach their full growth where the hope of a people for a better life has died. We must keep that hope alive. The free peoples of the world look to us for support in maintaining their freedom. If we falter in this leadership, we may endanger the peace of the world—and we shall surely endanger the welfare of this nation.[71a]

This policy soon became known as the Truman Doctrine. Now that this policy has been an integral part of American diplomacy for over a generation, now that it has in some respects become generally accepted and in certain other circles become the target of renewed criticism, it is important that this policy—and all that it implies for American diplomacy in Europe, in the Middle East and Africa, and in the Far East—be given its proper place in the great tradition of American foreign policy.[72a]

Although now generally accepted as sound and correct, the Truman Doctrine was at the time much criticized by many members of the President's own party and by certain leading political commentators —including Walter Lippmann—who, nearly twenty years later, now accept that policy fully, at least as adequate for that particular period.[73a] It should also be remembered—and this makes the formulation of the Truman Doctrine and of the policies based upon it an even more remarkable achievement—that these policies were formulated and carried out against a background of some of the most bitterly partisan debates in American history. If there was ever a period in recent American history when there was no real consensus on the place of America in world affairs or the circumstances that had brought the United States to its present condition, the immediate postwar years were such a period.[74a]

These debates, which went on for more than a decade and in certain quarters are still carried on, were both historical and political.

[71a] For a text of President Truman's address, see Commager (ed.), *Documents of American History*, II, no. 574. For the background of the President's address and his remarkable historical perception of the situation, see *Memoirs by Harry S. Truman*, II (New York, 1956), pp. 101ff.

[72a] Cf. Earle, "A Half-Century of American Foreign Policy," pp. 173–174, 175, 187. "Our present policies," wrote Professor Earle in 1949, "proclaim, as we have so frequently proclaimed in the past, that we have a sympathetic concern with the cause of freedom in the European world; but here again they go farther and (unlike President Monroe's declarations concerning Greece in 1822 and 1823) make it clear that we intend to translate that concern into political and economic support."

[73a] Walter Lippmann, "The American Ordeal," *Newsweek*, April 5, 1966.

[74a] If there was any kind of national consensus on foreign policy after the middle-late 1940's, it was probably less the result of the cogent arguments of Truman and other top government officials than of the continuing intransigence of the Soviet Union, which from its refusal to join the Marshall Plan in 1947 down to the outbreak of the Korean War destroyed all prospects of restoring the spirit of the wartime alliance and resolving the outstanding problems of East and West.

They began, soon after the defeat of Germany and Japan, with the politically inspired congressional investigation of the Japanese attack on Pearl Harbor—an attack, some politicians, publicists, and even a few historians seemed to suggest, that was actually desired, if not instigated, by Roosevelt, so that he could at long last involve the United States in the Second World War.[75a] There followed soon after a new debate about an alleged American (meaning again largely Roosevelt) "sell-out" to Russia at the Yalta Conference of early 1945;[76a] not long after that a venomous debate began, which spilled over into the presidential campaign of 1952, concerning American responsibility for the Communist victory in the Chinese civil war[77a]— a genuine civil war, in which President Truman had honored historic American foreign policy by not intervening militarily.

In the course of these debates the United States saw some of its most highly placed and respected political leaders attempting to rewrite the recent history of American diplomacy and to use these tragic events—and the deep passions they naturally aroused—to advance their own partisan purposes. "This is not history, but politics," wrote Hanson W. Baldwin, the military correspondent of *The New York Times* and no uncritical admirer of Roosevelt's diplomatic and foreign policies, "a particularly reptilian form of politics which would have us believe that our mistakes at Teheran, Yalta, and above all in our politico-strategic policies were part of a Great Conspiracy intended to hand the country over to Communism on a silver platter. The more quickly such drivel is dismissed the better; we should be able to recognize, pinpoint, and examine the mistakes of the past without indulging in generalized judgments condemnatory to the sincerity, patriotism, and integrity of all who played a role on the stage of history." [78a]

There can be little doubt that these (largely) Republican attacks on Roosevelt's foreign policy gained considerable reinforcement from the apparent disinclination of the late President's staunch supporters to admit any serious shortcomings in recent American foreign

75a See above, p. 3, note 10.

76a For a convenient, now somewhat dated, survey of the important literature on Yalta, see Richard F. Fenno, Jr. (ed.), *The Yalta Conference* (Boston, 1955), and also the discerning essays in John L. Snell (ed.), *The Meaning of Yalta* (Baton Rouge, 1956).

77a Cf. Pichon P. Y. Loh (ed.), *The Kuomintang Debacle* (Boston, 1965). "Not since Washington had assumed the duties of office in 1789," Norman A. Graebner has written, "has an event beyond the immediate involvement of the United States produced such extensive and vituperative debate as the fall of Chiang Kai-shek" (*The New Isolationism* [New York, 1956], p. 32).

78a Graebner, *The New Isolationism*, p. 44, quoting Hanson W. Baldwin, "Churchill Was Right," *The Atlantic Monthly*, July 1954.

policy;[79a] and there was not a little irony in the fact that it was the State Department's publication of its principal documents on the Yalta Conference—ordered by Secretary of State Dulles shortly after he came into office—that almost immediately took the wind out of the frequently repeated charges concerning gravely myopic or even treasonous American policy at the time of the second and last Roosevelt-Churchill-Stalin conferences.[80a]

Now that these debates—about the attack on Pearl Harbor, about the Communist triumph in China, and about the wartime summit conferences—have been largely stilled; now that the historical profession in the United States is engaged in a monumental project to publish the papers of the Founding Fathers and many other of the country's great political leaders; now that the revealing papers of Woodrow Wilson and many of his close associates are becoming available,[81a] and many other important facets of American diplomatic history are undergoing careful re-examination, one might hope that we could look forward to a more dispassionate assessment of the great tradition of American foreign policy and the meaning of that tradition in our own revolutionary age.

This does not, however, seem to be the case. As noted at the beginning of this essay, the very foundations of American foreign policy are under serious attack and if we examine more closely the nature of that criticism, we shall find that it is tied closely with a growing uncertainty and confusion over just what the tradition of American foreign policy is. In other words, the political division, the lack of

[79a] One of the most intriguing problems of the President's wartime diplomacy is the extent to which his policy toward the Soviet Union, especially his policy of promising military assistance to Russia immediately after the Nazi attack in June 1941, was the result of his own personal experiences and historical reflection. Since he served as Assistant Secretary of the Navy in the Wilson administration, it would be interesting to know to what degree his policies reflected Wilson's concern, in 1917, to keep Russia in the war, and to what extent Roosevelt reflected on Wilson's failure to require the Allied Powers to accept his war aims as a prerequisite for military assistance in 1917–1918. Cf. William L. Langer and S. Everett Gleason, *The Undeclared War, 1940–1941* (New York, 1953), pp. 787–798, 818ff; and Marvin D. Bernstein and Francis L. Loewenheim, "Aid to Russia—The First Year," in Harold Stein (ed.), *American Civil Military Decisions* (University, Ala., 1963), p. 120.

[80a] *The Conferences at Malta and Yalta, 1945* (Washington, D.C., 1955), ed. by William M. Franklin *et al.,* was the first of the important series of documentary volumes on the history of the wartime summit conferences, published by the outstandingly competent scholars of the Historical Office of the State Department. The second volume in the series, the massive and equally impressive two-volume collection *The Conference of Berlin (The Potsdam Conference), 1945,* ed. by G. M. Richardson Dougall *et al.,* appeared in 1960, and the third, *The Conference at Cairo and Tehran, 1943,* ed. by Franklin *et al.,* appeared in 1961. It is expected that additional documentary volumes on the important conferences at Casablanca and Quebec (1943, 1944) will be published in the near future.

[81a] *The Papers of Woodrow Wilson,* ed. by Arthur S. Link *et al.,* began appearing in the fall of 1966, and are being accompanied by supplementary volumes incorporating the important papers of some of the other leading political figures of this period, the first volume consisting of Raymond B. Fosdick's invaluable *Letters on the League of Nations,* cited above.

a prevailing consensus on foreign policy, is based in the first instance upon serious, even fundamental, differences of historical interpretation. Or, to put it another way, one of the principal reasons why the country seems, at the moment at least, to be experiencing so intense and divisive a debate about current American foreign policy is due in large measure to disagreements about the nature of the great tradition of this policy, the continuity of that tradition in the twentieth century, and how it should be applied in the contemporary world. This fundamental disagreement can best be illustrated, perhaps, by a brief look at the positions of three leading diplomatic commentators—George Kennan, Walter Lippmann, and Hans Morgenthau. While their personal backgrounds and intellectual development have been different, their present positions, as these have developed over a period of years, tell us a good deal about the fundamental relationship between historical consciousness and foreign policy.

It was Kennan, of course, then a comparatively little-known member of the new Policy Planning Staff of the State Department, who in an article, published anonymously in *Foreign Affairs* in July 1947, first stated explicitly the intellectual foundations of the new containment policy that lay at the heart of the Truman Docrine.[82a] It seems all the more surprising and important, therefore, that following nearly thirty years of distinguished diplomatic service, and after having written several widely acclaimed books on American foreign policy, he should now reveal himself, as he has on a number of recent occasions, as a sharp and incisive critic of current American diplomacy.

Yet if we take a closer look at the evolution of Kennan's historical opinions, at his interpretation of the American past as it can be traced from a number of his well-known books and other published remarks, it becomes evident that his current position is not surprising after all. While in the public mind Kennan has always been associated primarily with a policy that sought to take to its logical conclusion the historic American position of encouraging and supporting the spread and growth of constitutional, democratic, and liberal governments throughout the world, in fact he seems never to have had much faith in this particular philosophy of American foreign policy.

A deeply thoughtful, reflective, and sensitive man, Kennan was

---

82a "The Sources of Soviet Conduct," *Foreign Affairs*, XXV (July 1947).

born, it should be remembered, a decade before the outbreak of the First World War, that his formative years were overshadowed first by the enormous Wilsonian enthusiasm and then by the drastic deflation of that enthusiasm, that he entered the Foreign Service in the mid-1920's, a time when the hopes of building a new and better world upon the principles of idealism and morality were seemingly shattered for good, when the earlier noble efforts of Bryan and others to bring about a more peaceful world through international law were being imitated by mockeries such as the Kellogg-Briand Pact,[83a] and when the whole world was paying little attention to its growing economic and social problems—problems about which President Wilson had become increasingly concerned in the last years of his administration.

That Kennan did not share the underlying assumptions of this foreign policy first became clear in the Walgreen Lectures he delivered at the University of Chicago in 1950, which, subsequently published under the title *American Diplomacy 1900–1950*, have become one of the most widely read books on modern American diplomacy. The purpose of these lectures, as Kennan said, was "an attempt to look back from a present full of uncertainty and controversy and unhappiness, to see whether a study of the past will not help us to understand some of our present predicaments."[84a] Kennan evidently believed that such a historical approach to American foreign policy would be fruitful, and his lectures made it amply clear that he did not like what he saw in the record of the last half century.

Summing up his position, he said,

I see the most serious fault of our past policy formulation to lie in something that I might call the legalistic-moralistic approach to international problems. This approach runs like a red skein through our foreign policy of the last fifty years. It has in it something of the old emphasis on arbitration treaties, something of the Hague Conferences and schemes for universal disarmament, something of the more ambitious American concepts of the role of international law, something of the League of

[83a] Kennan is perhaps too harsh in lumping together the Bryan, Hay, Knox, and Root treaties on the one hand, and the Kellogg-Briand Pact on the other. Before 1914 there was some reason to believe that the Great (and lesser) Powers would take such treaties with the seriousness they deserved; after the First World War that hope was largely gone; and the hopes and energies that were wasted on the Kellogg-Briand Pact (and on some other new American arbitration treaties) would no doubt have been much better expended on improving the international economic climate, which proved so decisive in 1929 and after.

[84a] Kennan, *American Diplomacy 1900–1950*, p. 55. This and subsequent quotations from this work are reprinted by permission of the University of Chicago Press, © 1951 by The University of Chicago.

Nations and the United Nations, something of the Kellogg Pact . . . something of the belief in World Law and World Government.[85a]

And Kennan went on from there to excoriate the Open Door Policy in China and the broad range of American foreign policy from the First World War to the Second, the general theme of his remarks being that American foreign policy, both in the Far East and in Europe, was blinded by irrelevant considerations of ideology rather than informed by the evident needs for a continuing balance of power in various parts of the world. Kennan, it soon became clear, had no use whatever for President Wilson's view of international affairs, and he saw some of America's most serious subsequent problems in foreign policy stemming directly from the grave errors of that time—none of these more egregious than what Kennan called the illusory and dangerous insistence upon "total victory" and "unconditional surrender."

But where in his lectures at the University of Chicago Kennan had confined himself largely to the history of the last fifty years, in his Stafford Little Lectures, delivered at Princeton University in March 1954, his attack now covered the whole range of American foreign policy as it had developed since the eighteenth century. He denied, for instance, that the young Republic had "any real sense of responsibility for the trend of international life outside our borders."[86a] And he saw in "a rural America, an unmechanical America, an America of the barefoot boy and the whitewashed board fence . . . the America of the Webster cartoon" the real roots of its "exclusiveness and provincialism and an intellectual remoteness from the feelings and preoccupations of mankind generally.[87a]

From this view of the relation of society and diplomacy from Washington to Wilson, Kennan passed on to what he considered the cardinal error of American foreign policy. This error, he declared, elaborating on his Walgreen Lectures, was the attempt to inject morality into an area where it had no place—the realm of international affairs. "We Americans," he declared,

have evolved certain concepts of a moral and ethical nature which we like to consider as being characteristic of the spirit of our civilization. I have never considered or meant to suggest that we should not be concerned for the observation of these concepts in the methods we

85a *Ibid.*, p. 95.
86a George F. Kennan, *Realities of American Foreign Policy* (Princeton, 1954; 2nd ed., New York, 1966), p. 103. This and other quotations from this work are reprinted by permission of Princeton University Press, © 1954, 1966 by Princeton University Press.
87a *Ibid.*, pp. 109, 110.

select for the promulgation of our foreign policy. Let us, by all means, conduct ourselves at all times in such a way as to satisfy our own ideas of morality. But let us do this as a matter of obligation to ourselves, and not as a matter of obligation to others. . . . let us not assume that our moral values, based as they are on the specifics of our national tradition and the various religious outlooks represented in our country, necessarily have validity for people everywhere. In particular, let us not assume that the *purposes* of states, as distinct from the methods, are fit subjects for measurement in moral terms.[88a]

This is not to say that Kennan had any illusions about the Communist system or its prevailing attitude toward the West. He did not. He had no doubt about "the congenital and deep-seated hostility of the Soviet regime to . . . the western world . . . and particularly to the United States." This antagonism was rooted, for the most part, he said, in "the ideological prejudice entertained by the Soviet leaders long before they seized power in Petrograd in 1917."[89a] He had no doubt either about the subtlety, as well as the complexity, of the Communist challenge. "Of all the hopes in the Soviet breast," he said, ". . . the ones most formidable to us, center around this prospect for sowing disunity everywhere in the western camp, and particularly in every relationship that has anything to do with western strength. That means disunity within our own country as between classes, and races, and outlooks. It means disunity between ourselves and our allies. It means the disruption of the confidence of others in us. It means, above all, the disruption of our confidence in ourselves."[90a]

Nor did Kennan—who by the time he delivered these lectures had had a brief and unhappy ambassadorship in Moscow (a mission that ended abruptly when the Soviet government took umbrage at certain unflattering remarks he made about conditions in Russia at a stopover in Berlin while on a trip west)—have much hope that this deep-seated hostility and suspicion could soon or readily be removed. "We must recognize Soviet hostility," he said, "as something reflecting a deep historical and political logic; and we must not be moved by the silly suggestions, recurring from time to time in western opinion, that this hostility might easily be made to disappear if some of our statesmen were to make themselves personally agreeable to the Soviet leaders. This is a hostility that will not be caused to disappear by either cocktail or the vodka glass."[91a]

88a *Ibid.*, p. 47.
89a *Ibid.*, p. 68.
90a *Ibid.*, p. 71.
91a *Ibid.*, p. 69.

But it was one thing to analyze without false illusions the nature of our foreign adversary, and quite another to prescribe the principles upon which a proper response could be based. And here Kennan did not escape the logic of his previous position. As he had emphasized on previous occasions and was to do again many times in the future, if the United States did not, in fact, have a great tradition in foreign policy that it could fall back on, if there did not exist certain fundamental, continuing principles that had animated that policy over nearly two centuries and had on the whole guided it with remarkable success, then it followed that the best the United States could do in the contemporary world was to follow a policy of self-effacement and circumspection, devoting itself more fully to its myriad domestic problems, of which Kennan was acutely conscious and made frequent mention.[92a]

Ultimately, wrote Kennan, our principal task in the realm of foreign policy lies not abroad, but at home:

What seems to me to be of first and vital importance is something that we Americans have to do for ourselves and by ourselves, and that is to render our country fit and eligible for the sort of adjustment our foreign relationships are going to have to go through.[93a] To the extent that we are able to devise and implement programs of national action that look toward the creation of a genuinely healthy relationship both of man to nature and of man to himself, we will then, for the first time, have something to say to people elsewhere of an entirely different order than the things we have had to say to them hitherto. To the extent that we are able to develop a social purpose in our own society, our life and our experiences will become interesting and meaningful to peoples in other parts of the world.[94a]

So spoke Kennan in March 1954; and on republishing these lectures recently, he wrote that his remarks "stand as the most comprehensive statement I ever made of my outlook on the basic problems of American foreign policy in this postwar world."[95a] This is no doubt true, and it also goes far to explain his more specific views about the world around us in the 1960's, and more especially his quotation of a statement made by John Quincy Adams, one of our stalwart conservative continentalists, on July 4, 1821:

Wherever the standard of freedom and independence has been or shall be unfurled, there will be America's heart, her benedictions, and

92a *Ibid.*, p. 99.
93a *Ibid.*, p. 105.
94a *Ibid.*, p. 115.
95a *Ibid.*, p. viii.

her prayers. But she goes not abroad in search of monsters to destroy. She is the champion and vindicator only of her own. She is the well-wisher to the freedom and independence of all. [But] she well knows that by once enlisting under banners other than her own, were they even the banners of foreign independence, she would involve herself beyond the power of extrication, in all the wars of interest and intrigue, of individual avarice, envy and ambition, which assume the colors and usurp the standards of freedom. The fundamental maxims of her policy would insensibly change from liberty to force. . . . She might become the dictatress of the world. She would no longer be the ruler of her own spirit.[96a]

Whereas Kennan's ideas and general outlook were no doubt deeply affected by a lifetime spent in the Foreign Service, Walter Lippmann served in an official capacity only once, when for a short time in 1917–1918 he acted as secretary of the House Inquiry—although he was for a number of years close to Colonel House and his circle and for a time at least had a degree of influence at the White House. Lippmann was one of the brilliant young intellectuals who did so much to give the Progressive Era its striking and exciting character. But he was, even then, not one to share the great enthusiasms of the time; as can be seen from his first important published work, *Drift and Mastery* (1914), he was always inclined to be distrustful of prevailing ideas;[97a] and only for a brief period in the Wilson and Roosevelt administrations did he find himself supporting the prevailing course of American foreign policy.

Lippmann's great skepticism about the possibilities of an effective, instrumentalist foreign policy stems partly, it appears, from his profound doubt about the essential rationality of Political Man, about his ability to perceive his real needs and interests, and therefore his ability to respond accordingly. This skepticism, no doubt, was greatly increased by the events of the First World War; and the pessimism of his influential book *Public Opinion* (1922)[98a] and of his many important discussions of intellect and politics over the next two decades—including his revealing Phi Beta Kappa Oration at Columbia College in May 1932[99a]—were the continuing evidence of this skepticism.

[96a] "Kennan on Vietnam," *The New Republic*, Feb. 22, 1966, p. 22.

[97a] Charles Forcey, *The Crossroads of Liberalism* (New York, 1961), pp. 163ff. It seems clear that until the 1950's Mr. Lippmann was generally opposed to the centralizing tendencies of the Federal Government. Indeed, there is in his writings, from the Wilsonian period on, a strong emphasis on the things the Federal Government cannot or should not do; and this concern over such limitations in the realm of domestic policy has carried over, as will be seen, into a similar belief about the necessary limitations of American power in world affairs.

[98a] *Ibid.*, pp. 297ff.

[99a] "The Scholar in a Troubled World," *The Atlantic Monthly*, Aug. 1932.

Nor was this skepticism limited only to the realm of domestic affairs. Although he has spoken of it rarely in public, there can be little doubt that he was deeply disillusioned by the failure of the Wilsonian policies, with which he was for a time connected, and that this failure left a deep imprint on his thinking about foreign policy. "In my opinion," Lippmann wrote to Raymond B. Fosdick, then Under Secretary of the League of Nations and a strong supporter of President Wilson, in August, 1919:

the Treaty [of Versailles] is not only illiberal and in bad faith, it is in the highest degree imprudent. It is a far worse job, I think, than the Treaty of Vienna a hundred years ago, because the men who gathered at Vienna did honestly take into account the balance of forces in Europe. The men at Paris ignored these forces. . . . I am certain that the present League is in structure and function and ideal the enemy of a real League of Nations, and the greatest danger is that its failure, like that of the Holy Alliance before it, will disillusionize a whole generation.

You ask for my suggestions and I give them to you in the spirit you ask them. The first necessity is that the President, and if not he then Colonel House, should permit the whole world to know just what the dangers of this settlement are. . . . Until that primary act of honesty is committed we shall be living a lie and committing one immorality to cover another. The plain fact is that nobody can get away with this Treaty, and the sooner that is confessed so that all the world knows it, the better for the world.[100a]

This advice, however sound, the majority of Wilsonians had no intention of following. The result was not only that the treaty—including the League—failed of ratification in the Senate, but that there developed in this country, especially in intellectual circles, a new and widespread feeling of isolationism, an attitude of "a plague on both your houses." There developed, also, a strong feeling that there were distinct limitations to what the United States could—or should—attempt to achieve in the realm of international affairs. In Lippmann's case, it seems clear, this reluctance to see the United States become closely involved in European and Far Eastern problems soon fused with a belief—frequently reiterated in the 1930's—that there were distinct limits to the proper role that government could play in the realm of domestic recovery and reform. Seen from this vantage point, it becomes clear that Lippmann's current position that the United States cannot hope—and should not attempt—to play an effective

100a *Letters on the League of Nations from the Files of Raymond B. Fosdick* (Princeton, 1966), pp. 10, 12.

political and military role on the mainland of Asia is not, by any means, a new position.

It is interesting to recall, for instance, that in September 1931, when the Japanese were first beginning their efforts to take over control of Manchuria—efforts that are now widely regarded as the first phase of the Second World War in the Pacific—Lippmann wrote in the *New York Herald Tribune:* "It is disheartening to confess that the Powers are not in a position to do more to vindicate law and order majestically and set justice upon her throne. They are not. The Manchuria issue lies beyond the present resources of our civilization, and the fact that the League, under the guidance of Secretary Stimson, has recognized this limitation is not a sign that diplomats lack will, but that they are capable of acknowledging an unpleasant truth."[1b] But the only true conclusion the Japanese seem to have drawn from this particular episode and from similar ones later, was that they could defy both the United States and the other Great Powers with impunity, a conclusion that had as its final expression the attack on Pearl Harbor.

Not until the beginning of 1940, however, did Lippmann begin to revert to something like his position of 1917–1918, that the United States did have important interests outside her shores and that these interests lay both in the Atlantic and in the Pacific. He expressed his deep conviction on this subject in a moving passage of his book *U.S. Foreign Policy: Shield of the Republic* (1943), probably the most important of his later works. Discussing the tragic situation that obtained at the end of the First World War, he wrote that the American people had then not yet

had it demonstrated to them how much the defense of the Western hemisphere depended upon having friendly and strong partners in the British Isles, in the French ports on the Atlantic, at Gibraltar and Casablanca and Dakar; or how much the defense of the Philippines depended upon French Indo-China, and upon British Hong-Kong, Malaya, and Burma, and upon the attitude and strength of Russia and upon China in Eastern Asia. . . . Not until twenty years later, not until France had fallen and Britain was in mortal peril, not until the Japanese had surrounded the Philippines, did it become possible for the nation to perceive the hidden but real structure of America's strategic position in the world.[2b]

[1b] Quoted in Allan Nevins (ed.), *Interpretations, 1931–1932* (New York: The Macmillan Company, 1932), pp. 189–190. This quotation is reprinted by the permission of The Macmillan Company.

[2b] *U.S. Foreign Policy,* pp. 38–39. This and subsequent quotations from this work are reprinted by the permission of Atlantic-Little, Brown and Company, © 1943 by Walter Lippmann.

It cannot be said, however, that Lippmann long persisted in this new global view of American politics; indeed, he was—as is now generally overlooked—one of the most outspoken opponents of the Truman Doctrine, and he devoted a long and notable series of articles in the *New York Herald Tribune,* later published in book form as *The Cold War,*[3b] to a detailed critique of Kennan's recently published article "The Sources of Soviet Conduct," which, as already noted, set forth some of the principal intellectual, political, and strategic considerations underlying the Truman Doctrine.

More recently Lippmann has returned to his earlier grave doubts about the essential realism of the Wilsonian view of world affairs, and his scorn for a foreign policy based on moral considerations has, once more, become increasingly sharp. Thus he now speaks mockingly not only of "self-determination" (in quotation marks),[4b] but of "the myth, propagated since the first world war by the naive and idealistic followers of Wilson, that all sovereign states . . . are . . . alike in their right to exercise influence in the world."[5b] He believes that it is futile for the small countries on the periphery of Communist China to try to maintain an independent position of their own; and he regards as even more dangerous and foolhardy American efforts to bring about such a position.[6b]

While Lippmann's position on contemporary American foreign policy can, to a considerable extent, be explained by his reaction to his unhappy experience with the foreign policy of President Wilson, the ideas of Hans Morgenthau, now professor of modern history and political science at the University of Chicago, derive from a different background. Steeped in the juridical positivism and relativism of early-twentieth-century Central Europe, he has never, at least in the realm of international affairs, held a position that could, ideologically speaking, be described as liberal. In his first book published in the United States, *Scientific Man vs. Power Politics* (1946), he made it abundantly clear that he regarded liberalism as an illusory philosophy in the realm of international affairs and that the diplomats and statesmen that appealed most to him were those who—like Canning, Castlereagh, and Disraeli, and even Richelieu and Bismarck—recognized the intrinsic nature of power and its prime importance in the conduct of foreign policy.

3b New York, 1947.
4b "War in Asia," *Newsweek,* March 14, 1966.
5b *New York Herald Tribune;* see also his "The Frustration of Globalism," *New York Herald Tribune,* March 10, 1966.
6b "Snub from Peking," *New York Herald Tribune,* March 31, 1966.

This strong emphasis on the primacy of "national power" has long been the hallmark of Morgenthau's work. "I have always," he has written, "emphasized the importance of power in all its manifestations as an instrument of foreign policy."[7b] His view of American foreign policy, moreover, has in many ways been even more critical than that of Kennan or Lippman, but his criticism has taken a different and an important form. Whereas Kennan seemed to find the great aberration of American foreign policy in its "legalistic-moralistic approach to international relations" and dated the beginning of that approach from the turn of the century, in Morgenthau's frequently repeated view the United States once had a "realistic tradition" of foreign policy in the era of the American Revolution, but it was a tradition that came to an end with the passing of the generation of the Founding Fathers.[8b]

Like Kennan and Lippmann, then, Morgenthau denies the continuity of American foreign policy and that there is any such thing as a great tradition of American foreign policy. Nor is it only in the realm of diplomatic philosophy that the United States has been lacking. "The brilliance of the first decades of American diplomacy," he has written, was followed by a long period of mediocrity, if not ineptitude. . . .[9b] In its formative years the United States benefited from the services of an unusually brilliant diplomacy. From the Jacksonian era on, the eminent qualities of American diplomacy disappeared as the need for them seemed to disappear.[10b]

It goes without saying, then, that Morgenthau denies the two most important and striking features of American foreign policy—first, that it has an intellectual content distinctly its own, and, second, that there is an essential continuity in American foreign policy from the eighteenth century to the present. On the contrary, he writes, the American political mind is intoxicated with "moral abstractions" that have "become the prevailing substitute for political thought." [11b] The result has been that for more than

7b Hans J. Morgenthau, *Vietnam and the United States* (Washington, D.C., 1965), p. 5. This and subsequent quotations from this work are reprinted by permission of Public Affairs Press.

8b Cf. "The Mainsprings of American Foreign Policy—The National Interest vs. Moral Abstractions," *American Political Science Review*, XLIV (Dec. 1950), and "Another 'Great Debate'—The National Interest of the United States," *Ibid.*, XLVI (Dec. 1952).

9b Hans J. Morgenthau, *Politics Among Nations* (3rd ed., New York: Alfred A. Knopf, Inc., 1960), p. 142.

10b *Ibid.*, p. 549.

11b Hans J. Morgenthau, *In Defense of the National Interest* (New York, 1951), p. 4. This and subsequent quotations from this work are reprinted by permission of Alfred A. Knopf, Inc.

half a century American foreign policy has been burdened by "utopianism, legalism, sentimentalism . . . [and] neo-isolationism."[12b]

"The year 1917," he writes, "constitutes a turning point in the history not only of American foreign policy but of the American purpose as well." [13b] But far from being a change for the better, it was a change only for the worse, the effects of which are still felt today; for "Wilsonian globalism endeavored to bring the virtue of American democracy to the rest of the world. Contemporary globalism tries to protect the virtue of the 'free wrold' from contamination by Communism. . . . The anti-Communist crusade has become both the moral principle of contemporary globalism and the rationale of our global foreign policy." [14b]

The principles of self-government, self-determination, and non-intervention, then, obviously have a modest place in Morgenthau's scheme of things, for, like Kennan and Lippmann, he strongly condemns a foreign policy based on historic idealism and principles of international morality. It is not surprising, then, that, again like Kennan and Lippmann, he has been a strong critic of American diplomacy in the Far East. "The issue China poses," he writes, "is

political and cultural predominance. The United States can no more contain Chinese influence in Asia by arming South Vietnam and Thailand than China could contain American influence in the Western Hemisphere by arming, say, Nicaragua, and Costa Rica. . . . If we do not want to set ourselves goals which cannot be attained with the means we are willing to employ, we must learn to accommodate ourselves to the predominance of China on the Asian mainland. It is instructive to note that those Asian nations which have done so—such as Burma and Cambodia—live peacefully in the shadow of the Chinese giant.[15b]

In short, it is—as he said a long time ago—all a question of power, not of principle.

Taken separately or together, there can be no doubt that the arguments of Kennan, Lippmann, and Morgenthau have the ring of authority and that they have exerted—and continue to exert—a considerable influence on current American thinking about foreign policy. But since their approach is, in fact, historical, one is inclined

12b Ibid., p. 92.
13b Hans J. Morgenthau, The Purpose of American Politics (New York, 1964), p. 104.
14b Morgenthau, Vietnam and the United States, p. 82.
15b Ibid., pp. 63, 64.

to ask to what extent their judgments rest solidly on historical evidence, and to what extent they simply reflect personal opinion and preconception.

Looking at the general corpus of their writings, certain basic historical questions immediately arise. In the first place, there can be little doubt that their work ignores almost entirely the historical continuity of American thinking about world affairs and the unique character of much of that thinking over the last two centuries. In the second place, it seems clear that they see the course of European and American history and politics as intrinsically unchanged by the intellectual and political revolution of the eighteenth century, which demanded—though it did not achieve its demands at that time—that international politics be conducted in a new and different manner. It was in the United States that such thinking first found concrete expression in the foreign policy of the new Republic,[16b] but these ideas were kept alive in Europe also, and it was for that reason, among others, that President Wilson received such a tumultuous welcome when he arrived there in December 1918. It seemed for a brief moment as if the New World and the Old had joined in establishing a new foundation for international peace. This was not momentary intoxication; it was the expression, rather, of a deep feeling all over Europe, and it was the profound tragedy of the Wilsonian era that, since these feelings could not be realized fully and immediately, they soon stood more or less discredited.

Finally, there can be no doubt that our judgment of modern and contemporary American foreign policy is bound to be based upon our judgment of earlier diplomacy, European and American. But in applying such a yardstick, which is entirely legitimate, it is important to view these historical events, of a more or less distant past, with the utmost accuracy, clarity, and dispassionateness; and reading some of the most important and influential writings of Kennan, Lippmann, and Morgenthau, it is impossible to escape the impression that the evidence, in not a few instances, has been tailored to fit the judgment.[17b] A little historical knowledge is a dangerous thing, and one is bound to say that the writings of Professor Morgenthau, in par-

16b See above, pp. 5ff.

17b Mr. Lippmann, it must be said in all candor, has been especially guilty of this practice. "For the conduct of war and diplomacy," Lippmann wrote in mid-January 1966 ("The Guns-versus-Butter Stereotype," *New York Herald Tribune*), "it is most important to cultivate anti-stereotypes to protect us from resorting to decaying and dead patterns of conduct. The appeasement of Hitler was the work of Englishmen and Frenchmen who could not believe the Chancellor of Germany was a monster like Hitler. The frightful consequences of appeasing Hitler left behind them in the minds of men the great Munich stereotype. . . . Mr. Dean Rusk is the current user of the Munich stereotype." Reading

ticular, are shot through with historical inaccuracies and oversim-
plifications, large and small. This is especially dangerous because the
American public, although generally interested in what might be
called the "historical approach" to foreign and domestic policy, is not,
on the whole, a sophisticated audience. In short, it is easily impressed;
and Morgenthau's works tend to be impressive.

Nevertheless, much of what he writes, not only about American
thought on foreign policy in general but also about specific aspects of
that policy, is likely to come as a profound surprise to students of
American diplomacy. There is, for instance, his favorite generalization
—or at least one of them—according to which the United States had
a great tradition of "political realism" in foreign policy at the time of
the Founding Fathers but that this tradition was then dissipated after
they passed from the scene. Yet the fact of the matter is that
from Albert Gallatin to Hamilton Fish to John Hay, the United
States scored one important series of diplomatic victories after another; and this is not to be accounted for merely on the ground of
the nation's "unchallengable superiority in material and human resources"—a material superiority that "spoke its own language."[18b]

It is not only Morgenthau's view of earlier American diplomacy
that will not stand examination. His indictment of more recent
American foreign policy is equally doubtful. "When," he writes,
with great assurance,

the need for an active American foreign policy became manifest in
the late 1930's, there was nothing to build on but a mediocre foreign

this astounding statement one can only surmise that, either Mr. Lippmann's memory is
playing tricks on him or he simply does not know—what every reasonably well-informed
student of the Munich crisis has long known—that Chamberlain was, in fact, perfectly well
aware of the kind of man he was dealing with but that he believed, for a variety of reasons,
that he must make a deal with him at almost any price. The same was true, it is clear,
of M. Daladier and most of the other leaders of the British and French governments—as
the official documents and excerpts from Chamberlain's private diary and correspondence,
published over the last twenty years, clearly show. (Cf. Francis L. Loewenheim (ed.),
Peace or Appeasement? [Boston, 1965]). What the available evidence also shows—and what
Lippmann prefers to ignore—is that the British and French governments, and the United
States government too, could hardly have been surprised by the events of 1938. For like
the Communist Chinese and Russians today, Hitler never failed to broadcast his objectives
well ahead of time; his associates spoke frankly about them to foreign diplomats, and no
one who followed the twists and turns of official Nazi propaganda was likely to be left in
the dark about Hitler's future objectives. The failure in London and Paris and Washington
in the 1930's, then—the failure that was climaxed by the Munich disaster—was not at all a
failure of intelligence. It was an inability to respond properly to this challenge, an unwillingness to recognize that it was impossible to compromise with Hitler, above all, a
failure to project—to conceive—what kind of Europe would result if Hitler was not checked
properly and effectively. What President Johnson has been saying—what Vice-President
Humphrey and Secretary Rusk have been saying and what Lippmann does not like to hear—
is that they take the Chinese Communist threats for what they appear to be, and are
not inclined to wait until the decline in Western power produces another Munich-type
debacle.

18b *Politics Among Nations*, p. 142.

service, the condemnation of power politics and of secret diplomacy transformed into moral indignation at "aggressor nations," and the tradition of the big stick, which had worked so well in the Western Hemisphere. Thus it was the improvisations of President Roosevelt alone . . . that kept American foreign policy in tune with American interests. [But] When Roosevelt, who for twelve years had almost single-handedly made American foreign policy, left the scene, there was no man or group of men capable of creating and operating that intricate and subtle machinery by which traditional diplomacy had given peaceful protection and furtherance to the national interest.[19b]

Just how well President Roosevelt "kept American foreign policy in tune with American interests," especially before the outbreak of the Second World War, has already been noted but it makes, to say the least, a caricature of the history of the U.S. Foreign Service to so deride it in a period when its leading embassies, in Europe and in the Far East, were headed and staffed by such men as William C. Bullitt, William E. Dodd, Joseph C. Grew, Donald Heath, Loy W. Henderson, Herschel V. Johnson, Nelson T. Johnson, George F. Kennan, George C. Messersmith, and many others who made their reputations during and after the Second World War. And who, if one accepts Morgenthau's generalization and carries it further, was responsible for the great and enormously beneficial revolution in American foreign policy begun under President Truman after 1947—a policy that Morgenthau, to be sure, now dismisses as nothing more than an "anti-Communist crusade"? [20b]

The readers of Kennan, Lippmann, and Morgenthau's writings will be aware that they are "full of much what not to do." But there is toward the close of Morgenthau's best-known work, *Politics Among Nations,* a section that sheds considerable light not only on his understanding of modern European history but also on his whole approach to the relation of history and diplomacy. For it is at this point that he presents his model of the ideal kind of international diplomatic conference:

The outstanding example of a successful war-preventing diplomacy in modern times is the Congress of Berlin of 1878. By the peaceful means of an accommodating diplomacy, that Congress settled, or at least made susceptible of settlement, the issues that had separated Great Britain and Russia since the end of the Napoleonic Wars. . . . When British Prime Minister Disraeli returned from that Congress to London, he declared with pride that he was bringing home "peace . . . with honor."

19b *Ibid.,* p. 549.
20b Morgenthau, *Vietnam and the United States,* p. 82.

In fact, he had brought peace for later generations, too; for a century there has been no war between Great Britain and Russia.[21b]

About this statement it must be said that its only completely accurate portions are the quotation from Disraeli and the fact that there has, indeed, been no war between Britain and Russia since that time. But the rest of it is entirely, significantly, and, it must be added, dangerously inaccurate. The Balkan wars of 1875–1878, which were dealt with by the Congress of Berlin, were not, as Morgenthau appears to believe, primarily a confrontation between Great Britain and Russia. They were the outgrowth, rather, of an ever-mounting nationalism in that area, which imperial Russia sought to use for its advantage against Austria and Turkey, behind which stood, at a discreet distance, the Royal Navy.

Andrassy, Bismarck, Disraeli, and Gorchakov—the leading participants in the Congress—would no doubt have been amazed by Morgenthau's description of their work. Only Disraeli returned home in triumph, for, as Professor William Langer has pointed out, "The victory of England [at the Congress] spelled the defeat of Russia, and Russia had never since the time of Catherine the Great suffered so terrible a diplomatic setback."[22b] Gorchakov paid for the disaster with his job and reputation; and, as for Andrassy and the Austrians, they were confronted with near-uncontrollable Russian rage—so great that the Three Emperors League, which Bismarck had carefully constructed in 1872 to prevent the possibility of a Franco-Russian combination against Germany, was completely and, it seemed for a time, permanently ruptured.

And what of the people of the Balkans, about whose fate the Congress deliberated? For them, as Professor Carlton Hayes has rightly said, the conference was a disaster. "Disregard of the principle of nationality," he has written, "has often been cited as the most serious flaw in the Vienna peace settlement of 1815, following the Napoleonic Wars. But it was even more egregious in the Berlin settlement of 1878. National aspirations of all the Balkan countries were flouted. . . . Nationalism in the Balkans, instead of being assuaged, was raised to fever pitch. If before 1878 the 'Eastern Question' concerned one 'sick man' [Turkey], after 1878 it involved a half-dozen maniacs. For the Congress of Berlin drove the Balkan peoples mad.[23b]

21b *Politics Among Nations*, pp. 568–569.
22b William L. Langer, *European Alliances and Alignments, 1871–1890* (New York, 1931), p. 162.
23b Carlton J. H. Hayes, *A Generation of Materialism, 1871–1900* (New York, 1941), p. 33.

But the reason that the Congress of Berlin was *not* a success—why, as Professor Hayes has put it, "it drove the Balkan peoples mad"—brings us to the heart of Morgenthau's problem and that of modern American diplomacy as well. It was at that Congress—and at not a few others before and after it—that the wishes of the people immediately concerned, whether they lived in Europe, or in Africa, or in the Middle or Far East, were largely or entirely ignored. These people were indeed, as President Wilson had once said, handed about "as property"; and they were so bandied about because the Great Powers of Europe—England generally included—recognized fundamentally no other system of international conduct and diplomacy.

The United States did. That is why from the eighteenth century on, the American attitude toward foreign policy has indeed called for a "new diplomacy," and that is why the Wilsonian diplomacy was so revolutionary and conservative at the same time. It proposed, as already noted, to make at last an indissoluble connection between personal and political conduct, between the conduct of domestic and the conduct of foreign policy; and it proposed to apply to the European peoples (and to others, presumably, later) the same principles of self-determination and self-government upon which the United States was founded. There can be no doubt, of course, that the United States, as Wilson himself was frank enough to admit, had on occasion violated those principles; but they had remained fundamental American principles nevertheless. It was Wilson who sought, for the first time, to get the other Great Powers to accept this revolutionary change in international affairs. And to ignore that achievement—and the nature of the ideas with which it was concerned—is to do a grave disservice to the historical traditions of the United States. On such misunderstanding no sound interpretations of America's present role in world affairs can possibly be placed.

In closing this essay on the relation of historical consciousness and foreign policy since the eighteenth century, two other points must be made. In the first place, it would be manifestly inaccurate and improper to leave the impression that the nature of the debate about contemporary American foreign policy, its intellectual foundations and ultimate objectives, is based largely on the writings of a few prominent and influential commentators. This is, of course, not so. The fact of the matter is—and here we come to a far more troubling aspect of the relation between historical consciousness and political consensus—that the important dissent over foreign policy now being expressed by such leading commentators as George Kennan, Walter Lippmann, and Hans Morgenthau is not confined to a small handful of historical critics.

There are now large areas of American diplomatic history that are in a condition of serious intellectual disarray. There is hardly an important aspect of recent American diplomacy that has not come in for drastic—often far too drastic—reconsideration. From the voluminous writings of Professor William A. Williams and his school—who view American history in a far more doctrinaire fashion than Charles A. Beard and his supporters ever did[24b]—to the attacks now being leveled on American policy toward Russia since 1917[25b] on the policy of "unconditional surrender"[26b] and the decision to use the atomic bomb against Japan,[27b] on the efforts to bring about an independent and effective government in China[28b] and on the origins of the Cold War itself,[29b] there can be little doubt that the whole tradition and meaning of recent American foreign policy is increasingly called into question. Some of this criticism, as already noted, has come from certain extreme right-wing circles; some of it, with greater intellectual respectability (but often hardly more justification for that), has come from the extreme Left. The general result has been the growth of serious confusion and uncertainty. There is about much of this recent writing an air of morose self-criticism so characteristic of the 1920's and 1930's. No one who has read much of the recent "antiwar" literature will find there much that is new about the history and meaning of American foreign policy.

It is quite possible, of course, that history never repeats itself and that only historians do. Yet in stressing the apparent differences between the men and circumstances of the 1920's and 1930's and our own time, we ought not to overlook the wisdom so painfully acquired from those bitter days.[30b] Fortunately the student of modern

24b See, for instance, *Studies on the Left,* the historical journal issued since 1959 by Williams and his former students.
25b D. F. Fleming, *The Origins of the Cold War, 1917–1960* (2 vols., New York, 1961).
26b Anne M. Armstrong, *Unconditional Surrender* (New Brunswick, 1961).
27b Gar Alperovitz, *Atomic Diplomacy* (New York, 1965).
28b Tang Tsou, *The American Failure in China, 1941–1950* (Chicago, 1963).
29b Cf. Staughton Lynd, "How the Cold War Began," *Commentary,* XXX (Dec. 1960), and David Horowitz, *The Free World Colossus* (New York, 1965).
30b Prophecy is no part of the historian's business. But it is part of his task to remind his audience—whether his students, fellow scholars, general public, or members of the government—that the present world situation is not so unique as it sometimes appears to be. It is sometimes observed that contemporary events have a certain similarity to those of the 1930's and this may well be true. On the other hand, it seems quite likely also that the present world situation has a good deal in common with the time of extended wars and upheavals of the age of the Protestant revolution

American diplomacy who wishes to inform himself of how the country got where it is, is in a better position than his counterpart in any other country. Beyond the voluminous and ever-growing literature of memoirs and biography, beyond the rising number of specialized studies and general histories of these times, there is at hand that remarkable documentary series *Foreign Relations of the United States,* published annually now for more than a century, which allows us to study in its incomparable richness the historical record of modern American diplomacy, its principles and policies, its aims, frustrations, and achievements.[31b]

But whatever our view of these recent decades may be, there can be little doubt that the principal function of the historian at the present time is to bring history back into the lives of the people. Knowing from recent experience what the proper restudy of the United States' domestic history can do to bring about the diminution of ancient social wrongs and the establishment of a more perfect union, it is not too much to hope that from a renewed study of the U.S. record in world affairs, we may approach the events of our days with greater faith in the American tradition and through such faith reach out to build a better world in our time.

---

in the sixteenth and seventeenth centuries, and perhaps also with the era of the French Revolution and Napoleon (or what R. R. Palmer has called the Age of the Democratic Revolution). In short, in discussing the current world situation, it might be well to compare not only the doctrines of Hitler and Lin Piao but also, for instance, the history of the struggles of the Allied powers and revolutionary France. For an illuminating statement on the role of historical analysis see Ernest R. May, "The Relevance of Diplomatic History to the Practice of International Relations," with a commentary by Arthur Schlesinger, Jr. *Harvard Alumni Bulletin,* Nov. 27, 1965, pp. 208ff.

[31b] Anyone interested, for example, in the problems of constructing and living with a coalition government that includes Communists should not miss the recently published documents on the experiences of the Polish government in 1944 and the reaction of the United States to that experience. Cf. *Foreign Relations of the United States, 1944,* III (Washington, D.C., 1965), 1231ff.

Historical Thought and American Foreign Policy in the Era of the First World War

by Arno J. Mayer

THE BURDEN of this essay, which deals with the relation of historical thought, ideology, and foreign policy, is that Woodrow Wilson's statesmanship—in particular his statesmanship at the Paris Peace Conference—was an extension of his *Weltanschauung;* that this world view was similar to that of the "New Historians," who became prominent during the quarter century before World War I; and that the reformist world view of both these New Historians and Wilson crystallized in response to rapidly accelerating economic and social change and to the accompanying challenge of socialism.

In order to sustain this thesis I shall, first of all, touch briefly on the nature of *Weltanschauung* in general, basing myself on the views of Wilhelm Dilthey and Karl Mannheim. Second, I shall briefly sketch the world view of the prewar (or post-1890) historians. Third, I shall turn to Wilson's own world view, first as expressed in his important, but long overlooked, lecture on the nature of history delivered at the St. Louis Exposition of 1904 and later reflected in his political pronouncements and policies before the war. And finally, I shall examine the ways in which Wilson's world view guided, served, and limited his statesmanship at the Paris Peace Conference.

I

There can be little doubt that "static conditions make for attitudes of piety" and that within static societies—especially but not exclusively within static agrarian societies—the tensions and conflicts between generations are essentially nonpolitical, nonideological, and nonintellectual. But under the impact of a quickening tempo and exploding scale of social change the almost automatic adaptation to "traditional patterns of experience, thought and expression" ceases to be possible. A social-political—rather than biological—generation emerges when its members, following exposure to dynamic change, develop a distinctive style and outlook.[1] Needless to say, in response to rapid change, opposing world views not only take shape simultaneously but also crystallize in terms of each other. According to Mannheim, early in the nineteenth century "both the romantic-conservative and the liberal-rationalist youth belonged to the same actual generation, [and] romantic-conservatism and liberal-rationalism were merely two polar forms of the intellectual and social response" to a common historical experience.[2] By the end of the century these two polar responses were face to face with socialism.

This intellectual and political response does not take the form of a carefully constructed and logically consistent philosophic system. Both Dilthey and Mannheim conceived of a *Weltanschauung* as an amalgam of ideas and sentiments about life interwoven with a set of "purposes, preferences, and principles governing action and giving life [both] unity and meaning." They saw it as a still ill-defined "historic-philosophic vision" of the past, present, and future.[3]

The origins of the New Historical school in America were similar to those of European historicism. It actually did not exist until "history was written from the historic *Weltanschauung*." Not historiography brought forth historicism, but "the historic process through which we lived turned us into historicists." Accordingly, historicism itself is a *Weltanschauung* that conditions "inner reactions, external responses, and forms of thought."[4]

II

Between 1890 and 1917 America underwent both fundamental and rapid change on all major fronts: the rise to world power was accomplished; the national economy was thoroughly enmeshed with the world economy; the symbiotic growth of industrialization and urbanization was quickened; and the rate of immigration rose to unprecedented heights.

Of course these changes were not unilinear: in particular, the cyclical swings in both the national and the world capitalist economy became more frequent as well as more severe. However, falling employment and income during successive recessions merely stim-

1 Karl Mannheim, *Essays on the Sociology of Knowledge* (New York, 1952), pp. 302–310.
2 *Ibid.*, pp. 304, 314.
3 H. A. Hodges, *Wilhelm Dilthey: An Introduction* (London, 1944), p. 160, and Mannheim, *op. cit.*, p. 88.
4 Mannheim, *op. cit.*, pp. 85–86.

ulated popular impatience with existing political and economic institutions; these seemed incapable of smoothly accommodating and channeling this change, which the New Historians, all of whom were confirmed Progressives, conceived to be for the better. These historians now realized that the viewpoint and the methodology of Ranke and Fustel de Coulanges could not help them explicate the dynamics either of change or of resistance to change—in their own time or in the past.

In Mannheim's terms, then, the historical process precipitated this revolt against formalistic and narrative history. It took the form of a rebellion against surface political, constitutional, diplomatic, and military history. Whatever their underlying philosophical and methodological differences—and there were many—Thorstein Veblen (1857–1929), Frederick Jackson Turner (1861–1932), James Harvey Robinson (1863–1936), Charles A. Beard (1874–1948), and Carl L. Becker (1873–1945) were less concerned with what happened than with why it happened. Profoundly conscious of change, they set out in search of a theory of social change; and this search led them to study the economic, social, intellectual, and social-psychological forces—the dynamic forces—shaping the development of society and polity. All five thought and wrote in keen awareness of and in creative response to the Marxist world view and the Marxist theory of social change. Even though only Robinson formally accepted economic determinism, all were inclined to view ideas, beliefs, and institutions as significantly influenced by changing and transient historical conditions and, at this particular juncture, by changing economic conditions.

In 1891—hence shortly before the publication of *The Significance of the Frontier in American History*—Turner flatly declared, in anticipation of Croce (1866–1952), that "each age writes the history of the past anew with reference to the conditions uppermost in its own times." He proclaimed that in the contemporary era economic rather than political questions were becoming increasingly important; that the machine age was "also the age of socialistic inquiry"; that historical study would turn predominantly to "the study of social conditions and . . . [of] the economic basis of society in general"; that the causes of social change had to be understood; that local and national history should be "viewed in the light of world history" and in comparative terms.[5]

Not surprisingly, two years later, in advancing his frontier thesis,

---

[5] See Turner's essay "The Significance of History" (1891), in Fritz Stern (ed.), *The Varieties of History: From Voltaire to the Present* (New York, 1957), pp. 197–208.

Turner argued that America's democratic institutions were largely the product of a passing economic stage. Before long the New Historians shared the view that now that the continental frontier was irrevocably closed, America was about to leave behind its uniqueness and join the rest of the Western world in struggling with the unsettling consequences of rapid modernization.

Hence, when Beard published his *Economic Interpretation of the Constitution of the United States* in 1913, rather than claim special credit for his seminal study of interest politics, he simply professed kinship with those other historians who were rejecting "barren political history [in favor of] a study of the real economic forces which condition [not determine] great movements in politics." [6]

One other but central aspect of the position of these New Historians remains to be brought out. Since they considered themselves students of history rather than academic historians, they shared an unexamined faith in the utility of historical study and knowledge. At the core of their *Weltanschauung* was the belief, which they had in common with many European historicists, that the study of history was an essential aid to an understanding of the present; and possibly as an outgrowth of America's pragmatic tradition they passionately preached that the study of history held the key to the future. From their trend analysis they concluded that the reconciliation of political liberty with economic equality was the most urgent and just demand of the hour. To be sure, they were not about to renounce America's traditional political ideals and institutions. But unlike their equally self-conscious conservative opponents, they proclaimed that existing political, legal, and economic institutions would have to be significantly reformed in order to accommodate the surge of social forces unleashed by rapidly advancing industrialism.

Technically, then, they were students of the past; but their creed enjoined them to be first and foremost concerned with explicating the present and the future. For Veblen, who had an unsurpassed sensitivity to the changing social conditions of his time, the historical argument did not "enjoin a return to the beginning of things, but rather an intelligent appreciation of what things are to come to." [7] Turner proudly announced that historical study should give the community not reverence for the past but "new thoughts and feel-

---

6 Cited in Cushing Strout, *The Pragmatic Revolt in American History: Carl L. Becker and Charles A. Beard* (New Haven, 1958), p. 92.
7 Cited in Joseph Dorfman, *Thorstein Veblen and His America* (New York, 1934), p. 398.

ings, new aspirations and energies"; in turn, these thoughts and feelings would "flow into deeds . . . [for] better things and reforms." [8]
He advocated the study of the growth of European socialism in order to deal effectively and creatively with its challenge in America. Similarly, Robinson and Beard, in their *The Development of Modern Europe* (1907–1908), consistently subordinated the past to the present so that their readers "should know what was the attitude of Leo XIII toward the social democrats even if they forget that of Innocent III toward the Albigensens."[9]

III

The world view of Woodrow Wilson (1856–1924) does not emerge from his major written works in history and political science. With one exception these were completed before he assumed the presidency of Princeton University in 1902. In Arthur Link's judgment this first period of Wilson's adult life was "characterized by an academic sort of conservatism." As a full-time teacher and scholar he wrote history and political science in the spirit and style of the old rather than the New History.

It was only after 1902, when he began to shift his attention from scholarly and academic to practical affairs, that Wilson "became more intimately acquainted with the economic and political problems of his times." In the course of the following decade Wilson gradually switched from a "belligerent political and economic conservatism with regard to the important domestic issues . . . to militant progressivism." [10]

It was in September 1904—at the Congress of Arts and Science held in St. Louis to coincide with the Universal Exposition—that Wilson expressed his affinity for the New History. Wilson and Turner had seen a good deal of each other at Johns Hopkins, where Wilson went to lecture from Bryn Mawr; and thereafter they kept up a fairly steady correspondence. Even though it is difficult to determine accurately the care with which he followed the writings of Turner and his confreres, it seems safe to assume that Wilson kept up-to-date on important historical scholarship, certainly until 1902.

In any case, in St. Louis, Wilson defined the task of the historian in terms that Turner and Beard recognized as their own but that to this day historians continue to ignore to their own disadvantage.

8 Cited in Stern, *op. cit.*, p. 208.
9 *Ibid.*, pp. 204, 257.
10 Arthur S. Link, *Wilson: The Road to the White House* (Princeton, 1947), pp. 31–32.

[In the New History] . . . interest centers not so much in what happened as in what underlay the happening; not so much in the tides
as in the silent forces that lifted them. Economic history is of this
quality and the history of religious belief, and the history of literature,
where it traces the map of opinion, whether in an age of certainty or in
an age of doubt and change. . . . It is the honorable distinction of historical writing in our day that it has become more broadly and intimately human. The instinct of the time is social rather than political.
We would know not merely how law and government proceed but
also how society breeds its forces, how these play upon the individual,
and how the individual affects them. Law and Government are but one
expression of the life of society. They are regulative rather than generative, and historians of our day have felt that in writing political and
legal history they were upon the surface only, not at the heart of
affairs. . . . In whatever form, upon whatever scale you take it, the
writing of history as distinguished from the clerical keeping of the
records is a process of interpretation . . . [and of] conceiving imagination. . . . The historian is not a clerk but a seer: he must see the thing
first before he can judge of it. . . . We must all in our several degrees
be seers, not clerks. It is a high calling and should not be belittled.
Statesmen are guided and formed by what we write, patriots stimulated,
tyrants checked. Reform and progress, charity and freedom of belief,
the dreams of artists and the fancies of poets, have at once their record
and their source with us.[11]

By the time Wilson embraced this outlook the northern and urban
rather than the southern, rural, and populist forces were dominant
in the Progressive movement; the Socialist party had been organized
and had polled 400,000 votes in a national election; and the I.W.W.
had been formed. Shortly after St. Louis, Wilson declared that
whereas the "country 'need[ed] and would tolerate no party of discontent or radical experiment' it needed and would follow a party
of conservative reform, acting in the spirit of law and ancient
institutions."[12] Within a few years he had gone much further: "We
are in a temper to reconstruct economic society as we were once in
a temper to reconstruct political society, and political society may
itself undergo a radical modification in the process. I doubt if any
age was ever more conscious of its task or more unanimously
desirous of radical and extended changes in its economic and political
practice."[13]

11 Woodrow Wilson, "The Variety and Unity of History," in Howard J. Rogers (ed.),
Congress of Arts and Science: Universal Exposition, St. Louis, 1904 (Boston, 1906), II,
3–20. (See Appendix I.) Turner and Robinson also read papers on this occasion, as did
Karl Lamprecht, John B. Bury, and Adolf Harnack.
12 Link, *op cit.*, p. 96.
13 Cited by Kazimierz Grzybowski, "Woodrow Wilson on Law, State and Society," in
The George Washington Law Review, Vol. XXX, No. 5 (June 1962), p. 817.

Indeed, Wilson's shift to the New History had been a first step in the direction of his own progressive response to the radical upsurge. Before long Beard noted that as part of "a counter-reformation" against rising radical dissent President Roosevelt repeatedly "warned the capitalists that a reform of abuse was the price which they would have to pay in order to save themselves from a socialist revolution."[14] Except for the second half of his first administration, between 1912 and 1917 Wilson continued this "counter-reformation," without, however, accepting T.R.'s crude social Darwinism and his strident chauvinism. At first Wilson, like T.R. before him, restricted himself to regulating large corporations and banks; he also reduced the tariff. His prewar reforms, however, culminated in the elevation of Brandeis to the Supreme Court and in legislation for rural credit, workmen's compensation, protection of child labor, and the eight-hour workday.[15] The large corporations readily reconciled themselves to federal curbs that tended to amount to self-regulation detrimental to small business. But big and small business alike turned against Wilson once he moved to promote social-welfare legislation.[16] Thereafter he was suspected of and charged with socialist leanings even though it was perfectly clear that he considered moderate social legislation as an indispensable antidote to radicalism.

On the other hand, this same social legislation, cast in a liberal rather than in a nationalist ideology, style, and rhetoric, appealed not only to the crusading intellectuals, journalists, and social workers but also to the New Historians. In 1916 all alike deserted Roosevelt for Wilson. These intellectuals and literati, including the New Historians, gave intellectual and ideological expression to the pre-1917 pre-emptive reforms. "They criticized some of the more glaring evils of capitalism, but their political affiliations were never revolutionary."[17] Much the same can be said about the railway brotherhoods and the A.F. of L.

Whatever the underlying and immediate causes for America's entrance into the war on the side of the Allies—from the very start the New Historians vigorously championed the cause of the "democratic" Allies (excluding Russia) against autocratic and militarist Germany—this war became the nemesis of self-conscious

14 Charles A. Beard, *Contemporary American History, 1877–1913* (New York, 1914), pp. 303–304.
15 See Arthur S. Link, *Woodrow Wilson and the Progressive Era, 1910–1917* (New York, 1954), *passim*.
16 Cf. Gabriel Kolko, *The Triumph of Conservatism: A Reinterpretation of American History, 1900–1916* (New York, 1963), esp. pp. 279–287.
17 Morton White, *Social Thought in America: Revolt Against Formalism* (Boston, 1957), p. 45.

and pre-emptive reforms. Not that "progress" was halted: the stimulus of war cured the economy of a lingering sluggishness, provided full employment, and led to considerable advances in labor-management relations. But all these developments were unintended by-products of war-generated "prosperity," in America as well as in the other belligerent nations. Even the German General Staff advocated liberal labor and social policies in the interest of maximum war production.[18]

But this war-generated economic and social welfare, which temporarily checked popular pressure for reform, was accompanied by an overall hardening of the state. The spiraling corporate profits were not nearly so significant as the movement of business executives into sensitive federal posts and the launching of the fierce but inevitable loyalty campaign. In America as in all other belligerent nations, archconservatives promoted and took advantage of the jingoist groundswell to denounce, distort, and repress progressive and liberal views on political and economic issues unrelated to the war. Clearly the conservatives of both parties, but especially the Republicans, proposed to use the war to advance their cause: they did not want to dismantle the New Freedom, but they meant to stifle those forces that, with the end of the war, planned to expand it in the areas of lower tariffs, progressive income taxes, and labor legislation.

Wilson anticipated this war-induced hardening of the state, which by April 1917 had reached full expression in Britain, France, and Italy. But unlike Lloyd George, Briand, and Orlando, he would not wait until victory to countervail the antiprogressive and illiberal consequences of war.

IV

It was at this point that Wilson's *Weltanschauung* left its imprint. Had he still been a Rankean, he would have made a fetish of the primacy of foreign policy instead of bowing to it as an unfortunate wartime necessity; he would also have viewed the present struggle as a conventional though geographically inflated war between and among monolithic sovereign states. However, as a New Historian turned statesman, and with the Mexican experience behind him, he could not close his eyes to the fundamental internal social conflicts—remember, "the instinct of the time is social rather

18 Gerald D. Feldman, *Army, Industry and Labor in Germany, 1914–1918* (unpubl. diss., Harvard Univ., 1963).

than political"—behind this world war. The war was the onrush-
ing tide, and he looked for the silent forces that were lifting it.
Presently the onslaught of the Right in America, the revolution
in Russia, and the response to that revolution throughout Europe
confirmed him in his diagnosis that the external war between the
Associated and Central Powers was at the same time an internal
struggle between the forces of order and the forces of change,
an internal struggle the outcome of which would be significantly
influenced by the course of the war and the nature of the peace
settlement. Having long since rejected both American exceptional-
ism and isolationism, he realized that the seething civil war in
Europe was bound to have tremendous repercussions on this side
of the Atlantic: whereas reaction or revolution would be equally
fatal, the triumph of reformist liberalism and moderate socialism
would serve the cause of American progressivism. The Fourteen
Points were in large measure designed to help achieve this aim:
Wilson proposed to mobilize the reformism of the Old World—
which in 1917–1918 was considerably stronger than its American
counterpart—in order to breathe new life into progressivism in
the New World.

It is true that in 1917 Wilsonian idealism—no annexations, self-
determination, League of Nations—"became the ideological bridge
by which most of the progressive groups moved with their leader
from neutrality to intervention" and to crusading warfare.[19] It is
also true that Carl Becker, like so many other left-oriented intellectuals and literati, rushed to Washington to write propaganda
pamphlets for Creel's Committee on Public Information.[20]

The additional implication, however, that they lightly abandoned
their domestic progressivism for the deceptive promise of a distant perpetual peace is less tenable. In fact, they never separated
one from the other, any more than Wilson did. The collapse of
wartime idealism among anti-imperialist progressives and liberals
will never emerge in proper perspective unless this link between
a moderate peace abroad and reform at home is clearly recalled.
In all likelihood most progressives would more readily have sac-
rificed the League for domestic reforms than domestic reforms
for the League. And it goes without saying that Henry Cabot Lodge

19 Eric F. Goldman, *Rendezvous with Destiny* (New York, 1952), pp. 260–261.
20 See Arno J. Mayer, *Political Origins of the New Diplomacy, 1917–1918* (New Haven,
1959), pp. 349–350, and Carl L. Becker (ed.), *America's War Aims and Peace Plans,*
War Information Series, No. 21 (published by the Committee on Public Information,
Washington, D.C., 1918).

and his cabal were more concerned with keeping progressivism in check at home than they were with the defeat of the Covenant as such.

Not that the New Historians were satisfied with the vague and narrowly political and diplomatic terms of Wilson's wartime pronouncements; they were painfully aware that Wilson failed to formulate a social-economic platform to go along with his Gladstonian foreign-policy dicta. In mid-1917 Beard called on the administration to make it clear that

... by democracy we mean no shallow Manchesterism or empty Rousseauism, that we are aware of our own shortcomings. The world for which [progressives and socialists] are willing to die ... is not the world of Milner, Cecil, Maxse, and Balfour. The kingdom of heaven for Kerensky and Liebknecht is not described in Lochner v. New York. . . . All this simply means is that there are now currents of thought around the world which are not understood by Mid-Victorians.[21]

Nevertheless, when the Fourteen Points were issued, they dealt with free trade, self-determination, and the League, but not with labor and social questions.

Veblen was equally disturbed. He felt that "the heads of the Inquiry did not appreciate the economic realities involved in achieving an enduring peace."[22] However eccentric his ideas about the obsolescence of national frontiers may have been,[23] he quite sensibly insisted that if the administration was really serious about a people's rather than a victor's peace, the Inquiry would have to campaign for it in the United States, where George Creel was working in the opposite direction. Moreover, in striking out for such a peace, the Inquiry would have to opt for "the spokesmen of revision and adjustment within the established order" over the spokesmen "of vested interests and of the unqualified maintenance of the established order."[24] With revolutionary Russia as a backdrop, Veblen warned of the hazards of returning to the status quo ante: the war to make the world safe for democracy would also have to make America "safe for the common man."[25]

21 *New Republic,* June 2, 1917, p. 137.
22 Dorfman, *op. cit.,* p. 380.
23 See his "The Passing of the National Frontier" (originally published in *The Dial,* Apr. 25, 1918), reprinted in Leon Ardzrooni (ed.), *Thorstein Veblen: Essays in Our Changing Order* (New York, 1934), pp. 383–390.
24 "Suggestions Touching the Working Program of an Inquiry into the Prospective Terms of Peace," from *Essays in Our Changing Order* by Thorstein Veblen. Copyright 1934, 1962 by The Viking Press, Inc. Reprinted by permission of The Viking Press, Inc. (See Appendix II.)
25 "A Policy of Reconstruction" (originally published in the *New Republic,* Apr. 13, 1918), reprinted in Ardzrooni, *op. cit.,* pp. 391–398.

Even Frederick Jackson Turner, politically the most moderate of the New Historians, was moved to make a concrete and constructive suggestion for the updating of Wilson's mid-Victorian liberalism. He wanted the administration to consider giving the League a legislative body in which international parties would be represented. "The last tie that snapped before the [American] Civil War, was the party tie"; perhaps party ties could be used to prevent international disunion.

There is a distinct advantage in utilizing this party system in a League of Nations. . . . In essence it means the utilization of that body of internationalism already in evidence not only in such organizations as radical political parties, such as the International, the I.W.W., Socialists generally, etc., but also the opposite tendencies seen in international business combinations, scientific and educational organizations, and conservative forces generally. The class struggle, so called, is in fact not a national but an international struggle. If party organization is also dominated and shaped by some one or two nations, as Germany or Russia, it will be extended . . . to other countries in the form of secret, or intriguing societies, proceeding by revolutionary methods. . . . The labor groups have been more responsive to the policy of internationalism than . . . other groups. They have a measure of self-consciousness, partly because they have international organizations. There is no reason why similar organizations on an international basis might not be given to conservative parties. . . . We should have at least a rough estimate of the probable power and probable policies of the various groups. This I have not. So far as the special interests of the U.S., however, operate on the decision, she has less to lose by an improvement in the conditions of labor and wages in Europe or Asia than she has to gain. If such a legislative body, therefore, should gain even the power to standardize labor conditions, it must standardize them upward to avoid revolution, and this result, desirable in itself, does not diminish but rather increases the power of the United States to develop international commerce, etc., and makes plain our relatively higher standards.[26]

In spite of the fact that Wilson never formulated a social-economic program to complement his Fourteen Points—in part out of concern for his right flank—these continued to be extraordinarily serviceable. In defeated Europe he was really looking for interlocutors who would talk his language and share his values. Even during the pre-Armistice negotiations Wilson demonstrated

[26] Frederick Jackson Turner, "International Political Parties in a Durable League of Nations," November 1918, published in the *American Historical Review*, Vol. XLVII, No. 3 (Apr. 1942); reprinted by permission of the Henry E. Huntington Library. (See Appendix III.)

that his diplomacy would continue to take account of the inter-section of foreign and domestic affairs.[27] Rather than press for unconditional surrender, he offered negotiated terms in exchange for moderate political reforms in the vanquished empires. He resisted pressures for unconditional surrender not only because he thought it important to check the Associated jingoists on the eve of the Peace Conference but also because he meant to prevent needless suffering and humiliation from enthroning the Spartacists in Berlin.

Indeed, as of October 1918 Wilson knew that he would be caught between the political consequences of victory and defeat. During the preceding half century it had become increasingly apparent that under conditions of acute social conflict military victory tends to strengthen the state and the forces of order, whereas military defeat tends to both weaken the state and strengthen the forces of change. These dates need merely be cited: 1856, 1867, 1871, 1905, and 1917.

The political consequences of victory were in full ascendancy even before the Peace Conference convened. In America the Repub-licans won control of Congress, and the Red Scare was about to begin; in Britain the khaki elections gave the hard-faced men a sweeping majority in Commons; in France the Left-Radicals and the Socialists were in disarray; and in Italy Bissolati and Nitti were eased out of the Cabinet, in some small measure with the help of Mussolini's jingoist claque.

On his so-called triumphal tour of the Allied nations Wilson was cheered above all by the Socialists, laborites, and Left-Radicals, who were all but decimated by this khaki reaction. The roaring cheers never swelled his head precisely because he was fully aware of their tenuous political import. Of course he repeatedly con-sidered appealing to this democratic Left. But he kept postponing such an appeal: he was reluctant to offend the Allied governments and he had few illusions about the effective strength and resolve of his supporters. His Fiume appeal, when it came in late April, was a cry of despair rather than a call to arms. Needless to say, had the Wilsonian parties and factions in Britain, France, and Italy been more powerful, the settlement would not have become nearly so Carthaginian.

In the defeated empires, meanwhile, the situation was quite the

27 The following discussion of Wilson's diplomacy is based on my forthcoming study "The Politics and Diplomacy of Peacemaking, 1918–1919: First Phase of Containment."

reverse. As seen from Paris, Germany continued to be shaken by serious disorders, and the Dual Monarchy had dissolved into perilously unstable successor states. Especially some of Germany's key urban centers, as well as Vienna, repeatedly seemed to hover on the brink of revolution. And then, of course, there was sinister Russia. In Russia defeat, exhaustion, and famine had underwritten Lenin's triumph, and the specter of Bolshevism now haunted Central, Eastern, and East Central Europe.

The lesson of the Russian experience was not lost on Wilson. As a reformer he refused to brand revolution as a conspiracy to be crushed by force, notwithstanding his condonation of the Palmer Raids in America. In his eyes the Bolshevik Revolution was an infectious disease to be quarantined and cured by constant ideological radiation and by promises of economic aid with political strings.

Rather than give top priority to settling accounts with the vanquished and to drawing frontiers, Wilson gave precedence to the containment and prevention of revolution. Negatively this meant keeping Foch, Churchill, Sir Henry Wilson, and Sonnino from mounting a large-scale direct military intervention—with American men and arms. It also meant blocking the French from driving the Germans into either revolution or reaction with excessive territorial demands. Wilson's admonitions against renewing the diplomatic practice of 1871 struck home once Béla Kun came to power in the wake of the French-instigated Romanian advance into unmistakably Hungarian territory.

In positive terms he proceeded to use America's economic and financial resources to stabilize conditions in Germany, Austria, and all the successor states. The promise of food and supplies was held out even before the Armistice; Hoover and Hurley arrived in Paris shortly after Wilson himself; in late January Wilson extracted $100 million from the Congress for food to combat Bolshevism; and even though food and raw materials did not enter Germany before April, they reached all other critical areas as of the turn of the year.

Simultaneously Wilson threw his power and prestige behind the Covenant, the Mandates, and international labor legislation. The League, the Mandates, and the I.L.O.—as well as his opposition to further direct military intervention in Russia—served to bolster the sagging morale of Europe's democratic Left, without which he would have been completely isolated. Wilson needed the support of this Left if the peace treaty were not to turn out even worse than he knew it would. He also wanted to inoculate the left Socialists and syndicalists against the mounting Soviet propaganda.

Because of his training and experience as historian and scholar the American President was rather "formal, academic, and donnish" around the conference table; "the chiselled phrase of the written word expressed him better than the quick repartee of debate."[28] But there were compensations for this academic deformation. It helped Wilson in his efforts to see the present historical juncture "in the light of world history." Wilson was the "seer" of the American delegation, whereas the experts of the Inquiry were "clerks" who had a well-intentioned but nevertheless narrow as well as repeatedly biased concern with national borders. The Inquiry steered clear of such sensitive issues as intervention in Russia and political instability in Central Europe, in part because these were outside their jurisdiction; but it also avoided them because most of the experts, including the historians, were academic conservatives without vision and courage.[29] Undoubtedly the Inquiry, not unlike similar groups in the other major delegations and the statistical commission at the Congress of Vienna, provided essential information. But it goes too far to claim that the Inquiry tempered the President's idealism with "a realistic awareness of the serious obstructions in the path of a just and lasting settlement."[30]

These obstructions were just the sort that the Inquiry historians never even saw, either then or in their subsequent works or musings.[31] It is not that Wilson was blind to the difficulties of drawing

28 Arthur Salter, *Personality in Politics: Studies of Contemporary Statesmen* (London, 1947), p. 156.

29 Of the Inquiry historians, only Samuel E. Morison eventually resigned. He meant to register his protest against Wilson's violation of the letter and spirit of his own peace program. Significantly, since Morison was the Inquiry's "expert" on Baltic problems, he could not avoid coming up against such broader issues as containment and intervention. In fact, in a number of his memoranda he deliberately ranged way beyond the narrow aspects of boundaries and self-determination, and he found Wilson's recognition of Kolchak altogether intolerable. Incidentally, a week before America's declaration of war, this young Harvard historian had expressed his unqualified admiration for Romain Rolland, urging him to stay at his solitary post in Switzerland in order to "keep alive the sacred flame of truth and justice" (Morison to Rolland, March 25, 1917, in Romain Rolland, *Journal des années de guerre, 1914–1919* [Paris, 1952], pp. 1190–1192).

30 See Lawrence E. Gelfand, *The Inquiry: American Preparations for Peace, 1917–1919* (New Haven, 1963), esp. pp. 188, 211–212, 313.

31 Ray Stannard Baker, former muckraker and journalist who served as director of the American Peace Delegation's Press Bureau, all along recognized the nature of these obstructions, even though he repeatedly misjudged their components and scope. Among the studies by high-level participants Baker's *Woodrow Wilson and World Settlement* (3 vols., New York, 1922) stands out for its appreciation of the interplay of peacemaking and the attendant civil war. Again, it is noteworthy that Baker left behind an unpublished "Manuscript Material with Notes from the Peace Conference Records Regarding the Russian Problem as Presented at Paris." Baker himself confessed that "in writing *Woodrow Wilson and World Settlement,* I intended to have a chapter regarding Russia. Notes were made regarding the material we had; but when I came to write the chapter I found so many points where the record was not clear and where I knew there must be background material not in Mr. Wilson's files, that I did not

frontiers in an age of self-conscious nationalism. After all, these difficulties were merely symptomatic of the tortured condition of the postwar world. To paraphrase Wilson's lecture in St. Louis, "frontiers are but one expression of the life of society. They are regulative rather than generative, and historians of our day feel that in writing conventional diplomatic history they are upon the surface only, not at the heart of affairs.[32]

Even in the last prewar decade, on both sides of the Atlantic, liberalism and progressivism had been in retreat. The war merely accelerated the erosion and emasculation of the vital center without which the Wilsonian project could not be viable. In the wake of the Bolshevik Revolution the President's *Weltanschauung* and project were caught between the Scyllas of Revolution and the Charybdis of Counterrevolution. Of course Wilson put up a valiant and partly successful fight. In the last analysis, however, his was the fate of all reformists in revolutionary times: he became a reluctant but indispensable accomplice of political forces considerably more conservative than himself.

No doubt he prevented the worst in Germany; but in his eagerness to ward off Spartacism he condoned the Ebert-Hindenburg pact, the Legien-Stinnes agreement, and the use of the *Freikorps* in the Ruhr and in the Baltic.

Similarly, even though with the help of Lloyd George he forestalled the escalation of direct military intervention in Russia, he nevertheless played a consequential role in the battle against the Bolshevik Revolution. American troops stayed on in northern Russia and Siberia; U.S. money and supplies continued to be sent to the Whites; and America participated in the economic blockade of Soviet Russia. Moreover, U.S. assistance flowed freely to the

---

have and could not get that I dared not complete it. I therefore laid the chapter aside and it has never been printed" (Ray Stannard Baker Papers, Box 18, folders 1–3, Firestone Lib., Princeton Univ.). Meanwhile, in his published work Baker made his position perfectly clear: "At every turn of the negotiations there rose the spectre of chaos, like a black cloud out of the east, threatening to overwhelm and swallow up the world. There was no Russia knocking at the gates of Vienna! At Vienna, apparently, the revolution was securely behind them; at Paris it was always with them. . . . The effect of the Russian problem on the Paris Conference, which will be fully treated elsewhere [*sic*], was profound: Paris cannot be understood without Moscow. Without ever being represented at Paris at all, the Bolsheviki and Bolshevism were powerful elements at every turn. Russia played a more vital part at Paris than Prussia! For the Prussian idea had been utterly defeated, while the Russian idea was still rising in power. When it came to the crisis, then, the need to hold the world steady, keep order, and fight both extremes—militarism on the one hand and Bolshevism on the other—the responsibility of breaking up the Conference became too great. Accommodation became imperative" (*Woodrow Wilson and World Settlement*, I, 102; II, 63–64).
[32] See above, p. 78.

border peoples who, with Allied help, were setting up the ingenuous but Janus-faced *cordon sanitaire*.

This opening phase in the containment of Bolshevism was essentially successful. Even though the Allies failed to overthrow Lenin, they immobilized the Red Army during a crucial year of instability in Eastern and East Central Europe; and they left the revolution confined to a strategically truncated Russia. Wilson himself both promoted and approved this outcome. On the other hand, he was bound to regret the high diplomatic and political cost of containment. Poland and Romania received exorbitant territorial compensations for their part in the freedom fight; and within both countries, as well as in Finland and Hungary, autocratic right-wing parties thrived on this crusade against Bolshevism. Even if he had managed to bring America into the League, Wilson could not have relished the prospect of safeguarding the security and integrity of the regimes of Pilsudski, Brătianu, Mannerheim, and Horthy.

V

Certainly the New Historians should have known better than to blame Wilson for the Carthaginian peace and for the postwar reaction. Instead of intoning their disillusionment they might have set out to systematically analyze the historic vise in which both Wilson and they themselves were caught, in which their common *Weltanschauung* and values were threatened. Among American social scientists, only Veblen, Turner, Robinson, Beard, and Becker had the necessary historical imagination to study the war and its consequences "in the light of world history."

Although Becker never tackled this assignment he gradually admitted that if Wilson had been wrong-headed, he had been "wrong-headed in the right direction."[33] Eventually he even conceded that anger had interfered with his endeavor to understand Wilson until he realized that he was really angry with himself for having "failed to see that he must fail." The President had been caught in a dual power dilemma. Certainly he should not have tried to put over the treaty with the Senate and the people as a fulfillment of his promises. But what did "it matter anyway, [since] it won't last"?[34]

33 Cited in Strout, *op. cit.*, p. 121.
34 Becker to William E. Dodd, June 10, 1920, and Feb. 26, 1923; cited by Phil L. Snyder, "Carl L. Becker and the Great War: A Crisis for a Humane Intelligence," in *The Western Political Quarterly*, Vol. IX, No. 1 (March 1956), pp. 5, 7–8.

When hard pressed, Veblen also came to Wilson's defense. Not that he approved of the President's course. Just the same, he could not accept Keynes's widely acclaimed interpretation in which personal factors counted for so much and that hinged so heavily on a misreading of the President. Was Wilson really the "Nonconformist Minister . . . [whose] thought and temperament were essentially theological and not intellectual, with all the strength and the weakness of that manner of thought, feeling and expression"? Was it really true that it "was harder to de-bamboozle this old Presbyterian than . . . to bamboozle him"?[35]

In his retort, which even Hans Morgenthau might do well to ponder, Veblen looked behind the "smokescreen" of the Covenant:

> . . . [The] difficult but imperative task of suppressing Bolshevism . . . has no part in Mr. Keynes's analysis. . . . Yet it is sufficiently evident now that the exigencies of the Conclave's campaign against Russian Bolshevism have shaped the working out of the Treaty hitherto. . . . Mr. Keynes has much that is uncomplimentary to say of the many concessions and the comprehensive defeat in which the President and his avowed purposes became involved. . . . Due appreciation of this anti-Bolshevik issue, and of its ubiquitous and paramount force in the deliberations of the Conclave should have saved Mr. Keynes from those expressions of scant courtesy which mar his characterisation of the President and the President's work as peacemaker . . . so that a well-considered view of the President's share in the deliberations of the Conclave will credit him with insight, courage, facility, and tenacity of purpose rather than with pusillanimity, vacillation, and ineptitude which is ascribed to him in Mr. Keynes's too superficial review of the case.[36]

For Veblen, then, the tragedy of Versailles was rooted not in Wilson's betrayal but in the nascent civil war; and Wilson, whatever the limitations of his mid-Victorian liberalism, had known how to fight it. Veblen did not like the outcome, either abroad or at home, but he had to give grudging credit where credit was due.

Unfortunately the New Historians never came up with an incisive analysis of the era of the First World War. Meanwhile, however, they maintained their creatively critical posture and refused to turn their back on the central tenets of their *Weltanschauung*. After their unhappy experience with the Wilsonian orthodoxy, they be-

35 John Maynard Keynes, *The Economic Consequences of the Peace* (New York, 1920), pp. 42, 54–55.
36 "The Economic Consequences of the Peace" (first published in *Political Science Quarterly*, Sept. 1920), reprinted in Ardzrooni, *op. cit.*, pp. 462–470, esp. pp. 464–465, 468.

came doubly jealous of the scholar's right and obligation to dissent. Carl Becker was inclined to put a plague on both Democrats and Republicans. In the early thirties he confessed that in forty years he had voted eight times for a President, usually choosing between two men standing for the same thing by flipping a coin. Only twice did he make an intelligent choice. The second time was in 1920. It seemed to him that since "the position of Debs was distinctly different from that of any of the others . . . [he] voted for Debs, not because he was a Socialist, but because he was in jail. . . . Such opportunities to vote intelligently are unfortunately rare."[37]

This posture of skepticism and independence of mind sounds anachronistic to contemporary ears. Julien Benda quite accurately sensed that in the present day

the descendants of Erasmus, Montaigne, Voltaire have denounced humanitarianism as a moral degeneration, nay, as an intellectual degeneration, in that it implies a "total absence of practical common sense," [because] practical common sense has become the measure of intellectual values with these strange "clerks." . . . [Even for Machiavelli] evil, even if it aids politics, still remains evil. . . . The modern realists are the moralists of realism. For them, the act which makes the State strong is invested with a moral character. . . . The evil which serves politics ceases to be evil and becomes good. . . .[38]

In spite of the traumatic shocks and disappointments of the war, the peace, and the aftermath, most progressives and liberals remained faithful to the heritage of the Enlightenment. And until his premature death Woodrow Wilson stood squarely among them.

37 Becker to Dodd, June 10, 1920; cited in Snyder, *op. cit.*, p. 7, and Carl L. Becker, *Everyman His Own Historian* (New York, 1935), pp. 87–88.
38 Julien Benda, *The Betrayal of the Intellectuals* (Boston, 1955), pp. 61, 85.

Some Notes on Historical Record-keeping, the Role of Historians, and the Influence of Historical Memories During the Era of the Second World War

by Herbert Feis

NOW THAT MORE than twenty years have passed since the end of the Second World War—and that most pertinent documents, memoirs, and official histories have been published, and the political controversies about the diplomacy of the war have begun to subside—it is at last possible to examine the war in broader perspective.

Many of the problems that produced the war, and many of the problems that were created by the war, are still with us. In this essay I want to examine three aspects of the war that seem to me to be of special interest and that up to now have received little attention: first, the materials available for the historian of the Second World War and some of the special problems involved in writing—particularly—its history; second, the leading professional historians who served President Roosevelt in important diplomatic positions before and during the war; and finally what is, in many ways, the most interesting problem—the impact of what might be called "historical memories" on some of the outstanding decisions of American wartime diplomacy.

I

History, of course, is first of all a matter of evidence. What is the state of our records, and what evidence exists for writing the history of the Second World War and especially the history of American foreign policy during this period?

The first thing to be observed in this connection is that the military branches of the American government made better pro-

92   THE HISTORIAN AND THE DIPLOMAT

visions for historians to write the history of the Second World War than did the White House or the State Department.

In peacetime, military organizations are drilled in putting down their thoughts on paper and in retaining them carefully. The commanders of every section of every branch and base see to it that journals and logs are kept; and they submit to their superiors in turn systematic reports of their activities and needs. Ambitious officers are encouraged to devote themselves to analytic studies of past campaigns anywhere in the world and against any conceivable enemy. Each day intelligence officers turn out reviews of the military and political situation of other nations, enhanced by their surmises about prevailing or future tendencies and intentions. The Chiefs of Staff always have before them neat sheaves of "situation papers" submitted by trained subordinates.

These practices are, as far as possible, maintained in wartime. Even under fire, desk sergeants and junior officers try hard to keep a running record of every action. Generals and admirals or some staff or public-relations officer assigned to them continue to keep journals. They do so against the chance that if they are unfortunate they may face a court of inquiry after the war. Or if they are fortunate they may enrich their retirement by fighting their battles over again in print; they can look forward to a second career—in the battle of the books.[1]

During the Second World War these standard procedures for keeping records of the kind sought by narrators were supplemented by special measures. A corps of professional historians was recruited from the universities and installed in the Pentagon and in the Navy Department in Washington. Some were attached to the staff of the commanding officers in every important theater of ground operations. Others were given berths on naval flagships; admirals revealed battle plans to them and allowed them to perch perilously on the bridge during battle engagements. Still others were stationed at main air bases to keep account of its main

[1] I cannot refrain from noting also the efforts of officers concerned with supplying the armed forces (known as logistics) to keep continuous inventories of what is stored in thousands of warehouses and supply depots and records of what is used and what is lost. They strive valiantly to continue to do so in tense and dangerous conditions of war when every commander calls for all he can possibly get, when soldiers, sailors, and airmen think of themselves as fighters and not property custodians. Men in uniform of an earlier generation used to regale themselves with the tale of the laden mule who fell over a high cliff in the Philippines during the campaign against Aguinaldo; that wonderful beast was carrying on his back all the equipment—not to mention canned goods—that had been sent to the Philippines that supply sergeants and harried commanding officers could not locate. Never were reports sent back to the War Department so simple and all-inclusive, or so indisputable even by scrupulous historians.

plans and operations, and were now and again taken along on bombing missions. The governors of the Manhattan Project instructed Henry Smythe to keep a current history of the effort to produce atomic bombs and assigned a special reporter, William L. Laurence, to be on the spot in New Mexico and Tinian to witness and record the first tests of the nuclear weapon.

Together these assigned historians amassed a tremendous amount of documentation about the military effort of the United States and its Western allies. Moreover, since they had sat in on so many of the conferences and had become acquainted with many of the senior and junior officers and had witnessed combat operations, their personal impressions illuminated the written word. Their voluminous chronicles were animated by a sense of participation, which was not wholly erased by the committees that subsequently edited their books.

Historians had no such intimate entree into the White House or State Department during the war. None was privileged to have an office close to that of the President, from which vantage point he could obtain invaluable firsthand insight into contemporary American policy. There was no Arthur Schlesinger, Jr., in the Roosevelt or Truman administration.

The occupants of the White House did not have any set practice of making memos of their conversations. Usually they did not trouble to record their views or explain their decisions in writing. As for President Roosevelt, the historian can, of course, garner much from his public speeches, statements at his press conferences, and orders. But he cannot learn nearly so much as he might wish from the personal or official correspondence. Roosevelt was a sporadic letter writer, and most of those he did write are casual in tone and slight in substance. He rarely made written notes either before or after the thousands of his talks with colleagues, subordinates, and foreign representatives. He dashed off many short handwritten or dictated messages called "chits" to the officials who worked under him. In these he might respond to a suggestion, express an opinion, or give an order. But he used the telephone more naturally than the typewriter or pen. The historians of the Roosevelt administration, then, must search for and rely heavily on testimony of others for information about the President's thought and some of his acts.

Even after these are thoroughly explored, important gaps remain in the available records of presidential reasoning and actions. For example, how much fuller documentary information all researchers, including myself, long to have when they try to tell what happened in those ten days of November–December 1941 before Pearl Harbor. Roosevelt did not write down for posterity his impressions and expositions of his purposes and explanatory justifications for his activities during this period. The several subsequent versions of Hull's thoughts that he has bequeathed to us in his memoirs and testimony before the Pearl Harbor Committee are murky. Marshall's memory of what occurred is incomplete. The notes made by Hopkins are fragmentary. The diary kept by Stimson is perhaps the most systematic source of information, but it is hurried and patchy.

Similarly deficient were the arrangements for keeping an official American record of discussions between heads of state and their assistants at the momentous conferences at Casablanca, Quebec, Washington, Cairo, Tehran, and Yalta. The historians of the State Department, in their subsequent compilations of the record of these conferences, had recourse primarily to the summary notes which Charles Bohlen made in the course of his work as interpreter. Historians should be grateful to him for his conscientiousness in writing out these notes despite his weariness after a long day's tense work. But they cannot but wish that the available contemporary records of these conferences were more expansive, precise, and revealing. They sometimes leave the historian to conjecture about the reasoning of the chief figures and the course of their argument; and they seldom provide him with quotations with which he can adorn his tale.

Fortunately, at each of these conferences some other attendant member or members of the American delegation besides Bohlen jotted down, as he listened, fragments of what was said by the historic figures around the table or what he was told by participants while memories were warm. But all these are cryptic and chancy and may be deflected by the author's own temperament and wishes. Of those known to me, the notes made by Averell Harriman, who was at Quebec, Tehran, and Yalta, and who was intimate with both Roosevelt and Churchill, are the most informative. There are also the many books written by American officials who were present during the sessions of the conference—such as the ones by Admiral Leahy, Roosevelt's representative on the Chiefs of Staff, based on his files; those of Secretary of State Cordell Hull, based on his memories of the conference at Moscow; and those of his successor, Edward Stettinius, based on his memories and records of the Yalta conference; and those which Robert Sherwood wrote around the Harry Hopkins papers. Taken altogether, these still leave breaks in our knowledge and some decisions not clearly explained. As far as I know, the only American notes on the talks at Yalta between Roosevelt and Stalin about Far Eastern affairs were the brief ones Averell Harriman jotted down on his own initiative.

Even less is to be found in the official files of the private talks between Truman and Stalin at Potsdam. Those who would like to know exactly what the President told Stalin about the atomic bomb and what Stalin answered must be content with the sentence or two in Truman's *Memoirs,* pallid and laconic, and the terse comment he made to Churchill; for no other American record exists of the words spoken by either Truman or Stalin. As another example, how baffling all historians have found the task of giving a clear, full and reliable historical report and explanation of presidential policy during the Civil War in Spain (1936–1939).[2]

Moreover, the White House system for retaining and filing documents was rather casual. Retention of copies of notes made by Roosevelt and the White House staff and of incoming and outgoing communications was determined by their working needs rather than concern for maintaining a complete historical record. The system of filing was sufficient for the current conduct of affairs and convenience of these officials, but it was elementary and sometimes offhand. Yet all the while, Franklin Roosevelt was mulling over with pleasure plans for the erection of a library in Hyde Park to house the records of his working life and times—emulating, of all his predecessors, Herbert Hoover.

Some of the most important documents were placed in one or another special niche known only to Roosevelt or Hopkins or Missy LeHand or Grace Tully, and in a few instances papers were mislaid or forgotten. No one has yet found any American notes on Roosevelt's conversations with Chiang Kai-shek at Cairo in December 1943; yet it is probable that some were made by somebody.

Truman was able to acquaint himself with the text of the secret agreement about the Far East that Roosevelt had made with Stalin at Yalta in February 1945 only because Admiral Leahy remembered that he had the President's copy in his safe.

2 The best I have read are contained in F. Jay Taylor's *The United States and the Spanish Civil War* (New York, 1957) and Chap. 8 of Julius Pratt's *Cordell Hull, 1933–44* (New York, 1963).

The American government had to request the British government to provide it with a copy of the accord reached by Roosevelt
and Churchill at their second Quebec conference in August 1944
about the joint United States–British decisions in regard to the
development and use of atomic weapons.

The making and keeping of historical records in the State
Department was more regular than in the White House. But
even so, the system did not meet the desired standard of archivists
and historians. Most American ambassadors and consuls were
assiduous in reporting their observations, contacts, and actions. The
Secretary of State and most other senior officers of the department maintained tradition by making memos of their important
talks with foreign officials and representatives of other departments.
The Division of Communications and Records within the department customarily decided, under necessarily general instructions,
the distribution and routing of messages received from abroad
and those sent abroad. But the individual officer determined for
himself the routing of papers he originated and how long after
they had found their way back to him he would retain them in
his own divisional files.

Despite laxity in these procedures, they did not work too badly,
for at that time the number of officers in the State Department
who dealt with matters of significance, who made decisions, was
small—perhaps not more than twenty. And all were trained to
give and require responsible accounts of affairs of importance
that came to their attention and to preserve documents and
communications.

Thus the industrious historian will sooner or later be able to
extract from the archives of the State Department reliable—though
not always so complete or revealing as could be wished—knowledge of its activities and those of its diplomatic missions during the
Second World War. But, in my time, the search for a particular
message or memo or group of them might turn into a hunting
expedition in the black index books into which entries were made
as papers were dispatched to the files from other lairs in which
they had been reposing—perhaps for months or years. A long
time could elapse before papers that arrived in the central record
office were sorted out and properly indexed, since the amount of
money provided for these purposes was ridiculously meager. The
members of the small staff of this division were helpful hunters,
with memories of the location of thousands of papers that had

been placed in their custody during the decades in which they had worked in this division. One of these I particularly remember. He was an elderly Negro named Holmes, whose really happy home was among the filing cabinets, boxes, and shelves that contained both what was glorious and inglorious in our history.

The system allowed two possibilities that historians must lament. One was that the records of important missions in foreign countries might be mislaid. If and when these papers were sent back to Washington, they might long remain in their original packages before the small staff could dispose of them properly. I remember the disorder in which I found the records of the European Advisory Commission. The sides of their cardboard containers having been broken, they were strewn loosely along the lowest shelf in an unfrequented alcove in the files. Even more vivid in my memory is the location of the pile of unopened brown-paper bundles containing the originals of the messages exchanged between General Marshall, while special representative in China, and President Truman and Secretary of State Byrnes. These were heaped up in a small ground-floor den in the State Department building into which neither light nor air entered from outside. They were not hidden or lost. The Records Division simply did not have the time or space to house them better or the money or staff then to process them promptly.

Another defect in the system of making and keeping records was that senior officers, if they chose, could take, or even destroy, before or after they left office, papers in which their words, acts, or experiences were set down. They seldom did so, but instances were not unknown. Secretary of State Cordell Hull had the Secretary of the American delegation to the abortive Economic Conference in London in 1933 burn the minutes he had kept of the meetings of the American delegation. More frequently officers, on leaving the department, carried off originals of some official papers that were mingled with personal ones—but these were usually returned to the department later on. It may be noted also that some significant groups of State Department documents that had been sent to the White House for President Roosevelt's attention were kept there and sent along with presidential papers to Hyde Park, where they were found later on.

One vanished paper for which I searched eagerly when I was writing my book on the coming of the war[3] was a "chit"—well remembered by several of those who read it at the time—that

3 *The Road to Pearl Harbor* (Princeton, 1948).

Roosevelt in August 1941 had sent to the State and Treasury departments. This small piece of paper bore a blue check next to the entry "Freeze Japanese Funds"—an action that resulted in the cessation of all shipments of oil to Japan. But who knows, some day this may turn up in a trunk that is being cleaned out by the grandson of one of my former colleagues.

The whole system has been transformed, of course, since the days I am talking about. Now there are scores of regulations about the making and keeping of records, spacious storage rooms, standardized systems of routing, indexing, and filing, and a much larger staff to carry out these tasks and to assist both officials and historians to find them. However, there are much more severe security restrictions and formalities to hinder the historian and much more massive documentation to weary him. And for all I know someone more *au courant* than I with present-day experience will later confide to another audience that as many papers were extracted or went astray as before.

The records concerning the conduct of American foreign relations will be more scattered in separate libraries built to commemorate the services of Presidents, secretaries of state, and generals. No doubt these structures are preferable to solemn monuments or equestrian statues. But each will be guarded by official custodians. Some of these may deem that their first loyalty is to the image of their hero whose papers are in their care—at least while he is still alive. Or the trustees may want to protect his fame against possible tarnish or rust that might be caused by the probing of historians. And it is hard to learn whether some of the papers that ought to be in these commemorative collections have been held out by request or bequest. These are reasons for misgiving because the historical records of our times are being filtered through the screens of authorized guardians—the archivists and trustees of the memorial libraries and foundations.

There was in the State Department the Historical Division, in which a conscientious and qualified group of men worked industriously. However, they were engaged primarily in routine tasks. Their chief assignment was to collect and edit documents from the files to be printed in the annual publications of *Foreign Relations of the United States*. This procession of volumes followed the events recorded in them by about twenty years. The members of this division responded willingly to current requests of all other sections of the department for information regarding the previous history of situations and issues with which they were currently concerned. They also contributed material for speeches and for communications to foreign governments.

But members of the Historical Division were seldom, if ever, invited to be present during top-level discussions of contemporary affairs. Therefore they had little chance to secure firsthand knowledge of the historical events about which, many years later, they or their successors would collect and edit the documents. Even less frequently was their advice sought. In short, the influence of the Historical Division on the shaping of decisions was only in imparting educational information. Its contacts with officials responsible for decisions being remote and intermittent, the division could do little to ensure that current policy was in sound accord with past experience. Had it been able to be more effective in this respect, I believe some mistakes might have been avoided; for example, the American government might not have reposed exclusive confidence in China as a prospective postwar ally in Asia.

The office of the Legal Adviser was also a repository of information about the past, especially about the questions that involved treaties and international law. The Legal Adviser was often asked for his views on the legal aspects of a current question; he thus had considerably more chance to influence policy—that is, to make history—than the members of the Historical Division. But being by nature modest and careful to avoid trouble, his advice seldom contravened the views of his superiors; he usually provided reasons for what they wished to do instead of attempting to tell them what ought to be done.

I should pay homage to one member of the State Department whose memory was colossal and generosity inexhaustible. His name was Frederick Livesey. He was Assistant Economic Adviser, but his learning extended in every realm. Any State Department official who wanted to inform himself of the intricate history of an economic, financial, or commercial matter beat a track to his desk—at which he had sat for more than thirty years, peering through his thick glasses over the piles of papers and documents that were his constant companions.

There were two other clusters in the State Department that provided historical information. One was the small staff of the State-War-Navy Coordination Committee (SWNCC). This committee was composed of assistant secretaries of these three departments. The policy papers it produced were usually approved by the three department heads to which the committee reported and by the White House. SWNCC was created to deal with immediate questions arising in the course of the conduct of the war. However, its work and decisions brought about situations that could not easily be changed once the war was over. Its subcommittees sought to keep the committee aware of the historic past; the committee itself made history during and after the war.

One decision in which SWNCC had a leading part was the formulation of the economic, financial, and political policies to be pursued after Allied forces landed in North Africa and Italy. Another was the composition of the directive to General Eisenhower, Supreme Commander of Allied Forces in Western Europe. This document outlined principles to guide him in dealing with French civilian authorities as the Allied armies traveled across that country and in the exercise of his authority in Germany as the troops of the Western Allies advanced into that country. A third was the directive sent to General MacArthur, Supreme Commander of the Allied Forces in the Far East, to guide him in the control of Japan. Of course in the preparation of such primary instructions as these, SWNCC consulted many officials in all branches of government concerned—none more than the intelligence divisions of the Army and Navy—which compounded the pros and cons of every situation and contingency.

Then also there were the desk officers in the geographical divisions of the State Department. On questions ordinary and extraordinary they provided historical information. Many of them had been students and observers of, and had officially reported on, the previous development of questions in their area of responsibility. And most kept near at hand folders of pertinent information for which they might be asked at any moment. Because of their familiarity with issues and their involvement in the process of negotiation, it was they who wrote most of the briefing papers for the instruction and guidance of their superior officers who were about to engage in important diplomatic discussions and conferences.

Some decision-makers sometimes read through the whole text of these briefing papers. But more often they scanned only the summaries and conclusions. And not always that; some of the most thorough papers remained undisturbed in the black binders that the President and Secretary of State took with them when they went abroad. Those who wrote them usually had more time than those for whom they were written.

None of the top American decision-makers during this period was a habitual reader of documented books or memos. Each would rely for information and impressions primarily on personal talks and the summary notes handed to him by some associate in connection with their talk. Roosevelt, as President, paid more attention to memos and briefing papers originating in the military departments than to those originating in the State Department. Harry Hopkins was even more casual in his treatment of State Department memos. Both were loath to have their views blurred and their decisions blunted by notes written by officials of the State Department whose minds—and spirits—with few exceptions, they thought to be deadened by stale diplomatic routine. But the President found it hard to refuse to scan the sheaves that Secretary of the Treasury Henry Morgenthau—who frequently yearned to exercise the authority of the Secretary of State as well—left on his luncheon tray or desk.

Secretary of State Cordell Hull had had a decidedly studious bent as a young man and a senator. However, by the time he became Secretary of State his energies were waning. He was usually too beset by the demands of his office and the challenges to his authority to do more than read the memos on urgent business that his own staff sent to his desk. But that he did conscientiously. His successor, Edward Stettinius, was an affable man without intellectual depth or interest. He was content to rely on the verbal reports of facile minds about him. His willingness to adopt without question the views and wishes of Roosevelt and Hopkins was one of the reasons why he was selected for the office; he did not stay up nights reading Thucydides.

President Truman had a genuine interest in the history of national affairs and a lively memory of its figures and episodes. However, his knowledge of the previous history of international affairs was sketchy. During his first year in office he had little chance to do anything more than to acquaint himself with the records of the Roosevelt administration. He also was no longer, by this time, an intent reader of books or memos. He preferred companionship to the isolation of the study. As often as not, he pulled his decisions out of his hat rather than out of his files. The Secretary of State that served under him, James F. Byrnes, also a former senator, was a person of similar disposition and ways.

In this roving review of the sources of historical information, the intelligence section of the Office of Strategic Services should most certainly be included. Professor William L. Langer of Harvard was one of the main contributors to, and editor and author of, its confidential reports, which often reached back into the past as well as forward toward the future. These were well read and respected. But, regrettably, I have too slight firsthand knowledge or memory of its inner organization, methods of work, and of communication of its views to attempt to appraise the possible importance of its influence on policy-making.

Almost all the work of a historical character that I have reviewed up to this point was activated primarily by the need to deal with the questions that arose in connection with the conduct of the war—a war that was being fought by the United States as a member of a complicated coalition. But either later in 1942 or early in 1943 preparatory work was begun on issues that, it could be foreseen, would present themselves when the war was won and the Allies set about determining peace terms and postwar arrangements. The committee then formed to study the problems of peace was called the Advisory Committee on Post-War Foreign Policy.[4] Charles Dickens would have had another name for it. I believe Sumner Welles, the Under Secretary of State, was the prime mover in this undertaking. But Hull was designated chairman, out of regard for his sensibilities, and because of his interest in general principles. Hull was aggrieved at the freedom with which Welles used his privilege of direct recourse to Roosevelt; Welles was annoyed at Hull's caution and increasing vagueness.

The committee was a loose conglomeration. Some of its members were officials of the State Department, some were senators and congressmen—and along with these were a few eminent and qualified outsiders. The sessions I attended were drifting and depressing. The discussions were random and inconclusive. Neither Hull nor Welles, both of whom always had urgent demands on

---

4 For a detailed account of the personnel of this committee, of its subcommittees, and of the divisions in the State Department that contributed to it, and of the meetings, reports, and studies of each and all, see State Department Publication #3580 (1947), *Post-War Foreign Policy Preparation,* by Harley Notter. However, this account is an uncritical compendium that gives a misleading impression both of the value of the work done and of the influence of this whole conglomeration of committees and memo writers. The estimation of the importance of the work of the committee given in Chap. 22, "Planning for the Post-War World," in Julius Pratt's biography of Cordell Hull, also seems to me to be dubious. The one and only matter to which the committee made an effective contribution—the preparatory work for the formation of the United Nations—is singled out; the abortiveness of all the rest of the committee's work is barely noticed.

their time and energy, gave sufficient and steady guidance to the committee. The congressional members took no responsibility for its performance; some seemed to lack belief in the utility of the project, and they were wary lest they lose their future freedom to dissent from the decisions of the administration. In short, the committee had little cohesion and no authority.

Subcommittees were formed for the more intensive consideration of each prospective main problem. For their work many professional students of foreign affairs, including some historians, were recruited from outside the government. These subcommittees strove earnestly to supply recommendations—but only a few managed to progress beyond the point of identifying difficulties and alternatives.

Under the best auspices and most favorable circumstances the task of the Advisory Committee would have been one of great difficulty. But both were adverse. The President and Hopkins showed only incidental interest in its work.

Some of the settled policies of the administration compelled the committee to grope among conjectures; one policy in particular did so: Hull's opposition, with Roosevelt's assent, to making agreements with the United States' allies regarding postwar questions—especially territorial ones—while the war was still going on. This compelled the committee and its subcommittees to try to conceive recommendations for an undefined future time and an obscure future international scene. Before victory was won the armed forces of each of the Allies would have come into control of enemy territory; their diplomatic relations might have changed in ways that could not be foreseen, and conflicting desires, suppressed during the war, might be revealed. And while the committee was left to formulate policies and make plans for this uncertain future, the President and the military authorities, without consulting it, were making decisions that had immutable effects on the future.

No wonder, then, that the work of the Advisory Committee on Post-War Foreign Policy was futile and neglected. Only one effective contribution can be conclusively credited to it: it did sustain the impetus toward the formation of a collective organization to maintain peace after the war, and it kept the thinking of the American government toward that end in the lead.

It left one other important residue. To service the committee, the Division of Special Research was created within the State Department. This survived the demise of the parent committee and spawned several subdivisions of its own. Leo Pasvolsky was in charge of their zealous activities. He was a former professor, voluble and likable, whose ideas and ideals were always held in line with those of Secretary of State Hull. His patience was inexhaustible. He sat without wilting through any and all long and dull discussions and committee meetings. He wrote and rewrote, with no evident decline in zest, speeches and press statements for the Secretary of State in which the same principles and attitudes were reiterated over and over. For the rapidly expanding staff of the division he recruited many historians, economists, political scientists, and lawyers who were eager for a chance to play a part in shaping the future. The production of papers was an esteemed activity, which flourished mightily even as the Advisory Committee languished. I wonder in which special cavern in the National Archives repose undisturbed these mementos of studious eagerness to bring about a just and lasting peace.

II

Such were the many conduits within the government through which historical knowledge flowed. In addition I will write briefly about three leading professional historians who were appointed to important diplomatic posts.

William E. Dodd, soon to be elected president of the American Historical Association, was sent as ambassador to Germany in 1933. He was not happy in that post and his performance was ineffectual.[5] But I do not think the fault was mainly his. The heads of the Nazi government had neither admiration nor respect for men of academic learning—except for those few who nourished their inflamed spirits and ambitions. To Dodd the principles and actions of the Hitler regime were repugnant. He did not disguise his feelings or repress his views. But because during the period of his ambassadorship Hitler knew that the majority of Americans did not want to get dangerously involved in European questions, Dodd's criticisms and protests were usually ignored by the *Führer's* Chancellory and Ribbentrop's Foreign Office. Ironically, the same attitudes and qualities that alienated the German leaders caused Dodd to be depreciated by some of the officials in the State Department who were directly concerned with European affairs. They thought him too emotional and indiscreet. His wholesomely indignant

---

5 The reasons are not clear to me, and remain so even after reading his diary, *Ambassador Dodd's Diary 1933–38* (New York, 1941), William E. Dodd, Jr., and Martha Dodd (eds.).

reports from Germany alarmed rather than impressed them, for he served during those years when the wish to remain isolated and neutral governed American policy. Moreover, he offended influential financial groups and American holders of German bonds and other creditors by his reluctance to press their claims for repayment— on the whole fair claims, it may be remarked, and within the capacity of National Socialist Germany to pay had it not been spending such large sums on armaments. His study of history had confirmed his prejudice against banking interests, national and international.

Claude G. Bowers was a popular rather than an academic historian. He had friends and acquaintances in both the executive and congressional branches of government and was intimate with members of the Democratic National Committee. A Jeffersonian Democrat who espoused the ideas of the New Deal, he was appointed ambassador to Spain when that country had a leftist republican government. But events displaced him and he lost his chance to make history, for when civil war broke out in Spain in 1936, Bowers was at a summer resort near the French border. On instructions from Washington, he, along with most of his diplomatic colleagues, crossed over into France and spent the war years at Saint-Jean-de-Luz. Roosevelt and Hull favored his absence from Madrid since it made it easier for them to sustain their policy of detachment. In his frontier listening post, communication with Washington was more reliable than it would have been in Madrid. But regrettably, he was away from the scene of the war and out of personal touch with the leaders of both sides.

During the later years of the Second World War, Professor Carlton J. H. Hayes of Columbia University served as American ambassador in Madrid. Hayes was a gifted scholar with a wide and reflective knowledge of European history, a devout Catholic, and a conservative. Whether due to his professional training or his religious sympathies or his political judgments, he was a strong defender of Franco against those elements in the American government that wanted to down him after war broke out in Europe in 1939. While Hayes did not get along well with his British colleague, Sir Samuel Hoare, and although they were rivals for credit, their diplomatic objectives were similar and their efforts complementary. Hayes restrained the American government from taking actions that might have either forced Franco out of office or impelled him to respond to German overtures. His sympathetic attitude quite possibly encouraged those individuals and elements in the Spanish government that did not want to tie up with Hitler, and reconciled Franco to American criticisms. Although Carlton Hayes was a firm supporter of the Franco regime, he disliked both the Nazis and the Fascists.

In sum, professional historians were outside rather than inside the circle of those civilians who formulated policies and made decisions during the Second World War. Their influence was relatively slight and random. I can point to only one great decision that can be said to have flowed directly—perhaps primarily—from their studies and advice. Historians and their professional associates in law and political science did have much to do with the development of ideas regarding the need for and the nature of the collective security organization that was brought into existence—and the Charter of the United Nations.

III

In contrast, American policies during the Second World War were much colored by the recollections of the decision-makers of past experiences or events. But any attempt to trace how and how deeply they influenced actions must be conjectural.

Policies and decisions emerge from a fiery combination of circumstances and calculation, not from a quiet, thought-conditioned chamber. Then also, as Sidney Hook has remarked, ". . . In many situations it is not the actual past which determined the present as what people imagine the past to have been." Decision-makers, like the rest of us, are prone to screen their memories and enliven them with their emotions or imagination. And to compound the difficulties of correct inference, most decisions were the outcome of discussions and often compromises among several individuals, each of whom had his own span of historical recall. Different experiences were most alive in the experience of each.

Still, who can doubt that Roosevelt vividly remembered the tragic defeat of Woodrow Wilson's effort to have the United States join the League of Nations and win Senate approval of the Treaty of Versailles? Or that he had not forgotten the divisive argument over whether the British and French governments had unconditionally assented to Wilson's Fourteen Points as the basis of peace with Germany? Or that there rang in his head Hitler's repeated assertions that the Versailles treaty violated the principles stated in Wilson's declarations, and his shrieking accusations that Germany therefore had been tricked and most cruelly treated?

We know from his writings as well as from his stand on many issues of strategy during the Second World War that Churchill had a chilling remembrance of the agony and great loss of lives in a land war of direct confrontation—the appalling four years of trench warfare, 1914–1918. We know that he still thought back ruefully to what he felt had been a great mistake: that Britain did not carry through the assault against the Turks in the Dardanelles, a military venture that ended in disaster and interrupted his career.

In defense of his demands, Stalin repeatedly reverted to the events of 1918–1919, the stumbling efforts of the Western Allies to assist reactionary czarist generals to crush the Bolsheviks and their later support of Polish territorial claims.

Hull brooded anxiously over several upsetting occurrences during his years in the Senate and the State Department before the Second World War. He saw a warning in the uproar that had ensued when members of the Foreign Relations Committee of the Senate learned of the secret treaties that had been signed by the Allies before American entry into the First World War. He continuously connected the high trade restrictions that nations erected in the twenties and thirties with the trend toward war—almost as cause and consequence.

These few pointers to some of the front patches in the historical memories of these few decision-makers may suffice to suggest how greatly they varied from one another in scope, depth, and impact on their conduct during the Second World War.

Having emphasized that the influence of historical memory is contingent and hard to prove with precision, I will try to identify some elements of policy on which its impact seems to have been both evident and important.

First I will take one field in which the impress of memories of the First World War experience is clearly distinguishable: the nature of the financial relations between the United States and its Allies before and during the Second World War.

Before American entry into the First World War the British and French governments had sold several hundreds of millions of dollars of bonds to American banks and private investors and had also contracted large debts to them and to American munitions makers. Subsequently American critics alleged that the determination of the lenders not to lose their money—as they would have if Britain and France had been defeated—had been one of the main reasons why the American government was propelled into the war. This exaggerated emphasis still swayed enough Americans during the 1930's—when war in Europe loomed again—to lead to the enactment of laws forbidding loans to foreign governments for the purchase of munitions even while they were not engaged in war and the making of either public or private loans to governments when they were. During these years dependence of the governments fighting the Axis on American financial assistance was more acute than it had been during the First World War because in 1939 neither the British nor the French possessed nearly so great a sum of foreign investments that their governments could mobilize and sell as they had had in the earlier struggle.

The state of American opinion would have in any case debarred the government from giving its future allies the financial aid they urgently required, in the form of loans, even after the war broke out in Europe. Moreover, historical memory of the terse later quarrels caused by the subsequent demands by the American government for repayment of principal and interest on the loans it had made to its associates in the First World War produced a determination not to risk a repetition of this experience; for our former allies had regarded these obligations as having been incurred in a common cause to which they had suffered most in lives and material loss. Then during the depression they had defaulted. Isolationists and others in and out of Congress had maintained indignantly that the cessation of repayment was a mark of ingratitude. They averred that it was another proof of the wisdom of never again linking our political fortunes with those of other countries. Legislation was passed (the Johnson Act) banning loans to defaulting governments.

During his first two or three years in office Roosevelt had seemed to sympathize with this popular disapprobation of public lending to foreign authorities. He was caustic about the defaults and allied attempts to draw the United States back into European affairs by linking resumption of their payments to the United States on World War I debts with resumption of German reparations payments to them. The resulting dispute between the American and debtor governments had injurious effects on all, weakening the diplomacy of all, retarding their economic recovery, and digging a political ditch between them.

The rancor aroused by the refusal of our former allies to continue payments had debarred the granting of new loans to them during the 1930's, when the United States should have been aiding them to expand their industries and build up their military strength.

This financial negativism and our neutrality legislation caused Hitler to be more confident that Germany could make itself supreme in Europe. Only when the British Commonwealth was valiantly striving all by itself to maintain resistance against Germany and Italy, and in dire need of financial assistance to procure the means of doing so, did Roosevelt try to find a way to provide them. Then, still mindful of the grievous consequences of the system of lending during the First World War, he and his advisers devised the ingenious Lend-Lease basis of assistance.

In this connection Hull's view of historical experience came into play. He grasped what he thought an excellent chance to exact from the distressed beneficiaries of Lend-Lease pledges that after the end of the war they would cooperate to reduce trade barriers and forgo discrimination in trade. He considered equality of treatment in commerce to be one of the prime conditions of peaceful relations between nations. However, the British government would not, even under duress, renounce imperial preferences unconditionally. So after arduous argument Hull had to satisfy himself with a qualified promise. Since the French Committee of National Liberation (known more popularly as the Free French Provisional Government) was not recognized as the government of France until October 1944, no attempt was made to obtain a similar promise from it until much later. And because all of its foreign commerce was arbitrarily conducted by the Soviet government on what was essentially a barter basis, no way was worked out adopting the principle to its system of trade, no rule that the Soviet government could be expected to observe impartially.

How great a deviation from this policy of trade equality, which the American government so stubbornly persisted in before, during, and immediately after the Second World War, was its later enthusiastic endorsement of the preferential accords entered into by six countries of Western Europe, designed to create a common market. By the 1950's fear of Soviet Communism had become stronger than the lingering view of the historical effect of trade discrimination that had seemed so important to Hull and the negotiators of our trade agreements.

Recall of episodes in the past accounted in part for Roosevelt's stubborn sponsorship of the principle of "unconditional surrender." This terse statement of the only terms on which we would make peace did not mean, as has been alleged so often, that the Presi-

dent's military and political aims were unlimited and wholly
unsettled in his mind. It did mean that he did not want to bargain with either our allies or our enemies while the war was still
being fought. He wanted to retain the unimpaired right to formulate the actual terms to be imposed upon the enemy in the light
of prevailing circumstances at the end of the war. It is probable
that he did not foresee how drastically the scope of his opportunity to do so would be fenced in by military movements and
by political changes that occurred in the course of the war. By
1944–1945 both Roosevelt and Truman had to reckon with the
fact that in some situations possession was, if not nine-tenths of
the law, more than half of it.

Pressure to define our terms in advance first arose when, after
Mussolini had been displaced, the Italian government in September
1943 made overtures of surrender. The several emissaries sent to
General Eisenhower's headquarters in Africa tried to extract preliminary promises of leniency from him. Or rather, they were
brazen enough to wish that Italy be allowed to change its uniform
at once and, having been an ally of Germany, be accepted at once
as an ally of the West and be treated as such. Several statements
emanating from Eisenhower's headquarters had averred that the
Allies would not be vengeful or cruel or oppressive. But, regarding
formal obligations, Eisenhower summarily demanded and secured
an "unconditional surrender."

The same general course of reserving expressions of our precise
intentions was pursued in regard to Germany. But it was upset by
a curious episode. While meeting with Churchill in Quebec in
September 1944 Roosevelt impulsively approved a plan composed
in the Treasury Department and pushed forward by Secretary of
the Treasury Morgenthau. Neither Hull, whose historical memories
would have led him to oppose the plan, nor Stimson, who would
have resisted it because he would have foreseen the troubles it
would cause our army of occupation, was present. This drastic
program envisaged the permanent reduction of Germany's heavy
industries and the division of the country into several independent
states. The quick protests of Cabinet officers and the lively uproar
that arose when the plan became public knowledge caused both
Roosevelt and Churchill to retreat from it as fast as they could
without openly repudiating it.

Thereafter until his death, Roosevelt remained chary of all
proposals that our peace terms for Germany be discussed and

announced and settled before the demand for unconditional surrender was accepted. However, when Allied forces began to thrust
into Germany from the West, the President authorized Eisenhower
to assure the German people, in general terms, that they would
not be oppressed and kept in bond forever.

At Cairo in December 1943 Roosevelt did forewarn Japan
that it would be deprived of all its empire, and he promised Chiang
Kai-shek that the former Chinese territories conquered by Japan,
including Manchuria, would be returned. The President was impelled to do so by the wish to sustain Chinese resistance. In retrospect it is clear that this departure from the rule of vagueness
about our intentions was too lax. Otherwise Roosevelt refused to
define in advance or clarify American intentions in regard to Japan
after "unconditional surrender."

Truman—and I think this is also a matter for regret—resisted
pleas in the spring of 1945 that he reassure the Japanese people
that they need not fear extinction or inhumane treatment. He waited
until July 1945, after the atomic bomb had fallen on Hiroshima, to
promise in the Potsdam Declaration that their millions of soldiers
would be repatriated to Japan and not held as prisoners; that civilian
Japanese property would not be taken; and that the Japnese people
would be permitted to restore their economic life and after a while
to govern themselves. These assurances should have been given the
Japanese people months earlier—as Under Secretary of State Grew
had urged.

Several congruent reasons combined to make both Roosevelt and
Truman stubbornly resist pleas to make known well in advance the
terms to be imposed on our enemies, in order to allay their fear of
what might happen to them if they surrendered "unconditionally."
Some of these reasons were tactical, others due to recollection of
what had happened during and after the First World War.

The actual terms that Roosevelt and Stalin—and in most matters
Churchill as well—intended to exact were hard ones. They were not
inhumane. But it could be foreseen that enemies would not accept the terms until and unless they were decisively beaten and
virtually helpless: for Japan, for example, complete expulsion from
China and loss of its whole empire; for Germany, the loss of all
territories seized by Hitler, the compression of German frontiers,
prolonged occupation and control, and condign punishment of
Nazi leaders and war criminals. Hence, declaration of these intentions would not have evoked surrender. To have disguised our real

intentions, as Stalin suggested to Hopkins in April 1945, would have exposed the United States to future accusations of duplicity—such as were made about the Treaty of Versailles. It was judged more sensible to reserve our right to impose the terms in mind after "unconditional surrender." And in my judgment, in the case of Italy and Germany, this did not prolong their resistance. Mussolini could not have been induced to admit defeat. Hitler's control of Germany remained strong enough to the end to keep the Germans fighting on as long and as hard as they did, rather than accept the terms imposed on them later—especially since not only Hitler but also the German generals in command did not lose hope of making a separate peace with either the Western Allies or the Soviet Union.

This prudential reason for retaining the formula and principle of "unconditional surrender" was upheld and supplemented by several others in which historical recollection also played an active part. One was the real risk that if the Allies fell to arguing among themselves about the terms of surrender and peace, the alliance would be jeopardized. There were clear indications of divergent or even conflicting purposes and claims among its members. Attempts to settle them while the war was being fought might have regrettable consequences. They might adversely affect military cooperation or even cause a rupture in the coalition. Or they might, as happened at the end of the First World War, eventuate in interallied accords that were unclear and did not express genuine and definite agreement. Not forgotten were the arguments that had ensued over the meaning and validity of the reservations that the Allies had made in Wilson's Fourteen Points before they agreed to have them presented to Germany. These disputes had left a hazy area over which Wilson, Lloyd George, and Clemenceau had wrangled at length at the Paris Peace Conference.

A connected reason for stern adherence to the principle was the determination not to give our enemies any ground for claiming later that their surrender had been conditional on promises about the terms of peace. Commanding in Roosevelt's memory was the way in which the German government had argued—the government of Weimar moderately, Hitler vehemently—that the terms of the Versailles treaty, which Germany was compelled to accept, were a violation of the Allied proposals. From these contentions sprouted the legend that Germany had not really been defeated in the war but had been deceived by false promises to lay down its arms.

Thereby ground was laid for allegations that Germany was therefore justified in tearing up the Treaty of Versailles as soon as it dared.

Several members of the State Department present at a discussion in the White House remember Roosevelt's grimace as he read aloud an extract from Norman Davis' report of his first talk with the new chancellor, Hitler, in April 1933. "It was ridiculous," Hitler had exclaimed, "for France to have any fear of Germany. The only reason why France could have any apprehension of Germany was because she was doing an unjust thing to force Germany forever to live under treaty conditions which no self-respecting nation could tolerate. These conditions were not comparable with the promises which had been made Germany in the Fourteen Points of President Wilson on the basis of which she had agreed to lay down her arms."

This German contention had been fed by the work of Western writers, especially by John Maynard Keynes, in a most influential book, *The Economic Consequences of the Peace*, published in 1920. In this work he had deposed with ardor that the reparations settlement imposed on Germany was illegitimate and that it had doomed Europe to economic disaster. With indignation that turned into scorn, he blamed Wilson for his anguished departures from announced principles.

Revisionist historians, among whom two Americans, Sidney B. Fay and Harry Elmer Barnes, were in the forefront, disputed with weighty historical evidence the judgment written into the peace treaty that Germany was exclusively responsible for the advent of the war. Other historians criticized various features of the postwar treaties with Germany and the former Austro-Hungarian Empire—particularly the boundaries drawn in Central and Eastern Europe—and the seizure of all the German colonies as historically unwise or unjust. All the while, Communist journalists and professors spewed forth Marxist denunciations of the acquisitions and claims of the victorious Western Allies.

In sum, the revised versions of the causes of the war, conjoined with accusations that the peace settlements were not in accord with Wilson's prior pledges, served to undermine them. Some of his Fourteen Points had proved to be unsound, others not possible to put into effect. His idealistic effort to arrange a peace for the future by enjoining all countries to constrain themselves and deal tolerantly and justly with others failed. His attempt to do so had aroused division among the Allies and had given the Germans a reputable reason for violating the treaties it had signed. It is safe to sur-mise that Roosevelt pondered over this tragic experience of his former chief. And it made him the more determined not to give any future Italian, German, or Japanese government possible ground for similar accusations of bad faith in the aftermath of World War II.

However, Roosevelt and Hull did make notable efforts to gain advance assent to the broad principles to shape the peace and regu-late the conduct of nations after the war. Roosevelt first tried to do so even before the United States entered the war—in the joint declara-tion he issued with Churchill in August 1941, called the Atlantic Charter. As an almost daily exercise in exhortation, Hull propounded the rules of conduct ("Pillars of Peace") by which he was con-vinced that nations must abide if they were to live and prosper. Preachment of these he deemed so essential a preparation for effective action that he almost at times seemed to regard them as a substitute. The Secretary of State briefly believed that at the Conference of Foreign Ministers in Moscow in November 1943 he had won the reliable approval of even the Soviet government to his sensible—though too inflexible—principles. In his report to Congress on No-vember 18, 1943, he said that "As the provisions for the Four Nation Declaration are carried into effect, there will no longer be need for spheres of influence, for alliances, for balance of power or any other of the special arrangements through which in the un-happy past the nations strove to safeguard their security or to pro-mote their interest." [6]

Concordantly with its wish to keep the future open, the American government was inclined to abstain—while the war was being fought —from making agreements, open or secret, regarding territorial set-tlements. It also did its best to deter its allies from entering into them.

This policy, too, was sustained by historical memories. Roosevelt and Hull and many Democratic senators remembered the grievous consequences of Wilson's failure to challenge the secret bargains made by the European Allies during the First World War about their respective territorial claims, and his surprising later denial that he had been informed of them. Then at the Peace Conference in 1919 he had met stubborn rejections of his suggestion that some of the promises of these accords were inadvisable and in contra-

---

6 Hull's reminiscences of this conference are told in the second volume of his *Memoirs* (New York, 1948), p. 1312 *et seq.*

vention of the Fourteen Points. Opponents of American membership in the League of Nations had been able the more persuasively to argue that it would be foolish and wrong to pledge ourselves to maintain the territorial arrangements set down in these secret diplomatic pledges.

The memory of these developments bred a wish to postpone the determination of territorial settlements until the Allies met in formal conference after the war was won. Hull was as firm as he dared be on this issue. And Roosevelt was fairly steady in his support of the Secretary of State's position in regard to European boundary questions. But he did not adhere to it in regard to the disposition of territorial questions in the Far East.

As early as December 1943, Roosevelt breached the rule in the Cairo Declaration that specified which parts of the Japanese empire were to be transferred ("restored") to China. Then at Yalta in February 1945 he was drawn into a secret agreement with Stalin, endorsing Russian claims for various pre-eminent rights and privileges in Manchuria. His chief reason for both actions was military. But I believe he drew some measure of justification from historical memory. Had it not long been American policy to try to preserve the territorial integrity of China? Did he not also remember that Theodore Roosevelt had acted as intermediary in adjusting the rival claims of Russia and Japan over Manchuria at the Portsmouth Peace Conference? He must have known of the persistent past attempts of Russia—detailed in many briefing papers—to secure a dominant position in Manchuria. He may well have concluded, therefore, that it was advisable to get Russian claims defined and delimited before its armies invaded Manchuria rather than await that desired event. This deviation from the rules of postponement and "open agreements openly arrived at" was, I believe, a mistake. But how greatly its consequences have been magnified and distorted by partisan recrimination!

Far less attention has been directed to the question of whether by adhering to the policy of postponing negotiations about territorial questions in Europe Roosevelt and Hull may not have made the opposite blunder. It is quite conceivable that the U.S. government could have managed to secure more satisfactory settlements than those ultimately made while the war was being fought and its Allies—especially the Soviet Union—were crucially dependent on us. I have in mind particularly the Soviet-Polish-German boundaries and the Soviet-Finnish one.

At Yalta in February 1945 Roosevelt did talk over with Stalin and Churchill, in a preliminary way, the prospective postwar territories to be awarded to the Soviet Union, Poland, and Yugoslavia, those to be restored to Austria and Czechoslovakia, and the French wish to detach the Rhineland and place the Ruhr under international control. But he did not enter into any firm accords on any of these questions. By that time the Soviet Union was out of peril. It had regained strength and confidence and could foresee excellent chances to thrust forward in both Europe and the Far East. Stalin could and did stubbornly maintain his claims in both areas.

However, had the American government insisted, when the Soviet Union was still in dire peril, that it moderate its territorial demands, it would have had to take the risk that the Soviet government would prefer to try to secure what it wanted by making deals with Germany and Japan. Churchill and Roosevelt remembered the collapse of the Russian armies in 1917, the refusal of the troops to stay in the field, the triumph of the Bolshevik revolutionaries, and Lenin's acceptance of the terms of peace dictated by Germany—in the Treaty of Brest-Litovsk in 1918. They still shuddered when they recalled the week in August 1939 when Stalin, while fending off Anglo-French overtures for an alliance, had entered into a pact with Hitler.

Thus during the desperate years of 1940–1942, before Stalingrad, Churchill and his British colleagues were concerned that Russia might again collapse or withdraw from the war if its wishes were denied. They were willing, in connection with the Anglo-Soviet Treaty of Alliance negotiated in 1941, to consent to the comprehensive territorial claims that Stalin advanced. But Roosevelt, after wavering, upheld Hull's opposition to any such pledge. The President appeased Stalin by statements that could be construed as a promise that a second military front in the west of Europe would be created by the Allies in 1942 or 1943. But he refrained from any attempt to get Stalin to reduce his territorial demands as a condition of providing Lend-Lease and other military support. By failing to do so he may have lost a good opportunity, for I do not believe that Stalin would have dared to quit the war on the only terms that Hitler would then have granted as the price of peace. He would have bargained angrily and would certainly have refused to give up his wish to absorb the Baltic States. But I believe—although this is only surmise—he would have accepted a Soviet-Polish frontier line farther to the East and given up his demand for the northern part of East Prussia. In that event the claims of Poland for German territory in compensation for what it yielded to the Soviet Union might have been more restrained or restrainable.

Another area of policy influenced by historical recollection was the treatment of Germany. Here also the decision-makers might have been led astray by their memories of the past. They were so strongly swayed by the wish not to repeat the mistakes which, according to the prevailing judgment, had prevented victory in the First World War from resulting in prolonged peace that their vision this second time was blurred. The old adage has it that soldiers are apt to conduct campaigns with strategy and tactics that would have brought victory in the war before the one they were fighting. In this case Western political leaders pursued policies that might have brought tranquillity to Europe after the First World War but that could not do so after the Second World War.

The failure to invade and occupy the whole of Germany in the First World War had had regrettable consequences. This time, the decision-makers resolved that the Germans would not be able to salve their sense of national superiority by the myth that the war had really been lost not on the battlefield but because of a few cowardly traitors in their midst. This time the Germans would not be permitted to return to their former ways and retain their twisted mentality. This time they would not be given a chance to rearm secretly and to plot to cast off the restraints imposed upon them by the peace treaties.

Germany would be occupied and subjected to control as long as necessary to disarm the military, root out the evil leaders and organizations, cause the people to realize that their aggression and cruelty had brought grief to themselves as well as to others, and re-educate them so that they would become peaceful and democratic in spirit.

These were all healthy and just purposes. Occupation was essential to effect them. It had to be a joint occupation unless Germany were split into several national states. Moreover, it was hoped that the continuing cooperation of the four main Allies in control of Germany would be a guarantee that it would not again be able to play one against the other.

Such was the cluster of policies that grew out of the soil of historical recollection. To pursue them the decision-makers had to hope that one interfering historical hint would not turn out to be so true in the future as it had been in the past—that before the war the Western democracies and Communist Russia had never been able to cooperate trustingly with one another.

But more acute appraisal of the applicability of the historical experience of Europe in 1918 to the conditions prevailing in 1945 (and in prospect) might have caused the Western statesmen to contemplate a period of occupation just long enough to effectuate a few primary purposes, no longer. It should also have led them to insist on more conclusive stipulations that at the end of a comparatively short period (two to at most five years) of occupation, troops of all nations should be withdrawn from Germany and also from adjacent countries through which lines of military communication to Germany run. The agreement on control of Germany could have been buttressed by a treaty of the sort that Secretary Byrnes proposed at Stuttgart in 1947, pledging the four occupying powers to repress any future attempt of Germany to rearm and any future German aggression.

This problem illustrates the fact that historical recollection often— perhaps usually—gives conflicting reminders and suggestions to decision-makers. It may leave them in a quandary as to which to heed and which to reject or how to hedge between them.

I have referred to the supposition implicit in the plans for government occupation of Germany—that it was to remain a unified, though decentralized, state. Almost up to the time when this decision was made, historical recollection tempted the Allies to break that country up into a number of separate independent states. During the century preceding German unification and Bismarck, some students of history asked, had not the Germans lived most tranquilly? If separated into regional states, could and would they not do so again? Thus both Roosevelt and Stalin were attracted to plans to divide Germany into a number of independent states. But that intention yielded to remembrance of the trend that dominated more recent German history—the strong urge of the German people to unite in one political state. The heads of state correctly concluded that this desire would challenge any enforced separation and, after dangerous chaos, which might bring war, upset it. So they deferred to the established historical fact of German unity.

But the memories of the shrill insistence of Hitler that all Germans in Europe could live happily only within one German fatherland caused the Allies after victory to grant this wish in a grim fashion. It weakened possible protests against the expulsion of those millions of German origin who had been living in the areas in the east that were detached from Germany, including the territory absorbed in postwar Poland, the Sudeten area of Czechoslovakia, and East Prussia.

Regarding Austria, historical memory properly prevailed: Austria went back to being an independent state.

I turn last to the area of policy on which, I think, historians and historical memory had the most incisive impact—the formation and form of the United Nations. All members of the coalition against the Axis had agreed that they must undo their failure, after the First World War, to make the League of Nations an effective agency to keep the peace. The scrutiny to which historians had subjected the past had convinced almost all statesmen and peoples that national diplomacy alone would not protect them from the scourge of war, and that balance-of-power arrangements and vows of neutrality would also fail. What American opinion had denied to Wilson it was uncritically eager to bestow on Roosevelt and Truman.

History called for a renewal, with firmer will, of the effort to reform the society of nations and to create a new method of regulating their relations. But differences of judgment lingered until 1944–1945 as to how this should best be attempted.

Up to the convocation at Dumbarton Oaks, late in 1944, several appraisals of historical indications ran helter-skelter through Roosevelt's mind. His original one was more akin to that of Stalin than to those of any of his advisers except Harry Hopkins. The demonstrated frailty of pledges of great scope but diffused obligation, such as those contained in the Kellogg-Briand Pact and the Covenant of the League of Nations, seemed to him to be proof that accords not upheld by centralized power would prove of little value as a guarantee of peace. This opinion he derived from the failure of the many nations that were partners to these accords to take concerted action to prevent Japan from assaulting China, Italy from conquering Ethiopia, and Germany from smashing Austria and Czechoslovakia.

This train of historical judgment led him to the conclusion that the only sort of organization that might stand the strain was one in which commanding authority was centered in three or four great powers who would vow to act together to suppress any future act of aggression. He was thus inclined to the idea that three (or four, if China were included) great powers should be self-appointed "policemen" to supervise the conduct of nations and together enforce the peace. Stalin responded enthusiastically to this conception. But the comments of the Soviet dictator reveal that it was closely connected in his thoughts with an understanding between the policemen about their respective spheres of sovereignty and influence. Whether Roosevelt perceived that such an agreement was an almost necessary condition or accompaniment to the operation of any such plan of policing as he proposed is a matter of conjecture. Churchill, during this period, was undecided. He was not averse either to British acceptance of the responsibility of acting as one of the policemen or to an agreement on spheres of primacy. But he was doubtful about whether the smaller countries—especially the other members of the British Commonwealth—would join an international system in which they would be so decidedly subordinated.

Although neither Hull nor Eden openly opposed the idea of the four policemen, their own expositions had quite a different bent. And the permanent staffs of both the State Department and the Foreign Office disliked and distrusted the Roosevelt-Stalin conception.

Then, as his own trust in the good faith and reasonableness of the Soviet Union began to wane in 1944, the President became receptive to a quite different interpretation of history, which was conveyed to him by a score of advisers. They argued that the League of Nations had not failed because of intrinsic or insuperable faults in the Covenant. They attributed its default to the refusal of the United States to join it, the distrust between Western members and the Soviet Union, the restrictive commercial and financial policies of the democracies, their shrinking from the danger of possibly having to endure the agony of war again, and twinges of doubt about the fairness of some features of the Treaty of Versailles. They opined that few, if any, limited alliances of the kind implicit in the notion of the three (or four) policemen had endured. They forecast that the many smaller countries, even if they accepted membership in a proposed organization, would rebel against the domination of the few and connive to divide them.

Hull and other American officials and advisers who retained faith in the ideals of Woodrow Wilson, as well as English statesmen of similar mind, such as Robert Cecil, argued with fervor that peace must be based on principle and upheld by general consent. They recognized that the new organization might have to resort to collective force to deter or defeat aggression and that only its stronger members would be able to provide the required force. But still they contended that the arbiters of peace must be pledged by the new

Charter that was to be written to administer equal justice to all and that all countries, even the smallest, should have an adequate chance to influence the decision of the collectivity. Such were their ideals of universality and equal standing under a new law of nations that inspired the ultimate American proposals for the emergent international organization to keep the peace.

Whether historical recollection in this vital area was a wise or foolish instructor cannot now be foretold. We cannot even be sure that it has implanted deeply enough its one primary and indisputable lesson—that nations must discard the ways of the past and adopt more peaceful and unselfish ones. Mutual terror, due to the existence of thermonuclear weapons, which may annihilate them all, has been restraining them more effectively than the ominous reminders of history.

Historians of tomorrow must devoutly hope that they will not again be called on to recount how historical recollections influenced the policies of nations in another world war. They should be content with the more pleasant task of tracing how they contributed to the maintenance of peace.

The Cold War and American Scholarship*

by Louis Morton

I T IS A TRUISM to observe that we are living in a revolutionary
world. The remarkable developments in science and technology—as well as the legacy of two world wars within a quarter
of a century—have all combined to make it so. Yet for all the
revolutionary nature of the contemporary world, many of the problems that confront the world today are, in one way or another, much
the same as those that confronted the world before 1914 and 1939.
History, in short, has not become obsolete; historical experience has
not become irrelevant. This seems to me to be true of the history of
Europe and the Far East as well as of the history of the United
States.

It would be pleasant to be able to begin this essay on the role
of history and historians in American foreign policy in the era of
the Cold War by asserting that the prestige of history and historians
in this country has never been higher, that the historian shares with
the scientist and engineer a leading place in the high councils of
national policy. This is not the case, of course, even if historians are
invited, as they were during the debate over Vietnam and China policy, to offer their views before the Senate Foreign Relations Committee. And yet it is precisely because America's role in world
affairs today is so different from what it was twenty-five to fifty years
ago, because there is such widespread uncertainty as to where we are
in the world today and what role we can and ought to play in our
own times, that the historians have a distinct opportunity—indeed,
an obligation—to provide for their countrymen a meaningful account of the American past, so that they may better understand
how the United States reached its present position, the direction in
which it is moving, and where, with reason, it may hope to stand in
the years ahead. There has been much discussion in recent years,
for instance, about the nature of American foreign policy during the
Second World War. Yet the fact is that there is nothing approaching

* Portions of this essay were published under the title "History, Historians and
Foreign Policy," in *Union Worthies*, No. 20 (1966), a publication of Union College,
Schenectady, N. Y.

a national consensus on the meaning of this experience, with all that such a consensus would imply for the present and future conduct of American foreign policy.

For this state of affairs, it seems to me, American historians must assume at least some of the responsibility. Too few have dealt with the larger and more controversial issues of our times, for understandable reasons—the lack of adequate documentation, the limitations imposed by security considerations, personal involvement and commitment. The result, perhaps inevitably, has been that the public at large, and probably the government as well, has looked less and less at what the historians had to say about the recent American past and has turned instead to the work of others less concerned with perspective and objectivity. Valuable as this work has been, it has often failed to provide the sense of continuity, the link with the past, that is so vital an element of historical writing. But many of our leaders have retained this sense. President Truman was conscious of the weight of history, occasionally delivering himself of homilies on the subject,[1] and President Kennedy was well aware of the relevance of the American past to the American present—and future. Speaking at the University of Wisconsin in June 1958, when he was still a senator, he recalled an earlier day when the world of scholarship was not so far removed from the world of politics. "The duty of the scholar," Kennedy remarked, "is to contribute his objective views and his sense of liberty to the affairs of his state and nation." Scholars should be, in his words, "men who can ride easily over broad fields of knowledge and recognize the mutual dependence of the two worlds of politics and scholarship." [2] Arthur Schlesinger, Jr., writing from the vantage point of the White House, wrote that he had no doubt that the statesman must have a knowledge of history.[3]

In this essay I shall address myself to some of the principal questions relating to the recent history of American diplomacy and scholarship. What have been the main lines of American foreign policy since the Second World War, and in what sense do these constitute a departure from traditional American foreign policy? To what extent have the leaders of the American government—the Presidents and Secretaries of State and some of the leading diplomats —been aware of the importance and relevance of historical considerations in the making of American foreign policy? What are some of the most important and controversial issues in recent Ameri-

1 See Harry S. Truman, *Mr. Citizen* (New York, 1953), pp. 143–189, 209–218.
2 Quoted in John F. Kennedy, *The Strategy of Peace* (New York, 1960), p. 189.
3 Arthur Schlesinger, Jr., "The Historian and History," *Foreign Affairs,* April 1963, p. 496.

can foreign policy that have most concerned American historians, and what is the relevance of these problems to the development of contemporary American diplomacy? And, finally, what has been the impact of the Cold War on the American intellectual community in general, and what contribution is this community making, and can it hope to make, to the shaping of American foreign policy in the era of the Cold War?

Cordell Hull once remarked, quoting Justice Holmes, that a page of history was worth a volume of logic. I shall begin, therefore, by recalling some of the main events in American foreign policy since 1945, for there can be little doubt that it was the troubled course of events immediately after the war that led the United States to re-examine its position in the world and to develop in the years that followed a new foreign policy, entirely different from anything in the history of the Republic.

I

In the late summer and autumn of 1945 the American people had every reason to rejoice. Germany and Japan had been defeated, and American troops, victorious everywhere, would soon be returning home. Unprecedented evil had been overcome by the greatest display of force ever marshaled in the cause of human freedom, and the Allies had made pledges to one another in the United Nations. The future seemed assured; a new era of peace and international cooperation had dawned.

Yet even before the end of the year, the bright hopes for the future began to dim. Mounting tensions between the United States and the Soviet Union, signs of which had appeared during the last year of the war, raised disturbing questions about the intentions of our wartime ally. In his famous address at Fulton, Missouri, in March 1946, Winston Churchill referred to the "iron curtain" that had been drawn across Eastern Europe, from Stettin on the Baltic Sea to Trieste on the Adriatic, and called on the Western democracies to stand together.

Churchill's address produced no immediate change in Western policy toward the Soviet Union. But the continued growth of friction between the Western powers and Russia led, in the winter of 1946–1947, to a dramatic and unforeseen change in American foreign policy. This change was produced by, among other things, the struggle in Greece, where the national government sought des-

perately to cope with a Communist-supported revolutionary movement aimed at taking over the whole country (in violation of
Allied wartime agreements that had placed Greece in the Western
sphere of interest). It was in Greece, indeed, that one of the
historic results of the Second World War first became dramatically
apparent—the inability of Great Britain to extend any significant
assistance to friendly but embattled governments such as that of
Greece. The political and economic weakness of Great Britain in
the postwar period was to prove a development of first importance
to the future of American diplomacy.

The events in Greece, and Britain's admitted inability to cope
with them, presented the United States with a momentous choice:
whether to remain aloof from the struggle or to intervene in behalf
of the beleaguered Greek government. Faced with this choice,
President Truman did not hesitate. On March 12, 1947, he re-
quested the Congress to approve immediate American assistance to
Greece and Turkey in a speech that outlined the position the United
States was to follow throughout the Cold War. The Second World
War, he declared, had been fought to free the world from tyranny,
"to ensure the peaceful development of nations, free from coercion."
Reminding his listeners that tyranny was once more abroad, fasten-
ing its hold on the weak and threatening the peace of the world,
Truman announced the nation's intention to "assist free peoples to
work out their own destinies" without interference. "I believe," he
said, "that it must be the policy of the United States to support
free peoples who are resisting attempted subjugation by armed
minorities or by outside pressures."[4]

This statement, the so-called Truman Doctrine, established the
ideological basis of the struggle—a world divided between free and
oppressed nations, with the United States pledged to fight on the side
of freedom. The basis of the new American policy toward the Soviet
threat was supplied by George F. Kennan, Chief of the State Department's newly established Policy Planning Staff, in his famous memorandum on the nature of the Soviet system.[5] Arguing that the Soviet
Union bore within itself the seeds of its own decay, and that ultimately
the United States would prevail, he urged a policy of patience and
"firm and vigilant" containment. It should be the policy of the
United States, Kennan wrote, to oppose the Russians "with un-
alterable counter-force at every point where they show signs of

4 The speech was printed in its entirety in *The New York Times,* March 13, 1947.
5 Excerpts from the memorandum were published anonymously in *Foreign Affairs,*
July 1947, under the title "The Sources of Soviet Conduct."

encroaching upon the interest of a peaceful and stable world." In effect, what Kennan proposed and the policy that was adopted, was to set a line beyond which the Russians would not venture without risk of war with the United States. It was a clear and unambiguous warning, backed later by American troops and nuclear power.

The needs of Greece and Turkey were far less than those of other European nations devastated by the recent conflict. They needed a new, different, and completely unprecedented program of American economic assistance. Despite America's traditional attitude toward the Old World and its withdrawal from European affairs after the First World War, it was clear that the time had come for a change in America's historic policy toward Europe. It is ironic, perhaps, that the United States in the mid-1940's began increasingly to accept John Maynard Keynes's hypothesis of the economic interdependence of the Atlantic democracies—first put forth in 1919 in his famous work *The Economic Consequences of the Peace*—but there were few historians to suggest that had the United States recognized this interdependence after 1918, the events that brought on the Second World War might have been averted.

Unlike the Truman Doctrine, which was the rapid response of the American government to the collapse of British strength in 1946–1947, the Marshall Plan was the result of weeks and months of careful, detailed studies by the Policy Planning Staff, headed by Kennan. When Secretary of State George Marshall first proposed the idea of a large-scale program of American economic assistance to war-stricken Europe, at the Harvard University commencement in June 1947, he had in mind American assistance to all of Europe, including the Communist-controlled areas. The United States, said Marshall, would aid all nations to restore their economy, "without which there can be no political stability and no assured peace."[6] It soon became clear, however, that the Soviet Union would refuse to cooperate in any such recovery program, so the Marshall Plan came to have the effect of strengthening the European democracies (and the new West German state) against possible Communist inroads, and thus became a powerful contribution to the policy of containment. There can be little doubt that the Marshall Plan provided the basis of the remarkable postwar European recovery and that it was also responsible in large part for the development of a con-

6 The speech was delivered on June 5, 1947, and is reprinted in *The New York Times* for the following day.

siderable measure of economic integration—a tendency that many American policy-makers, and many Europeans also, hoped would become the basis of a politically integrated Western Europe.

The development of the Marshall Plan did not put an end to Soviet efforts to bring about a change in the European balance of power. Looking back now, it seems clear that 1948 and 1949 marked the high point of Soviet expansion. The Communist coup in Czechoslovakia in February 1948 left no doubt that the Soviet Union was now prepared to use force, when possible, to strengthen and expand its position in Central Europe. But an even more drastic confrontation between East and West began in June 1948, when the Soviet Union started a year-long ground blockade of Berlin.

The American response to these events was twofold. First, the United States undertook a massive airlift that successfully circumvented the Soviet blockade and that led in May 1949 to the Jessup-Malik agreement, formally lifting existing restrictions. Second, the United States repudiated one of its most enduring and hallowed principles of foreign policy—that the nation should avoid entangling alliances with foreign powers in times of peace. The immediate result of this dramatic shift in American foreign policy was the creation of the North Atlantic Treaty Organization in April 1949, an organization whose avowed purpose it was to maintain integrally the military security of the North Atlantic area in Europe and America. The main instrument of NATO was military, consisting of conventional forces, including American troops, to meet any initial aggression, and the nuclear weapons of the United States, also based in Europe and North America.

Hardly had this powerful new barrier to Soviet expansion in Europe been thrown up when the focus of the Cold War began to shift from Europe to the Far East. Having survived almost twenty years of Japanese aggression and occupation, the Chinese Nationalist government finally fell before the onslaught of its internal enemies in the spring of 1949. Chiang Kai-shek, whom the United States had supported for many years, now fled to Formosa, leaving the mainland to Mao Tse-tung and the new Chinese Communist government. Mao's victory gained for the Communist bloc control over 600 million adherents and a dominant position in Asia. It was the greatest Communist victory since 1917, far surpassing the territorial acquisitions of the Soviet Union in Europe and the Far East at the end of the Second World War. But a decade had scarcely gone by when the Chinese dragon was challenging the Russian bear for leadership of the Communist world. The split between the Soviet Union and Communist China radically altered U.S.-Soviet relations and greatly complicated the nature of international relations.[7]

Contrary to widespread criticism of American policy in the Far East the U.S. government had not been unaware of either the growing disintegration of the Nationalist government or the real character of the Chinese Communist movement. Yet it seems clear also that there was never any real prospect of direct American intervention in the Chinese Civil War; and when General Marshall's mission of mediation proved abortive, the ultimate outcome of the struggle seemed a foregone conclusion.

The triumph of the Chinese Communists was only one example of the growing power of the Communist movement in the Far East. A far more dramatic demonstration came with the North Korean attack on the Republic of South Korea in June 1950. It would be difficult to overestimate the significance of this attack. It has often been compared in importance to the German remilitarization of the Rhineland in March 1936, one of the turning points in the history of the Nazi era, and President Truman was to write later that he regarded his decision to support the Republic of South Korea as his single most important action in the White House.

This act, committed suddenly and without debate, represented the reversal of the long-accepted policy that the United States should not become involved with ground forces in the Far East unless its territory was attacked first. The decision to intervene in Korea was never fully understood or appreciated by the American people, and the conduct of the war, whose aims shifted with the tide of battle, created much confusion and controversy. It also aroused deep political passions and contributed in large measure to the overthrow of the Truman administration and the election of General Eisenhower in November 1952. But despite the dissension and confusion that marked this first effort to apply the containment policy in Asia, the conflict in Korea established the basis, through President Truman's historic intervention, for a new American policy in the Far East. No doubt it also affected Communist China's policy.

Although the end of the Berlin blockade did not bring with it any improvement in the Allied position in the former German capital, and despite the limited success of Allied action in Korea, the American

---

7 See Harry Schwartz, *Tsars, Mandarins and Commissars* (New York, 1964), and George F. Kennan, *On Dealing with the Communist World* (New York, 1964).

response to the challenge of world communism in the 1950's remained much the same as it had been since the first years after the war. This meant that in the Far East and elsewhere the United States reacted to the Communist threat by seeking to contain it, as it had in Europe, through a system of alliances. In the years that followed the North Korean aggression, as the number of threats increased throughout Southeast Asia, the Middle East, and Latin America, the United States took the lead in forming a number of multilateral and bilateral arrangements. By the end of the 1950's the United States, which throughout most of its history had assiduously avoided alliances with foreign powers, had concluded mutual-assistance pacts with more than fifty nations. But the changes in America's position did not stop there.

The consequences of bipolarity in an ideological conflict were already evident to the more discerning critics by the time of the Korean War. So high were the stakes, so irreconcilable the aims, so damaging the psychological effects of error or defeat that the dangers of a general war were enormously increased. The Korean conflict left an indelible impression on the American consciousness, and there seemed little likelihood that a similar resolution to a direct armed contest would be acceptable. "If we have another one," Walt Rostow told a congressional committee in 1956, "it is going to be big. . . . The impression is quite widespread around the world that the United States has interpreted the meaning of the Korean war in the sense that it wants no more of limited hostilities."[8] Bipolarity, reinforced by a policy of containment, had the effect also of multiplying alliances. The world became divided into friends and foes, and all who were friends or potential friends were converted into allies, with assurances of protection, even when the advantages of such alliances were minimal.

A fundamental element in this bipolar conflict, underlying every issue that arose and itself a major issue in the struggle, derived from the nature of the weapons available to both sides. The United States entered the Cold War with a distinct advantage, for it alone possessed the atomic bomb. This fact gave to American policy the sanction of force and to the American people a sense of security. Immediate postwar strategy viewed the next war, if any nation would be so foolish as to start it, as one that would be quickly decided by several atomic bombs dropped on strategic targets.

8 World Economic Growth and Competition, 84th Congress, 2nd session, Joint Economic Committee, Subcommittee on Foreign Economic Policy. *Hearings*, Dec. 10–13, 1956, p. 160.

But this sense of security was not to last long. In August 1949 the Soviet Union exploded its own atomic bomb, ending the American monopoly and exposing the United States for the first time in its history to direct attack from an overseas enemy. The psychological effects of the loss of the security that the United States had enjoyed for so long and that had shaped its relationship with Europe and Asia have yet to be fully explored. But the political and military consequences of the Soviet explosion were soon apparent. The certainty of American use of atomic weapons in defense of our allies diminished—or, in strategic parlance, the credibility of the nuclear deterrent was minimized—while the vulnerability of our bases in West Europe and North Africa increased. More important, however, was the fact that the cities of the United States were now exposed to attack, and this altered all its priorities and set as the first requirement of American strategy the deterrence of attack on the continental United States. As a result, the government took measures to strengthen the Strategic Air Command and decided to proceed with the development of a hydrogen bomb. Korea complicated matters by its requirement for conventional forces, but as long as the military budget could be maintained at the high figure of the Korean period—it rose from $13 billion in 1950 to $50 billion in 1953—the military could hope to meet both nuclear and conventional requirements.

The liquidation of the Korean War and the acquisition of the hydrogen bomb in 1953 gave the American people a renewed feeling of confidence in their military superiority. Taking advantage of this situation, the Eisenhower administration developed the New Look and massive retaliation—a matching strategy of complementary policies designed to achieve maximum security at minimum costs.[9] The results of these policies were less than satisfactory, however, since the Russians could scarcely be deterred, and the NATO allies reassured, by a threat that had little credibility, especially since the Russians successfully exploded a hydrogen bomb a year later. By this time the race for superiority in weapons and delivery systems was on in earnest, and the nuclear stockpile was growing rapidly. The problems created by the existence of these weapons was further complicated when England, and later France, acquired a nuclear

9 Paul Y. Hammond, Warner R. Schilling, and Glenn H. Snyder, *Strategy, Politics and Defense Budgets* (New York, 1962). The authors, in three separate studies, demonstrate that the New Look reflected President Eisenhower's views and was not, as was widely believed, the work of the economy-minded Secretary of the Treasury Humphry, supported by Secretary of State Dulles and Senator Taft.

capability. Then in August 1957 the Soviet Union forged ahead in the nuclear race when it launched an intercontinental ballistics missile, followed some months later by an earth satellite.

The marriage of nuclear warheads and missiles of intercontinental range, extraordinary speed, and great accuracy precipitated a comprehensive review of U.S. strategy and dramatically underlined what had already been evident for some time: that war between two superpowers armed with nuclear weapons could no longer serve as a means of resolving international conflict. Thus arose the supreme irony that the very weapons that made the United States and the Soviet Union superpowers, that gave them the ability to destroy completely any enemy in a matter of minutes, have become useless as instruments of policy. This is not to say that their possession is not essential, for without them the nation would be helpless indeed; but when both sides are equally capable of destroying the other side, then such weapons not only cease to further the ends of policy but also impose severe limitations on the freedom of action of those who possess them. Furthermore, the threat of force on a nuclear scale against a superpower becomes less plausible as the level of destruction increases; against a smaller power it becomes absurd. Of what use was the overwhelming force of the United States against Cuba? And how can nuclear weapons be utilized to further U.S. aims in Africa or in Southeast Asia? After all, you don't use a hand grenade to kill a fly in your living room, at least not without considerable damage to yourself and your house.

The bipolarity of the postwar world, which had struck most observers so forcefully, did not survive the 1950's; for the holocaust that had given rise to the two superpowers saw the destruction of old empires and the birth of a new nationalism in Asia and Africa. The revolution in military technology was now matched by an equally historic revolution created by the disintegration of the Western colonial empires. Out of the ashes of centuries of colonialism emerged a host of new nations, a "third world," painfully struggling to enter the twentieth century. In South and Southeast Asia, 600 million people gained their independence; the former British and Dutch colonies peaceably, French Indochina only after a costly civil war. In Africa, where in 1940 there had been only two free states, more than 100 million people became free. Between 1945 and 1961 a total of 42 independent states, with a population of nearly 1 billion, was established, leaving less than 2 percent of the world's population under colonial domination.[10] Aggressively nationalistic and economically underdeveloped, the new nations had little interest in the ideological conflict of the Cold War. From the rostrum of the United Nations they exercised collectively an influence in world politics out of proportion to their individual power and responsibilities. On the issues of peace and disarmament, self-determination, colonialism, and social and economic betterment, they stood together and spoke out in clear terms. But on the issues that divided the East and West, they remained uncommitted, neutral, thereby seeking to enhance (often successfully) their political influence in the Cold War.

In dealing with these former colonial peoples the American position was often difficult or uneasy. Although the United States had never been a colonial power in the traditional European sense of the word, it was tarred in the postwar era with the brush of imperialism. It was at a disadvantage, therefore, in the contest for the support of the Afro-Asian states, since it was not so free as the Soviet Union to throw its weight on the side of "liberation" or other revolutionary changes. Sometimes, almost against its deepest instincts, the United States found itself denying the principle of self-determinism and supporting the status quo in the interests of national security and containment. Here was a dilemma from which the United States found it difficult to escape and which restricted its freedom of action in dealing with nationalist revolutions. It was in response to this situation that the South East Asian Treaty Organization (SEATO) was established in the fall of 1954 in a vain attempt to check Communist penetration in South and Southeast Asia. The United States faced similar situations in Latin America, where the forces for change welled up from the deepest sources of poverty, exploitation, and misrule. Here again Washington found itself at a disadvantage, since it was not always easy to distinguish between Communist subversion and movements for social justice. Moreover, the American record of intervention in this region was scarcely calculated to reassure the peoples of Latin America.

The elaborate economic- and military-aid programs, designed to assist the emergent nations in their efforts to provide for their own security and develop into modern industrial and democratic societies, suffer from similar difficulties. The assumption of these aid

10 These were the figures President Kennedy used in his speech to the United Nations on disarmament on Sept. 25, 1961; *Public Papers of the Presidents: John F. Kennedy, 1961* (Washington, D.C., 1961), p. 624.

programs—that industrialization will transform an underdeveloped society into a democratic peaceful one—is by no means established. And there exists considerable criticism of the administration of the programs and the specific projects on which the money is spent. Billions of dollars have been expended on foreign aid, but despite growing opposition, it remains an essential element of the American response to the Communist challenge.

II

It is unnecessary here to trace in detail the complex and frustrating record of the past twenty years, with its succession of crises, which, we are frequently reminded, are unfortunately still with us. This "page of history" is already overlong. But even from this brief and vastly oversimplified recital we can identify those historic forces that give the postwar era its distinctive features and account for the change in America's role in world affairs since 1945. Clearly this is an age of revolution, of rapid and far-reaching changes in science and technology, military weaponry, international relations, diplomacy, and the rising expectations of hundreds of millions of depressed and deprived peoples. It is an age of so high a birth rate in some parts of the world as to justify the term "population explosion." It is an age of tension and conflict in which war with modern weapons has become unthinkable and peace hangs on a precarious balance of terror. Traditional values have become increasingly irrelevant to the great challenges of the times. Old empires have disintegrated, to be replaced by many new independent states; the center of world power has shifted from Western Europe eastward to the Soviet Union and westward to the United States. The bipolarization of the immediate postwar years has given way to a more complex world order as the new nations take their place in the sun and the two great blocs begin to split into their component parts.

Little in the history of the American people prepared them for the role they were to play in this age of revolution and crisis. They accepted leadership slowly and reluctantly. A century of isolation was no training for world leadership. To be sure, by 1945 most Americans realized that retreat into the Western Hemisphere was no longer possible, though they hoped, once the war was won, that whatever differences arose could be settled by the United Nations. Membership in that organization represented a triumph of history.

As Americans read the past, and as Europeans were so fond of telling them, the failure of the United States to join the League of Nations in 1919 had doomed that organization to impotence and had led to the outbreak of war in 1939. Had Hitler and Mussolini known that the United States would ally itself with Great Britain, the argument ran, they would never have embarked on aggression and the Second World War might have been avoided. Profiting from this bitter lesson that history presumably had taught, the American people strongly supported the efforts of President Roosevelt and President Truman to build a collective-security system for the post-war world.

But history does not repeat itself, and the world that rose from the ashes of World War II bore little resemblance to that of 1919. Ironically, the first war, which had been fought to change the European balance and remove the threat of Germany, had produced in the 1930's a situation little different from that of 1914; the second war, fought to restore an earlier world order, released revolutionary forces and led to a completely new world order. The balance of power in Europe, on which the nation had traditionally relied for its security, was gone, and the United States was forced, almost against its will, to move into the vacuum. It was the only nation with the power to stand against the Soviet Union. There was no choice; history had forced upon the nation leadership of the free world. The Truman Doctrine and the Marshall Plan signified acceptance of this role and marked the revolution in American foreign policy. Containment, collective security, economic aid, and nuclear weapons were designed to achieve the goals set for the free world. They proved remarkably successful in Europe. The Soviet Union was, in fact, contained, and remains today along the same line it held fifteen years ago.

The policies that worked so well in Europe, where the threat was overtly military, were less effective in Southeast Asia, the Middle East, Latin America, and Africa. In these parts of the world the policy of containment backed by military force proved inadequate to the more subtle challenge of political subversion and economic penetration. Nor did the alliances formed in these areas or the foreign-aid programs contribute substantially to the stability of these regions.[11] One can argue—indeed it has been argued by some scholars—that the funds pumped into the underdeveloped areas

11 Hans J. Morgenthau, "The Crisis of American Foreign Policy," Brien McMahon Lectures, Univ. of Conn., Feb. 22, 1960.

liberated and strengthened the forces of change rather than stability. And it is not at all certain that industrialization and higher standards of living lead to democracy in the Western sense or to a free-enterprise system. Finally, the policies designed in the 1950's to meet the threat of a monolithic, expansionist Communist bloc seem inappropriate in the mid-1960's, when the character of Soviet foreign policy and relations within the Communist camp, as within the Western orbit, have been so markedly altered.[12]

Greatly altered too were the structure and processes by which American foreign and military policies were made. World leadership and nuclear weapons required new ways of conducting diplomacy and utilizing military force. The President remained the final authority, but his responsibilities and staff were vastly increased. The National Security Council, established in 1947, advised him on security matters, and the Central Intelligence Agency and the military services gathered information, overtly and covertly, to assist him. In addition, he had a Special Assistant for National Security Affairs. The State Department, which in 1940 had fewer than 1,200 employees and an appropriation of $3 million, twenty years later had 23,000, with 16,000 of them overseas. The budget for 1960 was more than $200 million, in addition to the amount appropriated for foreign aid. Between 1945 and 1960 the United States spent abroad a total of $84 billion, two-thirds of which went for economic aid in the form of outright grants and credits and the remainder for military assistance. And by 1960 the Secretary of State had acquired an additional under secretary with two deputies, and eight more assistant secretaries.[13]

The defense establishment, consisting after 1947 of three departments unified under the Defense Department, grew correspondingly, reaching a size unprecedented in peacetime and gaining an influence that led some to wonder whether we were not becoming a garrison state. The Joint Chiefs of Staff acquired during these years a staff of several hundred and a chairman to advise the Secretary of Defense. Civilian employees of the Defense Department numbered more in 1960 than the entire federal civil service in the 1920's, and the military forces, which up to the Second World War had never been greater than 200,000 men (except in war), stood at almost 3 million. Military appropriations had risen from less than

12 Senator Fulbright expressed this view in an address to the Senate on March 25, 1964. The complete text was printed in *The New York Times,* March 26, 1964, p. 12.
13 Richard W. Leopold, *The Growth of American Foreign Policy* (New York, 1962), pp. 800–801, 805.

1 percent of the gross national product in the last century to 10 percent, accounting for more than half of the total federal budget.[14]

These facts provide some measure of the meaning of world leadership and the extent of the adjustment the United States has made to its new role. These adjustments have not, admittedly, come easily, and they have been shaped not only by external forces but also by peculiarly American attitudes that color and affect American policies. Among these attitudes have been a preference for total and simple solutions to complex problems; a tendency to see many issues as good or evil, black or white; a readiness to view war as an aberration, as a crusade against evil and an interruption of normal pursuits. With their strongly pragmatic and practical approach to problems, Americans refused to accept the fact that some problems were not solvable and sought to apply to social and political issues the techniques that served so well in the solution of scientific and technological problems. They searched for certainty in an uncertain world, absolutes in the realm of the relative. As Dean Rusk said, "We demand simple answers to the most complex questions confronting human intelligence. We expect consistency in policy, though the facts themselves are full of contradiction. We should like an easy way to carry a heavy burden, an agreeable way to perform disagreeable tasks, a cheap way to bring about an expensive result."[15]

III

These national traits are in large part the product of our history, the heritage of three and a half centuries of history, the first 150 years as a colony of Great Britain. And this brings us back to the general theme of the role of history and historians in American foreign policy.

We have noted before that historians as a professional group have had, on the whole, little effect on the formation of national policy. But this is not to deny the importance of history and of historical outlook and memories in shaping the United States' relations with other nations. Arthur Schlesinger, Jr., writing about his own involvement in public affairs as Special Assistant to President Kennedy, makes a useful distinction between historians and history that is

14 C. Vann Woodward, "The Age of Reinterpretation," *American Historical Review*, Vol. LXVI, No. 1 (Oct. 1960), pp. 4–5.
15 Quoted in Norman A. Graebner, *Cold War Diplomacy, 1945–1960* (Princeton, 1962) p. 10.

pertinent to this discussion. The historian as a professional, he has pointed out, is a member of a craft, "a quasi-priestly vocation," free of the passions of the day and dedicated to objectivity. His commitment is "to writing history rather than making it."[16] But the word "history" is Janus-faced, referring in one sense to the past itself and in another to the written record of that past as historians have set it down. Lingering too long on this distinction would necessitate raising certain philosophical questions, but the point here is that history, both as experience and as written record, influences the present and casts a long shadow into the future, though the historian himself remains aloof.

Not all would agree with this proposition. Some would stress the fact that we live in an age of revolution, when the pace of events is so swift, the break with the past so complete that history no longer has any relevance. It has nothing to tell us; its lessons, if it has any, are no longer applicable, and may even be misleading. The writing of history, they would assert, can be relegated to the antiquarian as an interesting but futile calling. Such criticisms reflect a naïve and uninformed view of the historian's task. He does not study history because of its utility or because it can tell him how to perform a job or what to do. History is not an exact science or even an inexact one. It is the record of man's past, and we study it partly out of curiosity, partly out of a deep need to search out our origins, and partly because we feel we should know where we have been to get some idea of where we are going. In its written form it is a record that the historian is constantly rewriting, using the strictest rules of evidence and with the highest regard for established facts. It can tell us much, but it cannot predict the future. To assume, as many do, that whatever value history may have lies in the discovery of those factors in the past that have remained constant, thereby making it possible to predict the future, is to expect too much from history. There are as many variables as constants in history, and the historian is too acutely aware of them to pose as a prophet. He is concerned with change, with the flow of events and the passage of time, with causes and consequences, with the origins of institutions, and with the role of chance and personality. Properly understood, history can do much for us. It can enrich our knowledge, put the present into perspective, and add another dimension to our thought. And these, I would suggest, are valuable intel-

16 Schlesinger, *op. cit.*, p. 491.

lectual tools for every man and indispensable for those who bear the responsibilities of leadership.

Most great national leaders are imbued with a strong sense of history and an acute awareness of its weight upon them. This is true, of course, of both American and European statesmen. We can see in Churchill, De Gaulle, and Khrushchev a feeling for the movement of historical forces and a conception of a world order. Perhaps the Communist leaders have this sense stronger than most, for they are fortified with a theory and a doctrine that put history on their side. In Marxism "God is personified History," and the Communists are the "bearers of History's will, beneficiaries of History's guarantees, executors of History's judgments."[17]

Most American leaders—certainly all the great ones—have been keenly aware of the American past, either from their own study or from the works of historians, and have related this awareness to their vision of the future. The examples of Jefferson, Lincoln, Wilson, and Franklin Roosevelt come quickly to mind. More recent Presidents have displayed equal sensitivity to the history and purpose of the nation, and their policies have reflected their view of the past. When President Truman called for aid to Greece and Turkey in March 1947, he appealed to moral principles and put his case on ethical grounds in terms that struck a responsive chord in most Americans. And in recalling his decision to intervene in Korea in June 1950, the former President spoke of the struggle between the strong and the weak, and reminded his readers of the fate of Manchuria, Ethiopia, the Rhineland, and Austria.[18] For him, history showed that each time the democracies had failed to act, the aggressors had been encouraged to move ahead.

President Eisenhower, as far as we know, did not steep himself in American history. Conscious as he is of his own place in history, as evidenced by his *Crusade in Europe* and more recent memoirs, he did not show much awareness of the traditions and continuities of the past in his state papers or public utterances as President. His usual reading was on the light side, but when he had a few spare minutes in his office, we are told, he might take from the shelves a volume of Jefferson or Lincoln. The latter was his favorite President. He painted him from a photograph and, it is said, urged members of his Cabinet to read the Civil War

17 Bertram D. Wolfe, "Communist Ideology and Soviet Foreign Policy," *Foreign Affairs,* Vol. XLI, No. 1 (Oct. 1962), p. 160.
18 Harry S. Truman, *Memoirs,* II (New York, 1958), 333. Truman frequently expressed his interest in history and referred to it on many occasions. See also his *Mr. Citizen.*

140   THE HISTORIAN AND THE DIPLOMAT

President as a way of sharpening their political insights.[19] There were a few occasions when Eisenhower sought to relate the American experience to contemporary problems. Once, in explaining to a group of reporters why Americans should not resent neutralism, he pointed out that "We were a young country once, and our whole policy for the first 150 years was, we were neutral."[20]

President Kennedy, speaking on the same subject to the United Nations General Assembly, declared, somewhat more accurately and elegantly, "My nation was once a colony, and we know what colonialism means: the exploitation and subjugation of the weak by the powerful, of the many by the few, of the governed who have given no consent to be governed. . . ."[21] Whatever the reaction of his African and Asian listeners, there can be no doubt that for Americans these words had deep meaning.

Unlike his immediate predecessors, Kennedy was a practicing historian, whose book *Profiles in Courage* won the Pulitzer Prize. In this respect, though less prolific, he was in the tradition of Theodore Roosevelt and Woodrow Wilson, both of whom had written a large number of historical volumes. At Harvard he wrote his senior thesis on the subject *While England Slept*, a book that met considerable critical approval when it was published in 1940. Recently reissued, it may still be read with pleasure and profit. One cannot but speculate on the lessons Kennedy might have learned as the son of the American ambassador in London, a man who, even after Munich, sought to improve German-American relations and who, in 1940, believed that Britain had little chance of survival, much less hope of ultimate victory, against the Nazi tyranny.

Kennedy never lost his interest in history. Biography was his favorite reading, and he is said to have followed historical literature more closely than many professional scholars. In 1963 he contributed an interesting review of the new edition of the *Adams Papers* to the *American Historical Review*; in January 1964 this leading American historical journal noted his tragic death:

No President since Wilson had such a disciplined interest in historical studies; and no President since Lincoln made history so organic a part of his political perspective. He saw the world as the historian should see it—not as warfare between good and evil, but as a complex

19 Robert J. Donovan, *Eisenhower, The Inside Story* (New York, 1956), pp. 206–207.
20 Ernest R. May (ed.), *The American Foreign Policy* (New York, 1963), p. 3.
21 Speech to the United Nations on disarmament, Sept. 25, 1961, *Public Papers of the Presidents: John F. Kennedy*, 1961, p. 624.

and obscure interaction of ideas and institutions. . . . His sense of history evidently reinforced his cool detachment in the midst of crisis, as his own instinct for the direction in which history was moving evidently fortified him for the hard decisions of his office.[22]

Kennedy's conception of the presidency was in the tradition of Lincoln, Wilson, and Franklin Roosevelt, a broad conception that viewed the office as a post of leadership for the representative of 180 million people. His writings display an admiration for those qualities that make for a strong executive, for boldness and initiative, and a clear understanding of the complex forces that shaped the nation. In his speeches are allusions to such figures as Jefferson, Webster, Tom Paine, Emerson, and Longfellow, and to the historians Herodotus, Gibbon, De Tocqueville, Parkman, Toynbee, and Churchill. To make his points, he refers to the Founding Fathers and the *Federalist Papers*, to "Pearl Harbor, Dunkirk, and Calais," the Great American Desert, the Webster-Ashburton Treaty of 1842, the Puritans in Massachusetts and the Mormons in Salt Lake City—all of which are familiar to most Americans. From these and other references emerges a view of the world deeply rooted in and strongly affected by his image of the American past. "No one who examines the modern world," he said at the University of California in March 1962, "can doubt that the great currents of history are carrying the world away from the monolithic idea toward the pluralistic idea. . . . No one can doubt that the wave of the future is not the conquest of the world by a single dogmatic creed but the liberation of the diverse energies of free nations and free men."[23]

This sense of history, this close link with the past, combined with a personal vision of a world order, is evident also in other high officials and policy-makers in all branches of government. Of the recent Secretaries of State, Dean Rusk and John Foster Dulles undoubtedly felt most the weight of the past. The first had delivered a series of lectures on the presidency to the Council on Foreign Relations, but plans for publication were canceled when he was appointed Secretary. Dulles, who as Secretary of State was largely responsible for the foreign policies of the Eisenhower administration, had also a close personal link with the diplomatic history of the United States. His grandfather, John W. Foster, had

22 *American Historical Review*, Vol. LXIX, No. 2 (Jan. 1964), p. 603.
23 *Ibid.* For a sensitive and thoughtful account of the late President's attitude to history and historians—and the relation of history to the larger problems of public policy —see Arthur M. Schlesinger, Jr., *A Thousand Days* (Boston, 1965), pp. 104–113.

been Secretary of State under President Benjamin Harrison, and an uncle, Robert Lansing, had been President Wilson's Secretary of State. It was Dulles' lifelong ambition to take his place with these distinguished ancestors, and no man in American diplomatic history prepared longer or harder for the post. Other members of his family had also been connected with the State Department, and as he was fond of telling people, there was probably no family in the United States that had been identified with foreign policy for so long. Dulles himself, as a young man, had served as a member of the American delegation to the Paris Peace Conference, and later, in the 1930's, he wrote a much-quoted book on the problem of "peaceful change." When foreign diplomats visited him in his office, he presented them with copies of the *Federalist Papers*, which he believed would help them understand his country.[24]

Yet Presidents Truman, Kennedy, and Johnson—whose evocation of our experience in the 1930's at home and abroad testify to his own distinct awareness of the relation of history, politics, and diplomacy—and Secretary Dulles have not been alone in their interest in history. Indeed, such preoccupation with history may be said almost to constitute a national trait affecting our policy at home and abroad often in subtle ways and not always in the best interests of the nation. The chief guide that Americans have in viewing the changed world about them is their own historical experience; and it is in that past that we must seek the explanation for their attitudes, beliefs, and hopes. Few people are as conscious of their history as Americans, refer to it so often, or know it so well. The reasons for its importance may be sought in a variety of factors—in its diversity, its brevity, its uniqueness.[25] The fact that so large a part of the population is only one or two generations removed from its Old World origins is certainly relevant, for behind much of the study of American history lies the strong urge to identify with the roots of the American past. Tests in American history are required for naturalization; courses in American history are mandatory in virtually all states on the primary and secondary levels and in many state universities on the college level. In a land where education is free and almost universal, this means that virtually every American has had repeated to him time and again the major facts about the history of his country.

24 Herman Finer, *Dulles over Suez* (Chicago, 1964), pp. 1, 519, note 16. *Department of State Bulletin*, Jan. 28, 1953, p. 239.
25 May, *op. cit.*, pp. 3–4.

For Americans, history also has a relevance, especially in foreign affairs, that it does not have for most other people. The past is closer to them in time and encompasses so wide a variety of experiences that there are few contemporary situations that do not remind them of similar experiences, whether accurately or not, in their own past. For the first 175 years of its history, while it expanded from the coastal plain to the Appalachians, the nation was a colony within the British Empire. It achieved its independence by revolution and force of arms, with military aid and assistance from the enemies of England. As a small new nation, it was caught in the struggle between France and England, two of the super-powers of that day, and it responded by declaring its neutrality and adopting a policy of isolation. Faced by a potential threat from the concert of Europe to the former Spanish colonies to the south, it proclaimed a doctrine of hemispheric solidarity that drew its force from British sea power. It survived the test of civil war and foreign intervention to become a great industrial power. By the beginning of the twentieth century, little more than one hundred years after independence, it had become a world power with colonies of its own. Two world wars, fought within the memory of many still living, destroyed isolationism and brought it to free-world leadership, with all its burdens and responsibilities.[26] Is it surprising, therefore, that Americans feel they can speak to the new nations of their colonial status and revolutionary heritage, that they claim affinity with the surge for freedom and the struggle for independence, that they profess to be tolerant of neutralism and to support the political, social, and economic development of the emerging nations of the world?

These claims are not always valid, and the resemblances are often superficial. Surface appearances can be deceptive. The American colonial experience was of a special kind, and few Africans or Asians would find many parallels in it to their own background. It can be argued also that the American Revolution was fought more to preserve something that already existed than to create something new.[27] In this respect it differs strikingly from present movements for independence and offers few signposts to the emerging states of Asia and Africa. The entire American experience as a colony was gained under a British rule that permitted a large

26 Charles Burton Marshall, *The Limits of Foreign Policy* (New York, 1954), Chap. 2.
27 In this connection, see Carl N. Degler, "The American Past: An Unsuspected Obstacle in Foreign Affairs," *The American Scholar*, Vol. XXXII, No. 2 (Spring 1963)— a perceptive article that discusses, at greater length, both this point and a number of others made above.

measure of self-government and the development of free institutions. It was the British effort to restrict the colonists that led to independence. In no sense was it a nationalist revolt by a backward people exploited by centuries of colonial domination. But the view of revolutions and independence movements that Americans have shapes their expectations of how other peoples will behave. That model is the American model, and when other revolutions differ from it, as they usually do, the American reaction is one of disappointment and rejection, an impatience with the failure to provide, as the United States did, for orderly government and free institutions.

The American attitude toward revolution is ambiguous. On the one hand, we view ourselves as inheritors of a revolutionary tradition and the example of the most successful experiment in self-government. It is in this tradition that Kennedy, in his inaugural, said, "We dare not forget today that we are the heirs of that first revolution."[28] Launching the Alliance for Progress in March 1961, he told his listeners that Americans welcomed the struggles for national independence and individual freedom, and that the revolution begun in 1776 was not yet finished. "Let us once again awaken our American Revolution," he said, "until it guides the struggle of people everywhere."[29]

On the other hand, the United States appears to many as the leader of antirevolutionary forces. "She now stands," wrote Arnold Toynbee, not long ago, "for what Rome stood for."[30] As defenders of the status quo, American leaders seemed to Toynbee to be playing the role of Metternich rather than of Lafayette. The old revolutionary zeal was gone, and in its place was the fear of change. Referring to the difficulties affecting U.S.-Latin American relations, in June 1961 one critic wrote: "Perhaps most important among these difficulties is our deep-seated uneasiness in the presence of revolution, actual or imminent. For ourselves and for others we prize stability, continuity, institutionalized change; we are distrustful of abrupt shifts, violent, radical departure."[31]

It is becoming increasingly fashionable these days to view the United States in its early years as an underdeveloped country

---

28 Inaugural address, Jan. 20, 1961, *Public Papers of the Presidents: John F. Kennedy, 1961*, p. 1.

29 *The New York Times*, March 14, 1961.

30 Arnold J. Toynbee, *America and the World Revolution* (New York and London, 1962), p. 92.

31 John N. Plank, an authority on Latin-American affairs, in *The New York Times*, June 11, 1961.

facing the same problems that the emergent nations face today, and solving them successfully under a system of free enterprise.[32] Like most historical analogies drawn from different times and places, this generalization, persuasive as it is, overlooks important differences in the two situations—great natural resources, access to foreign capital, land tenure, a skilled and growing population, exports, a home industry, a diverse economy, and a developed merchant marine. Unaware of these differences, Americans are unable to understand why other nations cannot emulate the American example. Disappointed when the reality falls short of expectations, they express their feelings in hostility and opposition to aid programs.

Feelings about imperialism strongly affect the American attitude toward the new nations. Despite its own imperialist adventures after 1898, the United States retains a strong aversion to colonialism that is rooted in its own colonial traditions and an expansionist policy that conferred self-rule and statehood. Americans see no contradiction in their record and their avowed sympathies. The Spanish-American War was fought to liberate Cuba; that it led to the acquisition of an empire in the far Pacific and the Caribbean was the result of other forces and only a temporary condition. Thus the surge for independence among the former colonies in Africa and Asia after World War II was greeted with favor by most Americans. Though U.S. support was limited by commitments to its European allies, condemnation of colonialism was made clear. This sympathy with the former colonial peoples did not always survive the realities of independence, but the distaste for imperialism nevertheless persists as an element in American foreign policy.[33]

The fact that the United States has not once been defeated or come under foreign domination, that it has never been invaded except briefly during the War of 1812, means that Americans view the contemporary world from a perspective different from that of most other people. The nation's remarkable growth and its geographical position, far from the centers of Europe, also color American views of the world today. Many of the nation's attitudes and policies were shaped in the nineteenth century, which was in many ways an

---

32 See, for example, Degler, *op. cit.*, p. 192, and Seymour M. Lipset, *The First New Nation* (New York, 1963).

33 Paul Seabury, *Power, Freedom and Diplomacy* (New York, 1963), pp. 58–63. All of Chapter 2, pp. 35–65, is particularly relevant to the present study. See also Herman Finer, *Dulles over Suez* (Chicago, 1964), p. 82, for Dulles' views on colonialism.

unusual period in modern history. In the century between Waterloo and Sarajevo, the concert of Europe maintained a balance and unity it had rarely achieved before and has lost since in the two world wars.[34] This experience, combined with uninterrupted and steady growth, geographical isolation, and a favorable and peaceful world environment, gave Americans the illusion that these were the normal conditions of society, and it was to this period that they wished to return in 1919 and 1945, after two interventions in the affairs of Europe.

One of the strongest and most persistent themes in American history is the tradition of isolationism.[35] Though it has been discarded in the Cold War, it continues to affect American attitudes toward Europe and the world in various ways. It has a nostalgic quality, reminding Americans of a happier, more carefree day when they did not bear such heavy burdens. To the discontented and the frustrated it offers a haven for retreat. But isolationism meant more than freedom from the concerns of Europe; it was a policy of unilateralism. It implied that the United States would act alone, relying on its own strength and resources. Even when the nation intervened in Europe or Asia or Latin America, it did so on its own, without reference to the policies or interests of others.

This habit of going it alone is still strong, and Americans find it difficult to adjust their policies to the needs of others. The Monroe Doctrine and the Open Door Policy are in this tradition. Both were unilateral statements deriving their sanction from an international situation that favored U.S. interests. In the case of Asia, the desire to go it alone persisted longer than it did in Europe because of a particular set of interests. As late as the Korean War, isolationist groups were able to argue for a separate American policy in the Far East without reference to the European allies. The Truman-MacArthur controversy, essentially such a debate, revealed the latent strength of isolationist sentiment.

The fact that the United States was settled largely by immigrants from all parts of Europe has also affected American foreign policy. Certainly it was an important element in isolationism and in American attitudes toward the Old World. The feeling of Irish-Americans toward Britain was a factor that always had to be taken into account in dealing with that nation. Ethnic and

---

34 Dean Acheson, "The Premises of American Policy," *Orbis,* III (Fall 1959), 268.
35 For a particularly useful account of this subject, see Selig Adler. *The Isolationist Impulse* (New York, 1953).

religious groups, with their traditional hatreds and loyalties, represent special interests in foreign policy that influence the policy-maker and the politician. Too close a relationship with one country may arouse opposition from one or more of these groups, creating conflicts and dissension in political life. Establishing a consensus for alliances under these conditions is difficult indeed. One of the reasons that our present alliance system has not produced internal schism may lie in its diversity. NATO, after all, offends no single ethnic group because it represents an alliance with all of the West European nations and is designed to contain the nation that has overrun the East European nations. Thus all groups can find grounds to support it.

Although the economic growth of the United States in the nineteenth century was due in part to foreign investments, labor, technology, and markets, Americans generally believed their blessings flowed entirely from the rich endowments of a beneficent nature and the unique virtues of American enterprise. Few were aware of the role of Europe and especially of England in the nation's economic development; for most Americans the remarkable growth of the nation was the result of a fortunate set of circumstances—great natural resources, an expanding frontier, internal free trade, and a large ready-made internal market. There was much truth in this view of a self-sufficient American economy contrasted with that of a European economy, forced to seek its markets and sources of supply outside, in Africa, Asia, the Middle East, and America. Such a belief reinforced the estrangement of Americans from Europe, fortified a protectionist policy, and provided additional justification for isolationism. This situation contains a paradox for an economy that viewed itself as self-contained and self-sufficient yet exerted in the twentieth century a profound effect on the world market through its trade policies, production methods, and technology. The result was a double image of the United States—a self-contained, isolationist America and an international America deeply involved in the world economy.[36]

Europe, with its secret diplomacy and frequent wars, represented for many Americans a decadent and corrupt society, a source of evil; the less we had to do with it, the better.[37] Iso-

36 For a fuller discussion of this subject, see Seabury, *op. cit.,* pp. 51–58.
37 Cushing Strout, *The American Image of the Old World* (New York, 1963); Erik von Kuehnelt-Leddhin, "America's Myths of Europe," *Southwest Review,* Vol. XL, No. 2 (Spring 1955), pp. 170–179. The image Americans have of themselves and of Europe is in itself a fascinating study, of interest not only to intellectual and social historians but also to other students of politics. The extent to which historians have contributed to this

lationism could thus be justified on moral as well as on political and economic grounds. The American viewed himself as uncomplicated, ingenuous, honest, and essentially good—a view that was reinforced by the historian Frederick Jackson Turner and his thesis of the role of the frontier in American history. This is a stereotype, of course, but it is not without effect. For a century and a half we could remain aloof from Europe, secure in the balance of power there. We had freedom to choose our course and to act unilaterally. When the balance was destroyed, so was our freedom of action, though we behaved as though we still had it. As late as the 1950's there were some, such as former President Hoover and Senator Taft, who talked still of returning to an earlier golden age by establishing a Fortress America and washing our hands of the affairs of Europe.

Americans tend also to think of themselves as a peace-loving people, never engaging in wars of conquest and fighting only to defend their shores and their sacred rights. Yet it is difficult to find any period in American history when the nation was not at war, and much of its territory was won by conquest. There is a contradiction here between the image and the reality that stems from the fact that Americans regard war as an evil in itself, as a moral offense against society. When political necessity or national interest required resorting to force, Americans sought to justify the action as self-defense. Thus the question of responsibility becomes a major issue with Americans, and the opening blow of the war assumes a significance scarcely warranted in the sequence of events that led to the war. It is a matter of prime importance for Americans to believe that the overt act was defensive and not aggressive.

The moral anxiety displayed by Americans toward the use of force finds expression in a concern over war guilt, in historical revisionism, and in our inability to understand how others can regard us as a military threat, despite the fact that we possess the most powerful military machine in history. We constantly assure others of our peaceful intentions while spending $50 billion a year for military purposes. "Our arms will never be used to strike the first blow in any attack," said President Kennedy in his special message to Congress in January 1961. "It is our national

---

image or have helped to create it has not yet been fully explored. If, indeed, this is the case, if the writings of Bancroft, Turner, Beard, and others have been an important factor in the shaping of the American image, their historical writing may be said to play a powerful role in foreign policy.

tradition." At the same time, Americans decry the use of force or the threat of its use by others. They know *they* have no aggressive intentions but assume that others who support powerful military forces do.

The American reluctance to resort to force bears no relationship to and has no effect on the degree of force exerted once hostilities begin. Lack of restraint in the use of arms is as characteristic of Americans as their concern about the overt act of aggression. Wars become crusades against the forces of evil. Thus in World War II we displayed no hesitation about burning and bombing the cities of Germany and Japan or dropping two atomic bombs on a nation that was already militarily defeated and seeking a way out of the war. And the Korean War, which was marked by self-imposed restraints, proved a traumatic experience for the American people.

The image we have of ourselves as a peaceful, freedom-loving and honest people is not always shared by others. And their picture of us shapes their policy toward us in the same way that ours does toward them. By some we are regarded as a people dedicated to the material things, placing undue emphasis on gadgets of all kinds—refrigerators, washing machines, television, and automobiles—devoid of culture and taste. We are viewed as a nation dominated by industry, dedicated to profits, characterized by a highly developed technology and mass production, and blessed with a high standard of living—a prosperous and luxury-loving nation seeking to preserve the status quo. This is a distorted image, of course, but it bears a close enough resemblance to reality to give it credence. Our dedication to equality and freedom must appear somewhat superficial to the peoples of the emergent nations of Asia and Africa, most of whom are colored, in view of the history of the Negro in America. And it is doubtful that others view the Negro problem, as we often do, as one peculiar to the American South. American protestations that they are doing everything possible to give the Negro equal status in practice as well as in law must strike Asiatics and Africans as hollow indeed. We tend to explain the Negro problem in historical and geographical terms, justifying it as the unfortunate result of slavery, southern prejudices, and sheer numbers. We forget, though others do not, that some nations with a similar history of slavery have absorbed the Negro into their culture, and that Europeans have displayed much greater racial tolerance than Americans. Here our own history is against us, affecting the attitudes of those whose support we seek and whose policies we wish to influence.

Americans tend, moreover, to think of their political system as superior to others and as a model for those seeking freedom and independence. Yet the basic American political documents—the Declaration of Independence, the Constitution, the Bill of Rights, and the *Federalist Papers*—are really not applicable to other peoples and other places. They are peculiarly American, based on a unique experience, and are not exportable. Yet we talk about them as though they constitute an ideology with universal appeal, comparable to Marxist-Leninist doctrine. The fact is that the United States has no ideology to compete with communism in the market place, no panacea to offer—only sympathy, economic aid, and military assistance when it is needed.

Americans believe also that their form of government, if adopted by others, would solve most of the world's problems. Federalism proved the solution to their situation in 1789 and made possible the extraordinary growth of the nation. Why, then, should not Europe adopt a similar system, since it has such clear and obvious advantages? Why not a united Africa of colored republics? Or a world government based on the American model to bring the blessings of peace and prosperity to all other peoples? But when such organizations produce results somewhat different from what we expected or create problems we did not anticipate, as is the case with the United Nations and the European Common Market, many express their disappointment in rejection and opposition.

Closely related to the American belief in the superiority of their system, what Charles Burton Marshall refers to as the tendency "to translate our individual characteristics into universals," is the faith that Americans have in the written document. The American experience provides ample justification for this confidence, for at the critical moments in our history stand the written agreements that embody our solutions to the problems of government. This faith in formal documents, projected into the realm of international politics, places an emphasis on the written word, on written agreements, that is unrealistic and unwarranted. Such agreements, Americans believe, have all the sanctity of a charter or a contract and thus can solve all their problems for all time. They overlook or are unaware of the differences between the conditions of domestic and international conflict. Our own system worked not only because of the wisdom of the Founding Fathers but also because of "a confluence of fortunate circumstances unique in the experience of nations."[38] Such favorable conditions are scarcely applicable to the world of international politics.

The roles of Congress and the public, combined with the dispersion of power in the American system, make the formulation of foreign policy a complicated and time-consuming process.[39] Americans feel strongly about the virtues of freedom of debate and believe that out of open discussion will emerge a consensus. Since there has never really been a fundamental difference among opposing groups in our history about the organization of our society—except during the Civil War—this belief has acquired the validity of a principle. We are impatient with those who see little merit in public debate, and we respond strongly to limits placed upon it. Since we have no experience with a hereditary aristocracy, an entrenched ruling class, or a strong proletariat movement, we are unable to understand societies with a rigid class structure where debate fails to provide consensus. In the liberal tradition, compromise and accommodation are always possible, and this view carried into foreign affairs tends to produce rarely fulfilled expectations.

It is a truism to observe that in the United States, debate over foreign policy is conducted in the open, and that for good or bad, public opinion plays a large role.[40] This is not always true, of course. President Kennedy consulted neither the Congress nor the public before he made his decision in the Cuban missile crisis, but it is inconceivable that he could have maintained his position for long against public opinion. President Roosevelt was unable to rally public support to quarantine the aggressor in 1937 and prudently withdrew. Strong leadership can shape public opinion, but must bow before it, too. The force of public opinion is ever a factor, influencing policies by the judgments made about it and making some policies impossible of fulfillment. Failure to heed it can destroy public figures. This is not always understood by others, either by our allies or by our adversaries, so that what is politically necessary or expedient at home often appears irrational or unwise abroad. Moreover, others may base their policies on an expectation of American reaction derived from official state-

38 Marshall, *op. cit.*, p. 56.
39 The author is indebted here, as elsewhere, to Stanley Hoffmann's discerning "Restraints and Choices in American Foreign Policy," *Daedalus* (Fall 1962), pp. 687–691.
40 For an interesting discussion of this point, see Ernest R. May, "Public Opinion and Foreign Policy," in William H. Nelson with Francis L. Loewenheim (eds.), *Theory and Practice in American Politics* (Chicago, 1964).

ments and attitudes only to find they have made a serious error. The North Koreans in June 1950 made such an error; perhaps so did Khrushchev in 1962 when he began to put intermediate-range missiles in Cuba. The Japanese in December 1941 miscalculated or underestimated the forces of isolationism in the United States and took at face value the statements of our leaders that an advance southward into the Indies would bring the United States into the war. Fortunately for the Roosevelt administration, the Pearl Harbor attack relieved it of the necessity of marshaling public opinion to oppose a Japanese advance into the British and Dutch colonies of Southeast Asia.

In a sense, Senator Fulbright's address to the Senate on March 25, 1964, on "Old Myths and New Realities" in foreign policy was directed against the constraints imposed on the policy-maker by public opinion.[41] American diplomacy, Fulbright charged, was to a large degree based not on the realities of international politics but on "myths," the most persistent and important of which was the belief that the Communist bloc was a monolithic power grouping involved in a vast conspiracy whose object is the destruction of the free world. But the policy-makers in both the executive and legislative branches of the government are in fact cognizant of the realities of international life and usually act on the basis of these realities. Senator Fulbright was well aware of this when he delivered his speech. But he knew, too, that most Americans continued to think in terms of the myths, and it was to them that his remarks were addressed, for their consent was essential. Providing the basis of popular support for foreign policy, it placed on the policy-maker the necessity for conforming or seeming to conform to the myth. As Richard Rovere pointed out, it becomes necessary to justify the realities of the 1960's with the Cold War rhetoric of the 1940's.[42]

Most educated Europeans know a good deal about countries other than their own and something about Asia and Africa, where they long maintained colonies, troops, and a civil service. But Americans, with their tradition of rejection of Europe, have shown less inclination, at least until recently, to learn about the Old World. Undoubtedly this lack of knowledge, first noted during World War II, has led to misunderstanding and made more difficult the tasks of foreign policy. This situation has been and is

41 *The New York Times*, March 26, 1964.
42 "Letter from Washington," in *The New Yorker*, April 11, 1964, pp. 149–155.

being corrected to some extent by an increased emphasis in colleges and universities on work in other areas of the world, in area study programs and in non-Western studies. Courses on Latin America and Asia are much more common now than they were a decade ago, and the study of Africa has become almost a new field of research.[43] Before the Second World War, there were comparatively few courses in Russian history; today courses on the Soviet Union are standard in most history departments. Perhaps the most spectacular advance on the academic scene in the post-war period has been the growth of area study programs. In 1946 there were 13 such programs, 6 on Latin America, 4 on the Far East, and 3 on Russia. Six years later the number had grown to 29, with 19 institutions represented. A survey by the State Department in 1960 listed 109 research projects concerned primarily with the study of foreign societies and regions, most of them based at universities. The largest number dealt with one or more countries of Asia, the smallest number with Africa and the Near East, where the number of scholars studying these areas was small. The Soviet Union and Eastern Europe provided the focus for more than 20 of the studies then in progress.[44]

IV

The search in the past for guidance to the solution of the problems of the Cold War may explain in part the popularity of historical works in recent years, as well as their titles. Much of this interest may represent simply a desire to return to an earlier and simpler day, but this, too, is essentially a reaction to the Cold War. It would be tedious to list titles, and publication figures may not mean much more than acceptance by a literary club. Still, the writings of George F. Kennan, who was in the unusual position of being both a historian and a policy-maker, are not without interest. The same can be said of Kennedy's *Profiles in Courage*, Arthur Schlesinger, Jr.'s, multivolume biography of Franklin D. Roosevelt, and, more recently, his account of the presidency of John F. Kennedy. Kennan's work, because of his position as head of the Policy Planning Staff, his experience as a Foreign Service officer, and the high quality of his historical writing, was particularly

43 See Robert I. Rotberg, "The Teaching of African History," *American Historical Review*, Vol. LXIX, No. 1 (Oct. 1963), pp. 47–63.
44 Louis Morton, "National Security and Area Studies," *Journal of Higher Education*, Vol. XXXIV, No. 3 (March 1963), pp. 142–143.

important. The Policy Planning Staff, established by Secretary Marshall in 1947 to study basic trends in international relations and to develop long-range American policies, became an influential group under Kennan and his immediate successor, and continued under Walt W. Rostow as an important center of intellectual activity within the State Department.[45] Like Kennan, other members of the group were experienced diplomats with great intellectual capacities, professional academic backgrounds, and an ability to express themselves forcefully and clearly in their writings. Among the group were Herbert Feis, Louis Halle, Charles Burton Marshall, Dorothy Fosdick, Paul H. Nitze, Robert Bowie, and others.

The attitude of this group toward foreign policy, best exemplified by Kennan and formulated in his *American Diplomacy 1900–1950* (1951) and *Realities of American Foreign Policy* (1954), was in the tradition of *Realpolitik* and emphasized the concept of national self-interest. This thesis was evident also in the works of Charles Burton Marshall, Dorothy Fosdick, and other former members of the Policy Planning Staff. The emphasis on national interest and realism was carried even further in the perceptive and brilliant works of Hans J. Morgenthau, professor of modern history and political science at the University of Chicago. Arguing from a strong historical basis, he asserted that American policy too often was based on moralistic considerations rather than on national interests. Isolationists and international utopians equally came under criticism in his work.[46]

The recent Civil War centennial produced a flood of literature on that conflict, but it is significant that as interest in it waned, there followed a rash of books on the First World War, in which Americans had shown little interest since the 1930's. Perhaps the most widely read book on the First World War was Barbara Tuchman's *Guns of August* (1962), which dealt in considerable detail with the events immediately preceding the war, the plans of both sides, and the first month of the conflict. There was a renewed interest also in the American Revolution[47] that took

---

45 Rostow succeeded McGeorge Bundy as Special Assistant to the President for National Security Affairs when Bundy resigned to assume the presidency of the Ford Foundation in the spring of 1966.

46 Hans J. Morgenthau, *In Defense of the National Interest* (1951). Morgenthau, a prolific author, has published a large number of excellent articles, many of which are collected in *Politics in the Twentieth Century* (Chicago, 1962). See also Robert E. Osgood, *Ideals and Self-Interest in America's Foreign Relations* (Chicago, 1953). Osgood was a colleague of Morgenthau's at the University of Chicago.

47 Book Review Section, *The New York Times*, March 29, 1964, for example, reviewed four new volumes on the Revolution. In late 1965 and early 1966 plans were being made for a bicentennial celebration of the American Revolution, and legislation was introduced in Congress to establish a commission, as had been done for the hundredth anniversary of the Civil War.

American readers back to their origins. Finally, serious historical biographies and memoirs by leading participants in the crowded events of the last decade found a wide audience. The list is an imposing one, including as it does the memoirs of two U.S. Presidents, numerous members of the Cabinet and of the Congress and ranking military men, together with the writings of their critics and supporters. If the country was not greatly stirred by many of these books—even those that dealt with such critical issues as the Suez Crisis of 1956 and the Cuban crisis of 1962 —at least it became better informed.

Considerably more important was the historical writing on the origins and history of the Second World War, and much of this was directly related to the important problems of the postwar world. A good deal of this scholarship was autobiographical and polemical, but a good part of it also represented solid historical research based on official records that had formerly been classified as confidential and thus unavailable. The review of America's entry into the war and its strategy during the conflict served to focus attention on postwar policies and to provide the basis for public debate and political controversy. Three issues, in particular, began to attract special attention—the Japanese attack on Pearl Harbor, American wartime diplomacy, with special reference to the Yalta Conference, and the loss of China to the Communists following the end of the war. Yalta became the symbol of surrender to Soviet blackmail, the rallying point for opposition to negotiation with the Russians. During the McCarthy era, the Communist Chinese victory was used as the basis for charges of treason and Communist infiltration of the State Department. The publication of the official Yalta documents by the State Department in February 1955 only added fuel to the fire and led to further charges and countercharges. Sober historical judgment based on a study of the conference records was seemingly lost in the heat of political controversy, but once the controversy began to pass, it became apparent to all but the die-hard Roosevelt detractors that the United States had not been betrayed, that it had not been the victim of a Communist conspiracy, and that the Russians probably would have intervened in the Far East regardless of the policy of the United States.[48]

Other aspects of World War II that came under scrutiny by

_____

48 The literature on Yalta is extensive. Most valuable is the official record of the Malta-Yalta conferences in the *Conference Series: Foreign Relations of the United States* (Washington, D.C., 1955). See also John L. Snell (ed.), *The Meaning of Yalta* (Baton Rouge, 1956).

historians included such controversial issues as the Germany-first strategy, the question of a Balkan invasion, and the decision by President Truman to drop the atomic bomb. The first could be used by those former isolationists and Anglophobes who were never reconciled to the close ties with Britain and France, and by the Asia-Firsters. General MacArthur was the idol of these people, and his removal from command in 1951 precipitated a debate over the basis of American foreign policy. The idea of an invasion of the Balkans in 1944, attributed to Winston Churchill and the British, was viewed in postwar terms as a lost opportunity to contain Soviet expansion in Eastern Europe and thus constituted a criticism of Roosevelt's wartime strategy. The decision not to cross the Elbe River in the spring of 1945 and to drive on to Berlin at the same time as the Russian troops was seen in the same light. But this decision never became the subject of wide controversy because it involved General Eisenhower and could not be pinned on a Democratic administration.

The debate over the decision to use the atom bomb against Japan involved a different set of issues and groups. It was the Left rather than the Right that criticized the decision, with the hope not of forcing a change from collective security to isolation or a firmer position toward the Soviet Union, but rather of securing a modification of our nuclear strategy and the adoption of measures leading to arms control and disarmament.[49]

Much of the writing on these and similar issues was partisan and political, but the writings of official civilian historians, working freely from classified documents, laid a firm foundation for the final evaluation. Here, as in other instances, the practice of employing civilian historians within the various government agencies proved a wise measure that paid large dividends. The official histories and the records of the wartime conferences published by the State Department ultimately furnished a detailed and objective account of wartime measures that made it indispensable for any study of the war. Though there had been historians in the State Department and several other government agencies before the war, the widespread use of historians in World War II represented an innovation. This system was retained in the post-

---

49 Some of these controversial decisions are treated in Kent Roberts Greenfield (ed.), *Command Decisions* (Washington, D.C., 1960). See also his *American Strategy in World War II* (Baltimore, 1963); Samuel Eliot Morison, *Strategy and Compromise* (Boston, 1958); Hanson W. Baldwin, *Great Mistakes of the War* (New York, 1950); Chester Wilmot, *The Struggle for Europe* (New York, 1952).

war period and extended to new offices and agencies as they were created. Already it has produced a volume on the history of the Atomic Energy Commission that provides the fullest account to date of the development of the bomb and its use in 1945.[50]

The work of these official and semiofficial historians represents a major historical achievement of the postwar period as well as a new approach to the writing of military history. Samuel Eliot Morison's fifteen-volume history of naval operations is the work of a professional and one of the great contributions to the historical literature of the war. The Army's series, prepared initially under the direction of Kent Roberts Greenfield, already numbers more than sixty volumes. Covering every aspect of the war in which the Army participated, it is an indispensable source for all students of the period and a guide to the records bearing on most controversial wartime issues. The equally professional Air Force history was written under the direction of Wesley Frank Craven of Princeton University and James Lea Cate of the University of Chicago. In addition to these and other official histories, there have been a number of first-rate scholarly studies, including those of Herbert Feis, on various aspects of the war, many of them dealing with those questions that continued to arouse controversy in the postwar period.[51]

Perhaps the most controversial of all wartime issues was the entry of the United States into the war, which isolationists used to create suspicion and sow mistrust of existing diplomacy, and the Republicans to discredit Roosevelt's programs and policies and with it "twenty years of treason." Revisionism is not new in American historical writing, and it has generally been useful in shedding light on the reasons why the United States has gone to war. The question of war guilt, an ever-present theme in American history, exercises a fatal fascination for historians. President Polk's policy toward Mexico in 1846, Lincoln's decision to send food to Fort Sumter, Wilson's decision to go to war with Germany have been re-examined in each generation. World War II provided only the most recent example of this search by historians for the truth, but in each case this search has been related to the questions of the day. The same was true in the post-World War II years.

The United States had scarcely emerged from the war when

50 Richard G. Hewlett and Oscar E. Anderson, Jr., *The New World, 1939–1946,* Vol. I of the official history of the U.S. Atomic Energy Commission (State College, Pa., 1962).
51 For a discussion of the literature on the war, see Louis Morton, "Sources for the History of World War II," *World Politics,* Vol. XIII, No. 3 (April 1961), pp. 435–453.

revisionist historians began to re-examine the events that had led to Pearl Harbor. Charles A. Beard led the attack with his *President Roosevelt and the Coming of the War, 1941* (1948), in which he argued with the skill of a lawyer and the techniques of a master historian that Roosevelt had exceeded his constitutional powers and had evaded his political commitments to take the United States into war. This same theme in various forms was repeated and enlarged on by others: Charles C. Tansill, George Morgenstern, William Henry Chamberlain, Harry Elmer Barnes, and Admiral Husband E. Kimmel. In its simplest form, this thesis may be stated as follows: President Roosevelt maneuvered Japan into attack by diplomatic and economic pressure, withheld vital information from the commanders at Pearl Harbor, and deliberately kept the Pacific Fleet at Pearl Harbor to invite attack and so bring the American people into the war united behind the administration. The reasons given for Roosevelt's actions varied, depending on the outlook of the authors, from a desire to aid Britain to an effort to cover up the failure of the New Deal.[52]

Twenty years later there was even more debate over the war in Vietnam. On this occasion, many intellectuals, including a large segment of the academic community, took a strong stand in opposition to the government's policy, challenging many of the assumptions on which this policy was based. Here the role of the scholar merged with that of the activist. Historians disputed the parallel drawn by administration spokesmen between Communist China (assumed to be the ultimate directing force in the conflict) and Nazi Germany as a justification for American involvement—a historical analogy that had been readily accepted when advanced by President Truman during the Greek and Korean crises. They also challenged the administration's analysis of the nature of the conflict, the relationship of the North Vietnamese government to Communist China on the one hand and to the Vietcong on the other, and the basis of U.S. policy in Southeast Asia. This is not to say that there was agreement among the intellectuals. Some favored immediate withdrawal; some, measures designed to limit escalation; others, negotiations with the Vietcong. But, united in their opposition to the expansion of the war, they played an increasingly important role in the debate, utilizing all the means at their disposal to bring pressure on the administration—full-page advertisements in newspapers, letters to the editor, pickets,

52 See Louis Morton, "Pearl Harbor in Perspective," U.S. Naval Institute *Proceedings,* Vol. LXXXI, No. 4 (April 1955), pp. 461–468; Arthur M. Schlesinger, Jr., "Roosevelt and His Detractors," *Harper's,* June 1950, pp. 62–68; Adler, *op. cit.,* pp. 384–389.

petitions, marches on Washington, and the "teach-in," a new technique that reached out to a national audience when various scholars and officials—including McGeorge Bundy—debated the issues on television.

The Senate Foreign Relations Committee, under the leadership of Senator J. William Fulbright, entered the debate also, contributing to the chorus of dissent with hearings that featured testimony by Dean Rusk, George Kennan, and General James Gavin. Central to the issues were the nature of American aims in Vietnam, the cost, the effect on allies and neutrals, the role of Communist China in the Vietnam war, and the fear that American policy in Vietnam might lead to war with that nation. To throw light on the little-understood but vitally important problem of China, Senator Fulbright invited a number of eminent scholars, including John F. Fairbank of Harvard and Doak Barnett of Columbia, to offer their views on America's China policy. Their testimony, generally advocating greater flexibility in the U.S. posture toward the Peking regime, made headlines in the national press and was followed by a statement signed by almost two hundred Far East scholars urging recognition of China, its admission to the UN, and other measures designed to draw Peking closer to the community of nations.

It is difficult to measure the impact of these efforts by the intellectuals to affect U.S. policy. There is little doubt that the intellectuals were largely instrumental in bringing the issues out into the open and forcing debate. Drawing on their knowledge of the area and its history, they were in a better position than other segments of the public to dispute administration statements that might otherwise have gone unchallenged. They provided, for a time at least, a counterweight to the pressure from the so-called hawks for stronger measures of an extension of the war, thereby contributing significantly to the shaping of foreign policy.

Two of the areas most closely related to the problems of the Cold War were diplomacy and military history. Both found larger followings in the postwar period among the reading public and among students at colleges and universities. The line dividing the two areas became less sharp, reflecting a growing awareness of the interrelationship between foreign policy and military force. Standard textbooks on American history, widely used throughout the country, devoted much more space to past wars than did texts of an earlier period. Professors T. Harry Williams, Richard N. Current, and Frank Freidel, in their two-volume *History of the United States*

(1959), devote three chapters to the Civil War, three to World War II (two of them on military operations), and one chapter, entitled "Nuclear Diplomacy," to the Cold War. Similarly, the standard books of readings and problems include documents and selections relating to Cold War issues.[53]

The same trend could be observed in textbooks on American diplomatic history. In the 1959 edition of his *Short History of American Foreign Policy,* Samuel Flagg Bemis sums up the impact of the last twenty years with the observation that "the new and foreboding picture of power and politics produced a diplomatic revolution in the history of the United States" (page 695). Several other recent general histories of American diplomacy, such as Richard W. Leopold's *The Growth of American Foreign Policy* (1963), have broken away entirely from the older narrative account of diplomatic events, administration by administration, to focus on issues, forces, and processes. Julius W. Pratt, in his *History of United States Foreign Policy* (1955), includes chapters on "The Tools of Diplomacy" and "The Tools of Force." "The average reader," he writes, "may or may not be aware that military force, whether used or held in reserve, is an indispensable instrument in the prosecution of foreign policy. . . . Since an acquaintance with this subject seems highly relevant to an understanding of foreign policy, [this] chapter summarizes the history of the military and naval policy of the United States" (page vii).

The impact of the Cold War on American society and its meaning in terms of American history have been of concern to many scholars. Historians have been more cautious than most in dealing with it in their professional capacity (though not as citizens), for the events are too recent for proper perspective. Still, Samuel Flagg Bemis, in his presidential address to the American Historical Association in December 1961, sought to relate American foreign policy to the nation's traditional policies and stressed "the unchanging value of our inheritance of freedom, as we confront the dilemma of our times."[54]

---

53 Texts examined include Harry J. Carman, Harold C. Syrett, and Bernard Wishy, *A History of the American People* (New York, 1961); Dumas Malone and Basil Rauch, *Empire for Liberty* (New York, 1960); Richard Hofstadter, William Miller, and Daniel Aaron, *The American Republic* (New Jersey, 1959). Readings examined were Sidney Fine and Gerald S. Brown (eds.), *The American Past* (New York, 1961); Abraham S. Eisenstadt (ed.), *American History, Recent Interpretations* (New York, 1962); Merrill Peterson and Leonard W. Levy (eds.), *Major Crises in American History* (New York, 1962). In this connection, see Louis Morton, "The Historians and the Study of War," *Mississippi Valley Historical Review,* Vol. XLVIII, No. 4 (March 1962), pp. 599–613.
54 "American Foreign Policy and the Blessings of Liberty," *American Historical Review, Vol.* LXVII, No. 2 (Jan. 1962), p. 305.

C. Vann Woodward approached the task in a different manner, suggesting that events since 1945 raised new questions about the past and required reinterpretation of large areas of history. In support of his thesis, Woodward referred to the evolution in military technology that had destroyed the security of the United States, likening it to the disappearance of the frontier and free land at the turn of the century. He noted also the relationship between free security and American attitudes toward war and power, its view of itself as an innocent nation in a wicked world and its demagogic diplomacy. "The heritage of free and easy security," he wrote, ". . . can almost certainly be discerned at work in the tendency to plunge into wars first and prepare for them later."[55]

Woodward called also for a reinterpretation of the whole of military history in the face of the revolution in military technology since 1945. "We are now able," he observed perceptively, "to view the past in a new perspective, to see that the great battles of World War II represented not a new age but the ending of a very old one."[56] Noting the decline in importance of Western Europe and the rise of nationalism in Asia and Africa, Woodward suggested that the time had come to stop viewing history in terms of Europe. "One of the historical results to flow from the confrontation between East and West should be a new and revised view of world history. The ethnocentric, or Europocentric, view that has been held for so long a time in the West can hardly be expected to survive the sweeping change in East-West relationships."[57] Perhaps, in the long run, this will be the most significant result of the postwar period.

V

After this brief examination of the nature of the world crisis and the role of history (and of historians as recorders of the past) in the shaping of foreign policy, it would be of interest now to broaden somewhat the scope of this inquiry to examine the effects of the Cold War on scholarship generally and on the intellectual community.[58] The most obvious effect is the new relationship of scientists to government in their capacity as researchers and as policy advisers.

---

55 Woodward. *op. cit.,* pp. 6–7.
56 *Ibid.,* p. 11.
57 *Ibid.,* p. 16.
58 The discussion that follows is based on research done under a grant from the Carnegie Corporation of New York to Dartmouth College. The results of the research have been published in Gene M. Lyons and Louis Morton, *Schools for Strategy—Education and Research in National Security Affairs* (New York, 1965).

The revolution in military technology has given to research in weaponry a prominence it never had before and has elevated the scientist to a new position in government. With these developments has come the application of scientific methods to decision-making, thereby enhancing further the position of the scientists and elevating the behavioral sciences. Not only the President but also the secretaries of State and Defense have Scientific Advisers. The head of the Policy Planning Council in the State Department under President Kennedy and for a time under President Johnson was an economic historian, the Comptroller of the Department of Defense until recently was an economist, and until recently the Special Assistant to the President for National Security Affairs was a former Harvard dean. Numerous academicians travel frequently to Washington to advise on matters of policy and security, and sit on a variety of advisory and *ad hoc* committees. Others perform research at their universities under government contract or work for private nonprofit research corporations that subsist almost entirely on federal funds. The professionalization of the Foreign Service has placed new demands on universities, and the most promising officials at mid-career are given opportunities for advanced work at large graduate centers throughout the country. A new professionalism in the federal service, created largely by the needs of the Cold War, has opened up new challenges for higher education.

The increasing concern of scholars with the problems of the Cold War was partly a response to the needs of the policy-makers, partly the result of an awareness of the opportunities and challenges presented by a new field of study, and partly the product of their own concern with the grave threats of the nuclear age.[59] The implications of the new military technology were as yet only dimly perceived; the political, economic, and social consequences of the great changes wrought since World War II needed to be explored; and the changed role of the United States in world affairs demanded increased attention. In all of these areas, the scholar could be of assistance to the hard-pressed official, overcome with the burdens of day-to-day operations. He could provide background and historical perspective, analysis of existing policies, and exploration of alternative policies. There was a need also for trained and disciplined minds in the public

59 Serious scholarly concern with the causes of war and the problems of national security can be traced back to the post-World War I era, to the studies at the University of Chicago during the 1920's under Quincy Wright, and to the seminars at Princeton in the late 1930's and early 1940's under Edward Mead Earle. The first led to the monumental two-volume *Study of War* (Chicago, 1942), recently published in an abridged edition; the latter to *Makers of Modern Strategy* (Princeton, 1943).

service. Expanded government activities in the fields of planning and intelligence required the skills and knowledge of social scientists. For these reasons increasing numbers of academicians found their way into the government after 1945, some on a level where they could participate directly in the shaping of policy.

From the start the federal government assumed primary responsibility for marshaling scientific resources for research in and the development of weapons systems and detection devices. As a result, the number of academic research programs in science and technology has grown at an astonishing rate and constitutes a major contribution of the universities to national security in the Cold War.

The study of related political, economic, and social problems has proceeded at a much more modest pace and with much less direct relationship between government and the universities. Still, in the last decade there has been a remarkable increase in the number of seminars, centers, and institutes concerned with foreign affairs and national security. Most of them are affiliated with academic institutions; others have only a tenuous university affiliation or are entirely independent. There are such centers at Harvard, Princeton, Massachusetts Institute of Technology, Columbia, Chicago, Ohio State, Stanford, California, Duke, North Carolina, and Pennsylvania. Similar activity is carried on at the Council on Foreign Relations, the Brookings Institution, the Stanford Research Institute, and government-organized institutes, such as the RAND Corporation and the Institute of Defense Analyses. Most of the academic programs are supported by one or more foundations; some work for one or more government agencies; and other programs, whether organizationally independent or affiliated with a university, derive the bulk of their funds from government contracts. Still others, such as the Council on Foreign Relations, are entirely independent, and some are largely paper organizations created to funnel funds from outside sources into the academic community for the purpose of stimulating research.

Any precise measurement of the growth of research and teaching in this area is extremely difficult. Not only does the decentralized character of American higher education and research make it difficult to assemble precise statistics, but the diverse nature of the programs also creates a problem of classification. Still, one can get some sense of the magnitude of the effort by viewing the statistics. In the spring of 1963, for example, the State Department listed more than 400 research projects relating to arms control and disarmament. A privately supported compilation in 1960 listed 21 major research institutions directly engaged in problems of world order and conflict. Finally, a survey undertaken at the U.S. Air Force Academy late in 1962 indicated that out of 115 colleges and universities responding to a questionnaire, 23 offered courses in national security and 25 declared they had plans to do so.[60] When compared to the number of courses and amount of research in the field in 1950, a real change in the academic scene is evident.

The programs and methods of operation of these centers and institutes vary widely. All serve the purpose of furthering research and teaching in different disciplines concerned with problems related to the Cold War. They serve also to bring together scholars in different fields to discuss issues of common interest, thereby creating in effect a community of experts in the Cold War. As part of all the programs, there are meetings, conferences, and study groups through which scholars from different institutions meet with one another and with policy-makers and politicians to review their own work or to concentrate on a single issue of current importance. Equally at home in Washington and on the campus, they acquire information not available to the public and filter it through to the academic community at large. Their number is small, but as a group their influence can be large when it is brought to bear upon a single issue. In an informal way they serve as a bridge between the world of scholarship and the world of policy. The group also provides a training ground for public servants and a source of potential policy-makers. The Kennedy administration, when it assumed office, drew on the group for several key appointments in the areas of foreign policy and national security. Paul H. Nitze and Roger Hilsman were active members of the Johns Hopkins Washington Center for Foreign Policy Research; Walt W. Rostow came from the Center for International Studies at MIT, Charles Hitch and others from RAND.

The scholar also contributes to policy formulation in his role as critic. A good example is the extended debate over the policy of massive retaliation that took place during the Eisenhower administration. Opposition to that new policy from within the government came largely from the Army, but it had the strong support of scholars and other intellectuals, many of them members of aca-

---

60 Colonel W. C. McDonald and Captain L. J. Larsen, *National Security Policy*, U.S. Air Force Academy, 1962 (mimeograph); *Current Thoughts on Peace and War*, Vol. I, No. 1 (Winter 1960); *Arms Control and Disarmament*, Bureau of Intelligence and Research, Department of State, May 1963.

demic centers and institutes. One of the most penetrating analyses of the doctrine came from William W. Kaufmann, then a member of the Princeton Center of International Studies, and more recently of MIT.[61] This analysis was extended by Robert E. Osgood, of the Center for the Study of American Foreign and Military Policy at the University of Chicago, in his book *Limited War—the Challenge to American Strategy* (1957), and by Henry A. Kissinger in his *Nuclear Weapons and Foreign Policy* (1956), an outgrowth of discussions and studies at the Council on Foreign Relations. Kissinger was later appointed a professor at Harvard and an associate director of its Center for International Studies.[62] Still another interesting example of such scholarship was The Twentieth Century Fund's study of American civil-military relations, directed by Professor Harold Stein at Princeton. Out of this work came a large volume of case studies dealing with military decisions from 1930 to 1950 and an analytical volume on civil-military relations in the same period.[63]

One of the direct results of scholars' interest in the problems of the Cold War has been the creation of a considerable body of specialized literature. Some of the published work extends existing research, and some of it, as in the area of military strategy, represents the opening up of a new field of scholarly inquiry. Much of this literature is the product of academically based research centers and institutes, some of it of private research groups or government-supported institutions. It would be difficult to estimate the extent of this body of published material, but in the field of national security a recent select bibliography filled thirty pages.[64]

The effect of these writings has been and continues to be important. They have provided the basis for informed public discussion on such issues as containment, political and economic development, Soviet policy, limited war, and arms control, and for further academic research and teaching. They have also had an indirect effect on policy-making, first by introducing fresh ideas into the discussion and second by focusing attention on certain aspects of an issue or on alternative approaches. In some cases, such as the books of Henry Kissinger and Herman Kahn, the work of scholars has received

---

61 Kaufmann had done his graduate work at Yale with the diplomatic historian Samuel Flagg Bemis; his first book was a study of British policy and the independence movement in Latin America in the 1820's.

62 Director of the Center was Robert R. Bowie, formerly Head of the Policy Planning Staff of the State Department, and now Counselor of the State Department.

63 Harold Stein (ed.), *American Civil-Military Decisions* (University, 1963); Walter Mills, Harvey Mansfield, and Harold Stein, *Arms and the State* (New York, 1958).

64 Samuel P. Huntington, *Changing Patterns of Military Politics* (New York, 1962), pp. 235–266.

wide attention and precipitated a public debate that has done much to clarify the issues. One of the most important and influential writers on military subjects was Walter Millis, formerly with *The New York Herald Tribune* and now a staff member of the Center for the Study of Democratic Institutions. After World War I Millis joined the ranks of the revisionists but supported Roosevelt's foreign policy in the bitter debate that followed World War II. A strong critic of the Eisenhower administration's defense policy, he has in recent years devoted his energies largely to the causes of disarmament and the possibilities of a world without war.[65]

In addition to the creation of a large and growing body of literature on all aspects of the Cold War, scholars and intellectuals contribute indirectly to the formulation of policy in a variety of ways—through personal relationships with political and career executives, through special studies prepared at the request of policy-makers and legislators, and in their capacity as consultants and advisers to committees and agencies of the government. The Rockefeller Committee on Defense Organization in 1953, the Gaither Committee on Civil Defense in 1957, and the Draper Committee on the Military Assistance Program of 1958–59 all had scholarly representation on both the committee and staff levels. Congress, too, has sought the advice of scholars and has reached out beyond its own membership and staff to enlist assistance. The most notable example is that of the Senate Foreign Relations Committee, which in 1959 commissioned thirteen reports from as many academic and private research groups. The result was a series of studies examining a number of basic problems in the field of foreign policy: administration of the State Department, basic aims of the United States, the role of ideology, the military implications of technology, and other subjects.[66]

In the field of military strategy, a central concern in the Cold War, scholars have made some notable contributions. In this field much of the thinking has of necessity had to be theoretical, since there is no experience with nuclear warfare and only limited opportunity for testing and maneuver. Further, the complexity and expense of the new weapons systems and the choices that had to be made dictated the use of intellectual tools in the use of which the military was not trained. These conditions placed a premium on the talents

65 Though not an academician, Walter Millis has written several outstanding works on American military policy and history, including *The Martial Spirit* (New York, 1931), the best study of the Spanish-American War, and *Arms and Men* (New York, 1956).

66 These studies were issued as committee prints during the 86th Congress, 1st session (1959) and 2nd session (1960). See also Jay H. Cerf and Walter Pozen (eds.), *Strategy for the 60's* (New York, 1961).

of scholars who more than any other group in our society were skilled in theoretical analysis and in the use of those intellectual tools and devices that could be useful in the selection of weapons and strategies. The decade of the 1950's witnessed the increased importance of the intellectual in strategy-making and an accompanying decline in the once pre-eminent role of the military in this field. William Kaufmann must be given credit for exploring the concept of credibility in relation to deterrence. Henry Kissinger and Robert Osgood were the first to show the importance of limited war in the nuclear age. Herman Kahn emphasized civil defense and forced many to think about the unpleasant and even "unthinkable" possibilities of a nuclear war. Thomas Schelling, Louis Sohn, Charles Osgood, and a host of other scholars made constructive contributions to the field of arms control. Roger Hilsman analyzed the relationship between strategic intelligence and policy, and was one of the first to emphasize the importance of internal war. And Samuel Huntington, in addition to his other perceptive analysis of security, set forth a new theory of civil-military relations.[67]

The new role of scholars and scientists in policy formulation, exercised in a variety of ways, creates a number of problems. Though these are not the central concern here, it is not altogether irrelevant to raise questions about the limits of their role. The objectivity to which the scholar rightly attaches so much importance visibly diminishes with his personal involvement, and his value judgments and unconscious biases need to be scrupulously examined. Are the views of scholars and scientists on issues that affect them deeply any more valid than those of other men? They may be, but less because of the objectivity and accuracy of the scholarship than of the quality of mind and depth of analysis.

Yet, because of the needs of the policy-maker, there is a strong tendency to orient scholarship toward current problems and to use the products of scholarship in support of policy. When the scholar deliberately chooses to work on current issues in an effort to influence the decision, to become in effect a "policy scientist," he is operating outside his field of special competence. Moreover, he rarely has all the data available to the responsible official. The result is neither scholarly nor useful, but, cloaked in the garb of academic

67 See William W Kaufmann (ed.), *Military Policy and National Security* (Princeton, 1956); Henry A. Kissinger, *Nuclear Weapons and Foreign Policy* (New York, 1957); Robert E. Osgood, *Limited War* (Chicago, 1957); Herman Kahn, *On Thermonuclear War* (Princeton, 1960); Roger Hilsman, *Strategic Intelligence and National Decisions* (Glencoe, 1956); Samuel P. Huntington, *The Soldier and the State* (Cambridge, Mass., 1957); Bernard Brodie, *Strategy in the Missile Age* (Princeton, 1959).

distinction, it may carry more weight than it deserves. Fed into the policy process, his work may have an unfortunate effect on the choice of policies adopted, or, in the political process, it may be used for partisan purposes with the same result.

These limitations do not nullify the function of scholarship in contributing to an understanding of Cold War problems and to the search for solutions; it only underscores the importance of objectivity and careful selection of appropriate areas of research. Within these limits, the independent scholar can and does make an important contribution to the clarification of broad policy alternatives and their long-range political and social alternatives and their long-range political and social implications.

The role of history and historians, in this effort, is fundamental. Despite continuous and rapid change, there is in American history a remarkable continuity.[68] There is much discussion these days of our national purpose, and various efforts have been made—including the creation of the Presidential Commission on National Goals in 1960 and the publication of essays by a group of prominent Americans under the sponsorship of *Life* Magazine and *The New York Times*— to define these goals. Invariably these efforts have failed. The reasons are clear. The United States subscribes to no single ideology, and its most striking characteristics are experimentation and diversity. But the failure to emerge with a single statement of purpose does not signify a lack of purpose and basic principles. These can be found in the historic documents of the American past from the Mayflower Compact to Franklin Roosevelt's Four Freedoms. How closely related these purposes and principles were to contemporary problems, how persistent had been the efforts throughout American history to define the national purpose and identify the distinctive character of the American nation, was skillfully portrayed by Oscar Handlin. He reached back into American history to illustrate the theme touched on by each of the ten essays prepared for *Life*. The result was a rich collection of documents dating from the seventeenth century, all relating to the issues facing the American people in the middle of the twentieth century. Emphasizing vividly the continuity of American history, these documents demonstrate clearly the relevance of the past to the present and the future.[69] More than three centuries separate John Winthrop, governor of the Massachusetts Bay Colony, and

68 This point is discussed in Marcus Cunliffe, "American Watersheds," *American Quarterly*, XIII (1961), 479–494.
69 Oscar Handlin (ed.), *American Principles and Issues: The National Purpose* (New York, 1961).

John F. Kennedy, but only a difference in style differentiates the words of the late President's inaugural address from Winthrop's thoughts, written in 1630: "We must be knit together in this work as one man," he wrote, "we must entertain each other in brotherly affection, we must be willing to abridge ourselves of our superfluities for the supply of others' necessities. . . . For we must consider that we shall be as a city upon a hill, the eyes of all people are upon us."[70] Indeed, even more now than ever before, the eyes of all people are upon us.

70 *Winthrop Papers*, II (Boston, 1931), 295; quoted in Handlin, *op. cit.*, p. 34.

Appendix I

The Variety and Unity of History*
by Woodrow Wilson

We have seen the dawn and the early morning hours of a new age in the writing of history, and the morning is now broadening about us into day. When the day is full we shall see that minute research and broad synthesis are not hostile but friendly methods, cooperating toward a common end which neither can reach alone. No piece of history is true when set apart to itself, divorced and isolated. It is part of an intricately various whole, and must needs be put in its place in the netted scheme of events to receive its true color and estimation; and yet it must be itself individually studied and contrived if the whole is not to be weakened by its imperfection. Whole and part are of one warp and woof. I think that we are in a temper to realize this now, and to come to happy terms of harmony with regard to the principles and the objects which we shall hold most dear in the pursuit of our several tasks.

I know that in some quarters there is still a fundamental difference of opinion as to the aim and object of historical writing. Some regard history as a mere record of experience, a huge memorandum of events, of the things done, attempted, or neglected in bringing the world to the present stage and posture of its affairs—a book of precedents to which to turn for instruction, correction, and reproof. Others regard it as a book of interpretation, rather, in which to study motive and the methods of the human spirit, the ideals that elevate and the ideals that debase; from which we are to derive assistance, not so much in action as in thought; a record of evolution, in which we are not likely to find repetitions, and in reading which our inquiry should be of processes, not of precedents. The two views are not, upon analysis, so far apart as they first appear to be. I think that we shall all agree, upon reflection and after a little explanation of the terms we use, that what we seek in history is the manifestation and development of the human spirit, whether we seek it in precedents or in processes.

All of the many ways of writing history may be reduced to two. There are those who write history, as there are those who read it, only for the sake of the story. Their study is of plot, their narrative

* First published in Howard J. Rogers (ed.), *Congress of Arts and Science: Universal Exposition, St. Louis, 1904* (Boston, 1906).

goes by ordered sequence and seeks the dramatic order of events; men appear, in their view, always in organized society, under leaders and subject to common forces making this way or that; details are for the intensification of the impression made by the main movement in mass; there is the unity and the epic progress of *The Decline and Fall*, or the crowded but always ordered composition of one of Macaulay's canvases; cause and effect move obvious and majestic upon the page, and the story is of the large force of nations. This is history embodied in "events," centering in the large transactions of epochs or of peoples. It is history in one kind, upon which there are many variants. History in the other kind devotes itself to analysis, to interpretation, to the illumination of the transactions of which it treats by lights let in from every side. It has its own standard of measurement in reckoning transactions great or small, bases its assessments, not upon the numbers involved or the noise and reputation of the day itself in which they occurred, so much as upon their intrinsic significance, seen now in after days, as an index of what the obscure men of the mass thought and endured, indications of the forces making and to be made, the intimate biography of daily thought. Here interest centres, not so much in what happened as in what underlay the happening; not so much in the tides as in the silent forces that lifted them. Economic history is of this quality, and the history of religious belief, and the history of literature, where it traces the map of opinion, whether in an age of certainty or in an age of doubt and change.

The interest of history in both kinds is essentially the same. Each in its kind is a record of the human spirit. In one sort we seek that spirit manifested in action, where effort is organized upon the great scale and leadership displayed. It stirs our pulses to be made aware of the mighty forces, whether of exaltation or of passion, that play through what men have done. In the other sort of history we seek the spirit of man manifested in conception, in the quiet tides of thought and emotion making up the minor bays and inlets of our various life of complex circumstance, in the private accumulation of events which lie far away from the sound of drum or trumpet and constitute no part of the pomp of great affairs. The interest of human history is that it is human. It is a tale that moves and quickens us. We do not approach it as we approach the story of nature. The records of geology, stupendous and venerable as they are, written large and small, with infinite variety, upon the faces of great mountains and of shadowed cañons or in the fine shale of the valley, buried deep in the frame of the globe or lying upon the surface, do not hold us to the same vivid attention. Human history has no such muniment towers, no such deep and ancient secrets, no such mighty successions of events as those which the geologist explores; but the geologist does not stir us as the narrator of even the most humble dealings of our fellow men can stir us. And it is so with the rest of the history of nature. Even the development of animal life, though we deem its evolution part of ours, seems remote, impersonal, no part of any affair that we can touch with controlling impulse or fashion to our pleasure. It is the things which we determine which most deeply concern us, our voluntary life and action, the release of our spirits in thought and act. If the philosophers were to convince us that there is in fact no will of our own in any matter, our interest in the history of mankind would slacken and utterly change its face. The ordered sequences of nature are outside of us, foreign to our wills, but these things of our own touch us nearly.

It is the honorable distinction of historical writing in our day that it has become more broadly and intimately human. The instinct of the time is social rather than political. We would know not merely how law and government proceed but also how society breeds its forces, how these play upon the individual, and how the individual affects them. Law and government are but one expression of the life of society. They are regulative rather than generative, and historians of our day have felt that in writing political and legal history they were upon the surface only, not at the heart of affairs. The minute studies of the specialist have been brought about, not merely by the natural exigencies of the German seminar method of instruction, not merely by the fact that the rising tide of doctors' theses has driven would-be candidates for degrees to the high and dry places, after all the rich lowland had been covered, but also by a very profound and genuine change of view on the part of the masters of history themselves with regard to what should be the distinctive material of their study. Before our modern day of specialization there was virtually no history of religion, or of law, or of literature, or of language, or of art. Fragments of these things were, of course, caught in the web of the old narratives, but the great writers of the older order looked at them with attention only when they emerged, gross and obvious, upon the surface of affairs. Law was part of the movement of politics or of the patent economic forces that lay near the interests of government. Religion was not individual belief, but as it were the politics of an institution, of the church, which was but the state itself in another guise. Literature concerned them only as it became the wind of opinion beating upon the laboring ship of state, or when some sudden burst of song gave a touch of imaginative glory to the domestic annals of the nation which was their theme. Art came within their view only when it was part of the public work of some Pericles or became itself part of the intricate web of politics, as in the Italian states of the Renaissance. Language concerned them not at all, except as its phrases once and again spoke the temper of an epoch or its greater variations betokened the birth of new nations.

And all this because their interest was in affairs of state, in the organized and coordinated efforts of the body politic, in opinions and influences which moved men in the mass and governed the actions of kings and their ministers of state at home and abroad. In brief, their interest was in "events." It is curious and instructive to examine what we mean by that much-used word. We mean always, I take it, some occurrence of large circumstance—no private affair transacted in a corner, but something observed and open to the public view, noticeable and known—and not fortuitous, either, but planned, concerted. There can, properly speaking, be no "event" without organized effort: it is not a thing of the individual. Literature is excluded, by definition, and art, and language, and much of religion that is grounded in unobserved belief, and all the obscure pressure of economic want. A history of "events" cannot be a history of the people; it can only be a history of the life of the body politic, of the things which statesmen observe and act upon.

The specialist has taught us that the deepest things are often those which never spring to light in events, and that the breeding-ground of events themselves lies where the historian of the state seldom extends his explorations. It is not true that a community is merely the aggregate of those who compose it. The parts are so disposed among us that the minority governs more often than the majority. But influence and mastery are subtle things. They proceed from forces which come to the individual out of the very air he breathes: his life is compounded as the lives of those about him are. Their lives play upon his, he knows not how, and the opinion he enforces upon them is already more than half their own. And so the analysis of the life of the many becomes part of the analysis of the power of the few—an indispensable part. It is this that the specialist sees. He sees more. He sees that individual effort as well as aggregate must be studied, the force that is in the man as well as the air that is in the community. The men who give voice to their age are witnesses to more things than they wot of.

Mr. Ruskin, in the preface to the little volume on Venetian art to which he has given the name *St. Mark's Rest*, propounds a theory which will illuminate my meaning. "Great nations," he says, "write their autobiographies in three manuscripts—the book of their deeds, the book of their words, and the book of their art. Not one of these books can be understood unless we read the two others; but of the three the only quite trustworthy one is the last. The acts of a nation may be triumphant by its good fortune; and its words mighty by the genius of a few of its children; but its art only by the general gifts and common sympathies of the race. Again, the policy of a nation may be compelled, and, therefore, not indicative of its true character. Its words may be false, while yet the race remains unconscious of their falsehood; and no historian can assuredly detect the hypocrisy. But art is always instinctive; and the honesty or pretense of it are therefore open to the day. The Delphic oracle may or may not have been spoken by an honest priestess—we cannot tell by the words of it; a liar may rationally believe them a lie, such as he would himself have spoken; and a true man, with equal reason, may believe them spoken in truth. But there is no question possible in art: at a glance (when we have learned to read), we know the religion of Angelico to be sincere, and of Titian, assumed."

Whether we agree with all the *dicta* of this interesting passage or not, the main truth of it is plain. It is to be doubted whether the "genius of a few of its children" suffices to give a nation place in the great annals of literature, and literary critics would doubtless maintain that the book of a nation's words is as naïf and instinctive as the book of its art. Here, too, the sincere and natural is easily to be distinguished ("when we have learned to read") from the sophisticated and the artificial. Plainly the autobiography of Benjamin Franklin is separated by a long age from the autobiography of Benvenuto Cellini, and the one is as perfect a mirror of the faith of the man and the manner of the age as the other. But these questions are not of the present point. Undoubtedly the book of a nation's art and the book of its words must be read along with the book of its deeds if its life and character are to be comprehended as a whole; and another book, besides—the book of its material life, its foods, its fashions, its manufacturers, its temperatures and seasons. In each of these great books the historian looks for the same thing: the life of the day, the impulses that underlie government and all achievement, all art and all literature, as well as all statesmanship.

I do not say that the specialists who have so magnified their office in our day have been conscious of this ultimate synthesis. Few of them have cared for it or believed it. They have diligently spent their intensive labor upon a few acres of ground, with an exemplary singleness of mind, and have displayed, the while, very naïvely, the provincial spirit of small farmers. But a nation is as rich as its subjects, and this intensive farming has accumulated a vast store of excellent food-stuffs. No doubt the work would have been better done if it had been done in a more catholic spirit, with wider sympathies, amidst horizons. The broader the comprehension the more intelligent the insight. But we must not ask for all things in a generation or expect our own perfection by any other way than the familiar processes of development.

Perhaps we are near enough the time of synthesis and coordination to see at least the organic order and relationship of the several special branches of historical inquiry which have been grouped in this Division of our Congress. All history has society as its subject-matter: what we ponder and explore is, not the history of men, but the history of man. And yet our themes do not all lie equally close to the organic processes of society. Those processes are, of course, most prominent in political and economic history, least prominent, perhaps, in the history of language. I venture to suggest that the organic order is: Politics, economics, religion, law, literature, art, language. So far as the question affects religion and law, I must admit that I am not clear which of the two ought to take precedence—in modern history, certainly law; but most history is not modern, and in that greater part which is not modern clearly religion overcrows law in the organic, social process.

I know that the word religion, in this connection as in most others, is of vague and mixed significance, covering a multitude of sins; but so far as my present point is concerned, it is easy of clarification. Religion, as the historian handles it, involves both a history of institutions, of the church, and a history of opinion. As a history of opinion it perhaps lies no nearer the organic processes of society than does the history of literature; but from the beginning of recorded events until at any rate the breaking up of foundations which accompanied and followed the French Revolution, it concerns the church as an institution as definitely as the history of politics, with its various records of shifting opinion, concerns the state, and the organic life of the body politic. In such a view, religion must take precedence of law in the organic order of our topics. From the remotest times of classical history, when church and state, priest and judge, were hardly distinguishable, through the confused Middle Age, in which popes were oftentimes of more authority than kings and emperors, down to the modern days, when priests and primates were, by very virtue of their office, chief politicians in the plot of public policy, the church has unquestionably played a part second only to the state itself in the organization and government of society, in the framing of the public life.

Law occupies a place singular and apart. Its character is without parallel in our list. It has no life of its own apart from the life of the state, as religion has, or literature, or art, or language. Looked at as the lawyer looks at it, it is merely the voice of the state, the body of regulations set by government to give order to the competitive play of individual and social forces. Looked at from the historian's point of view, it consists of that part of the social thought and habit which has definitely formed itself, which has gained universal acquiescence and recognition, and which has been given the sanction and backing of the state itself, a final formulation in command. In either case, whatever its origin, whether in the arbitrary will of the lawmaker or in the gradually disclosed and accepted convenience of society, it comes, not independently and of itself, but through the mouth of governors and judges, and is itself a product of the state. But not of politics, unless we speak of public law, the smaller part, not of private, the greater. The forces which created it are chiefly economic, or else social, bred amidst ideas of class and privilege. It springs from a thousand fountains. Statutes do not contain all of it; and statutes are themselves, when soundly conceived, but generalizations of experience. The truth is that, while law gets its formulation and its compulsive sanction from the political governors of the state, its real life and source lie hidden amidst all of the various phenomena which historians are called upon to explore. It belongs high in the list I have made, because it so definitely takes its form from the chief organ of society.

To put literature before art in the organic order I have suggested, is not to deny Mr. Ruskin's *dictum,* that art more than literature comes "by the general gifts and common sympathies of the race," by instinct rather than by deliberation; it is only to say that more of what is passing through a nation's thought is expressed in its literature than in its art. As a nation thinks so it is; and the historian must give to the word literature a wider significance than the critic would vouchsafe. He must think not merely of that part of a nation's book of words upon which its authors have left the touch of genius, the part that has been made immortal by the transfiguring magic of art, but also of the cruder parts which have served their purpose and now lie dead upon the page— the fugitive and ephemeral pamphlets, the forgotten controversies, the dull, thin prose of arguments long ago concluded, old letters, futile and neglected pleas—whatever may seem to have played through the thought of older days.

Of the history of language I speak with a great deal of diffidence. My own study of it was of narrow scope and antedated all modern methods. But I know what interest it has for the historian of life and opinion; I know how indispensable its help is in deciphering race origins and race mixtures; I know what insight it affords into the processes of intellectual development; I know what subtle force it has had not only in moulding men's thoughts, but also their acts and their aspirations after the better things of hope and purpose. I know how it mirrors national as well as individual genius. And I know that all of these data of organic life, whether he take them at first hand or at second, throw a clarifying light upon many an obscure page of the piled records that lie upon the historian's table. I fancy that the historian who intimately uses the language of the race and people of which he writes somehow gets intimation of its origin and history into his ear and thought whether he be a deliberate student of its development or not; but be that as it may, the historian of language stands at his elbow, if he will but turn to him, with many an enlightening fact and suggestion which he can ill afford to dispense withal. It is significant, as it is interesting, that the students of language have here been definitely called into the company of historians. May the alliance be permanent and mutually profitable!

My moral upon the whole list is, that, separated though we may be by many formal lines of separation, sometimes insisted on with much pedantic punctilio, we are all partners in a common undertaking, the illumination of the thoughts and actions of men as associated in society, the life of the human spirit in this familiar theatre of cooperative effort in which we play, so changed from age to age and yet so much the same throughout the hurrying centuries. Some of the subjects here grouped may stand high in the list of organic processes, others affect them less vigorously and directly; but all are branches and parts of the life of society. In one of the great topics we deal with there is, I know, another element which sets it quite apart to a character of its own. The history of religion is not merely the history of social forces, not merely the history of institutions and of opinions. It is also the history of something which transcends our divination, escapes our analysis—the power of God in the life of men. God does, indeed, deal with men in society and through social forces, but he deals with him also individually, as a single soul, not lost in society or impoverished of his individual will and responsibility by his connection with the lives of other men, but himself sovereign and lonely in the choice of his destiny. This singleness of the human soul, this several right and bounden duty of individual faith and choice, to be exercised oftentimes in contempt and defiance of society, is a thing no man is likely to overlook who has noted the genesis of our modern liberty or assessed the forces of reform and regeneration which have lifted us to our present enlightenment; and it introduces into the history of religion, at any rate since the day of Christ, the master of free souls, an element which plays upon society like an independent force, like no native energy of its own. This, nevertheless, like all things else that we handle, comes into the sum of our common reckoning when we would analyze the life of men as manifested in the book of their deeds, in the book of their words, in the book of their art, or in the book of their material arts, consumption, needs, desires; and the product is still organic. Men play upon one another whether as individual souls or as political and economic partners.

What the specialist has discovered for us, whether he has always discovered it for himself or not, is, that this social product which we call history, though produced by the interplay of forces, is not always produced by definite organs or by deliberation: that, though a joint product, it is not always the result of concerted action. He has laid bare to our view particular, minor, confluent but not conjoint influences, which, if not individual, are yet not deliberately cooperative, but the unstudied, ungeneraled, scattered, unassembled, it may be even single and individual expression of motives, conceptions, impulses, needs, desires, which have no place within the ordered, corporated ranks of such things as go by legislation or the edicts of courts, by resolutions of synods or centred mandates of opinion, but spring of their own spontaneous vigor out of the unhusbanded soil of unfenced gardens, the crops no man had looked for or made ready to reap. Though all soils from which human products suck their sustenance must no doubt lie within the general sovereignty of society, and no man is masterless in our feudal moral system, these things which have come to light by the labor of those who have scrutinized the detail of our lives for things neglected have not been produced within the immediate demesnes of the crown. Historians who ponder public policy only, and only the

acts of those who make and administer law and determine the relationships of nations, like those who follow only the main roads of literature
and study none but the greater works of art, have therefore passed them
by unheeded, and so, undoubtedly, have missed some of the most interesting secrets of the very matters they had set themselves to fathom.
Individuals, things happening obscure and in a corner, matters that look
like incidents, accidents, and lie outside the observed movements of
affairs, are as often as not of the very gist of controlling circumstance and
will be found when fully taken to pieces to lie at the very kernel of
our fruit of memory.

I do not mean to imply that the work of the specialist is now near
enough to being accomplished, his discoveries enough completed, enough
advertised, enough explained, his researches brought to a sufficient point
of perfection. I daresay he is but beginning to come into his kingdom:
is just beginning to realize that it is a kingdom, and not merely a con-
geries of little plots of ground, unrelated, unneighborly even; and that
as the years go by and such studies are more and more clarified, more
and more wisely conceived, this minute and particular examination of
the records of the human spirit will yield a yet more illuminating body
of circumstance and serve more and more directly and copiously for the
rectification of all history. What I do mean, and what, I daresay, I am
put here to proclaim, is, that the day for synthesis has come; that no
one of us can safely go forward without it; that labor in all kinds must
henceforth depend upon it, the labor of the specialist no less than the
labor of the general historian who attempts the broader generalizations
of comment and narrative.

In the English-speaking world we have very recently witnessed two
interesting and important attempts at synthesis by cooperation in Mr.
H. D. Traill's *Social England* and Lord Acton's *Cambridge Modern History,* the one now complete, the other still in course of publication. We
have had plans and proposals for a somewhat similarly constructed
history of the United States. Mr. Justin Winsor's *Narrative and Critical
History of America* hardly furnishes an example of the sort of work
attempted in the other series of which I have spoken. Aside from its lists
and critical estimates of authorities, it is only history along the ordinary
lines done in monographs, covering topics every historian of America
has tried to cover. Mr. Traill's volumes, as their general title bears
evidence, run upon a wider field, whose boundaries include art, literature,
language, and religion, as well as law and politics. They are broader,
at any rate in their formal plan, than Lord Acton's series, if we may
judge by the three volumes of the *Cambridge Modern History* already
published. The chapter-headings in the Cambridge volumes smack much
more often of politics and public affairs than of the more covert things
of private impulse and endeavor. Their authors write generally, however,
with a very broad horizon about them and examine things usually left

unnoted by historians of an earlier age. The volumes may fairly be taken, therefore, to represent an attempt at a comprehensive synthesis of modern historical studies.

Both Mr. Traill's volumes and the *Cambridge Modern History* are constructed upon essentially the same general plan. The sections of the one and the chapters of the other are monographs pieced together to make a tessellated whole. The hope of the editors has been to obtain, by means of carefully formulated instructions and suggestions issued beforehand to their corps of associates, a series of sections conceived and executed, in some general sense, upon a common model and suitable to be worked in together as parts of an intelligible and consistent pattern; and, so uniform has been our training in historical research and composition in recent years, that a most surprising degree of success has attended the effort after homogeneous texture in the narrative and critical essays which have resulted; a degree of success which I call surprising, not because I think it very nearly complete, but because I am astonished that, in the circumstances, it should have been success at all and not utter failure.

It is far from being utter failure; and yet how far it is also from being satisfactory success! Allow me to take, as an example of the way in which these works are constructed, my own experience in writing a chapter for the volume of the *Cambridge Modern History* which is devoted to the United States. In doing so I am far from meaning even to imply any criticism upon the editors of that admirable series, to whom we are all so much indebted. I do not see how, without incredible labor, they could have managed the delicate and difficult business intrusted to them in any other way; and I am adducing my experience in their service only for the sake of illustrating what must, no doubt, inevitably be the limitations and drawbacks of work in this peculiar kind. I can think of no other way so definite of assessing the quality and serviceability of this sort of synthesis. I was asked by Lord Acton to write for his volume on the United States the chapter which treats of the very painful and important decade 1850–1860, and I undertook the commission with a good deal of willingness. There are several things concerning that critical period which I like to have an opportunity to say. But I had hardly embarked upon the interesting enterprise, which I was bidden compass within thirty of the ample pages of the Cambridge royal octavos, before I was beset by embarrassments with regard to the manner and scope of treatment. The years 1850–1860 do not, of course, either in our own history or in any other, constitute a decade severed from its fellows. The rootages of all the critical matters which then began to bear their bitter fruitage are many and complex and run far, very far, back into soil which I knew very well other writers were farming. I did not know what they would say or leave unsaid, explain or leave doubtful. I could take nothing for granted; for every man's point of view needs its special

elucidation, and he can depend upon no other man to light his path
for him. I therefore wrote a narrative essay, in my best philosophical
vein, on the events of the decade assigned me, in which I gave myself
a very free hand and took care to allow my eye a wide and sweeping
view upon every side. I spoke of any matter I pleased, harked back to
any transaction that concerned me, recking nothing of how long before
the limiting date 1850 it might have occurred, and so flung myself very
freely—should I say very insolently?—through many a reach of country
that clearly and of my own certain knowledge belonged to others, by
recorded Cambridge title. How was I to a.oid it? My co-laborers were
not at my elbow in my study. Some of them were on the other side of
the sea. The editors themselves could not tell me what these gentlemen
were to say, for they did not know. The other essays intended for the
volume were on the stocks being put together, as mine was.

I must conjecture that the other writers for that volume fared as I
did, and took the law into their own hands as I did; and their experience
and mine is the moral of my criticism. No sort of cunning joinery
could fit their several pieces of workmanship together into a single
and consistent whole. No amount of uniform type and sound binding
can metamorphose a series of individual essays into a book. I may
be allowed to express my surprise, in passing, that some individual
historians should have tried to compound and edit themselves in the
same way, by binding together essays which were conceived and executed as separate wholes. The late Mr. Edward Eggleston furnished
us with a distinguished example of this in his *Beginners of a Nation,*
whose chapters are topical and run back and forth through time and
circumstance without integration or organic relation to one another,
treating again and again of the same things turned about to be looked
at from a different angle. And if a man of capital gifts cannot fuse his
own essays, or even beat and compress them into solid and coherent
amalgam, how shall editors be blamed who find the essays of a score of
minds equally intractable? No doubt the Cambridge volumes are meant
for scholars more than for untrained readers, though Mr. Traill's, I
believe, are not; but even the docile scholar, accustomed of necessity
to contrast and variety in what he pores upon and by habit very patient
in reconciling inconsistencies, plodding through repetitions, noting variations and personal whimsies, must often wonder why he should thus
digest pieces of other men's minds and eat a mixture of secondary authorities. The fact is, that this is not synthesis, but mere juxtaposition.
It is not even a compounding of views and narratives. It is compilation.
There is no whole cloth, no close texture, anywhere in it. The collected
pieces overlap and are sometimes not even stitched together. Events
—even events of critical consequence—are sometimes incontinently
overlooked, dropped utterly from the narrative, because no one of
the writers felt any particular responsibility for them, and one and

another took it for granted that someone else had treated of them, finding their inclusion germane and convenient.

But if we reject this sort of cooperation as unsatisfactory, what are we to do? Obviously some sort of cooperation is necessary in this various and almost boundless domain of ours; and if not the sort Mr. Traill and Lord Acton planned, what sort is possible? The question is radical. It involves a great deal more than the mere determination of a method. It involves nothing less than an examination of the essential character and object of history—I mean of that part of man's book of words which is written as a deliberate record of his social experience. What are our ideals? What, in the last analysis, do we conceive our task to be? Are we mere keepers and transcribers of records, or do we write our own thoughts and judgments into our narratives and interpret what we record? The question may be simply enough asked, but it cannot be simply answered. The matter requires elaboration.

Let us ask ourselves, by way of preliminary test, what we should be disposed to require of the ideal historian, what qualities, what powers, what aptitudes, what purposes? Put the query in another form, more concrete, more convenient to handle: how would you critically distinguish Mommsen's *History* from a doctor's thesis? By its scope, of course; but its scope would be ridiculous if it were not for its insight, its power to reconceive forgotten states of society, to put antique conceptions into life and motion again, build scattered hints into systems, and see a long national history singly and as a whole. Its masterly qualities it gets from the perceiving eye, the conceiving mind of its great author, his divination rather than his learning. The narrative impresses you as if written by one who has seen records no other man ever deciphered. I do not think Mommsen an ideal historian. His habit as a lawyer was too strong upon him: he wrote history too much as if it were an argument. His curiosity as an antiquarian was too keen: things very ancient and obscure were more interesting to him than the more commonplace things, which nevertheless constitute the bulk of the human story. But his genius for interpretation was his patent of nobility in the peerage of historians; he would not be great without it; and without it would not illustrate my present thesis.

That thesis is, that, in whatever form, upon whatever scale you take it, the writing of history as distinguished from the clerical keeping of records is a process of interpretation. No historical writer, how small soever his plot of time and circumstance, ever records all the facts that fall under his eye. He picks and chooses for his narrative, determines which he will dwell upon as significant, which put by as of no consequence. And that is a process of judgment, an estimation of values, an interpretation of the matter he handles. The smaller the plot of time he writes of, the more secluded from the general view the matters he deals with, the more liable is he to error in his interpretation; for this little part of the human story is but a part; its significance lies in its relation to the whole. It requires nicer skill, longer training, better art and craft to fit it to its little place than would be required to adjust more bulky matters, matters more obviously involved in the general structure, to their right position and connections. The man with only common skill and eye-sight is safer at the larger, cruder sort of work. Among little facts it requires an exceeding nice judgment to pick the greater and the less, prefer the significant and throw away only the negligible. The specialist must needs be overseen and corrected with much more vigilance and mis-giving than the national historian or the historian of epochs.

Here, then, is the fundamental weakness of the cooperative histories of which I have spoken by example. They have no wholeness, singleness, or integrity of conception. If the several authors who wrote their sections or chapters had written their several parts only for the eye of one man chosen guide and chief among them, and he, pondering them all, making his own verifications, and drawing from them not only but also from many another source and chiefly from his own lifelong studies, had constructed the whole, the narrative had been everywhere richer, more complete, more vital, a living whole. But such a scheme as that is beyond human nature, in its present jealous constitution, to execute, and is a mere pleasing fancy—if anyone be pleased with it. Such things are sometimes done in university seminars, where masters have been known to use, at their manifest peril, the work of their pupils in making up their published writings; but they ought not to have been done there, and they are not likely to be done anywhere else. At least this may be said, that, if master workmen were thus to use and interpret other men's materials, one great and indispensable gain would be made: history would be coherently conceived and consistently explained. The reader would not himself have to compound and reconcile the divergent views of his authors.

I daresay it seems a very radical judgment to say that synthesis in our studies must come by means of literary art and the conceiving imagination; but I do not see how otherwise it is to come. By literary art, because interpretation cannot come by crude terms and unstudied phrases in writing any more than pictorial interpretation can come by a crude, unpracticed, ignorant use of the brush in painting. By the conceiving imagination, because the historian is not a clerk but a seer: he must see the thing first before he can judge of it. Not the inventing imagination, but the conceiving imagination—not all historians have been careful to draw the distinction in their practice. It is imagina-tion that is needed, is it not, to conceive past generations of men truly in their habit and manner as they lived? If not, it is some power of the same kind which you prefer to call by another name: the name is not what we shall stop to discuss. I will use the word under correction. Nothing but imagination can put the mind back into past experiences not its own, or make it the contemporary of institutions long since passed away or modified beyond recognition. And yet the historian must be in thought and comprehension the contemporary of the men and affairs he writes of. He must also, it is true, be something more: if he would have the full power to interpret, he must have the offing that will give him perspective, the knowledge of subsequent events which will furnish him with multiplied standards of judgment: he should write among records amplified, verified, complete, withdrawn from the mist of contemporary opinion. But he will be but a poor interpreter if he have alien sympathies, the temperament of one age when writing of another, it may be contrasted with its own in every point of preference and belief. He needs something more than sympathy, for sympathy may be condescending, pitying, contemptuous. Few things are more benighting than the condescension of one age for another, and the historian who shares this blinding sentiment is of course unfitted for his office, which is not that of censor but that of interpreter. Sympathy there must be, and very catholic sympathy, but it must be the sympathy of the man who stands in the midst and sees, like one within, not like one without, like a native, not like an alien. He must not sit like a judge exercising exterritorial jurisdiction.

It is through the imagination that this delicate adjustment of view is effected—a power not of the understanding nor yet a mere faculty of sympathetic appreciation, or even compounded of the two, but mixed of these with a magical gift of insight added, which makes it a thing mere study, mere open-mindedness, mere coolness and candor of judgment cannot attain. Its work cannot be done by editorship or even by the fusing of the products of different minds under the heat of a single genius; its insight is without rule, and is exercised in singleness and independence. It is in its nature a thing individual and incommunicable.

Since literary art and this distinctive, inborn genius of interpretation are needed for the elucidation of the human story and must be married to real scholarship if they are to be exercised with truth and precision, the work of making successful synthesis of the several parts of our labors for each epoch and nation must be the achievement of individual minds, and it might seem that we must await the slow maturing of gifts Shakespearean to accomplish it. But, happily, the case is not so desperate. The genius required for this task has nothing of the universal scope, variety, or intensity of the Shakespearean mind about it. It is of a much more humble sort and is, we have reason to believe, conferred upon men of every generation. There would be good cause to despair of the advance of historical knowledge if it were not bestowed with some liberality. It is needed for the best sort of analysis and specialization of study as well as for successful synthesis, for the particular as well as for the general task. Moreover, a certain very large amount of co-operation is not only possible but quite feasible. It depends, after all, on the specialists whether there shall be successful synthesis or not. If they wish it, if it be their ideal, if they construct their parts with regard to the whole and for the sake of the whole, synthesis will follow naturally and with an easy approach to perfection; but if the specialists are hostile, if their enthusiasm is not that of those who have a large aim and view, if they continue to insist on detail for detail's sake and suspect all generalization of falseness, if they cannot be weaned from the provincial spirit of petty farmers, the outlook is bad enough, synthesis is indefinitely postponed. Synthesis is not possible without specialization. The special student must always garner, sift, verify. Minute circumstance must be examined along with great circumstance, all the background as well as the foreground of the picture studied, every part of human endeavor held separately under scrutiny until its individual qualities and particular relations with the rest of the human story stand clearly revealed; and this is, of necessity, the work of hundreds of minds, not of one mind. There is labor enough and honor enough to go around, and the specialist who puts first-rate gifts into his task, though he be less read, will not in the long estimate of literature earn less distinction than the general historian. It is a question of the division and cooperation of labor: but it is more; it is also a question of the spirit in which the labor is done, the public spirit that animates it, the general aim and conception that underlies and inspires it.

As a university teacher I cannot help thinking that the government of the matter is largely in the hands of the professors of history in our schools of higher training. The modern crop of specialists is theirs: they can plant and reap after a different kind if they choose. I am convinced that the errors and narrownesses of specialization are chiefly due to vicious methods and mistaken objects in the training of advanced students of history in the universities. In the first place, if I may speak from the experience of our American universities, students are put to tasks of special investigation before they are sufficiently grounded in general history and in the larger aspects of the history of the age or nation of which they are set to elaborate a part. They discover too many things that are already known and too many things which are not true—at any rate, in the crude and distorted shape in which they advance them. Other universities may be happier than ours in their material, in the previous training of the men of whom they try to make investigators; but even when the earlier instruction of their pupils has been more nearly adequate and better suited to what is to follow, the training they add is not, I take the liberty of saying, that which is likely to produce history, but only that which is likely to produce doctors' theses. The students in their seminars are encouraged, if they are not taught, to prefer the part to the whole, the detail to the spirit, like chemists who should prefer the individual reactions of their experiments to the laws which they illustrate.

I should think the mischievous mistake easy enough of correction. It is quite possible to habituate students to a point of view, and to do so is often, I daresay, the best part of their preparation. When they come to the advanced stage of their training, at which they are to be set to learn methods of investigation, they should not be set first of all to the discovery or elaboration of facts, to the filling in of the hiatuses easily and everywhere to be discerned, by their preceptors at any rate, in the previous study of detail. They should, rather, be set to learn a very different process, the process of synthesis: to establish the relations of circumstances already known to the general history of the day in which they occurred. These circumstances should not all be political or economic or legal; they should as often concern religion, literature, art, or the development of language, so that the student should at once become accustomed to view the life of men in society as a whole. Heaven knows there is enough original work waiting to be done in this kind to keep many generations of youngsters profitably employed. Look where you will in the field of modern monographs, and it is easy to find unassociated facts piled high as the roofs of libraries. There is not a little fame as well as much deep instruction to be got out of classifying them and bringing them into their vital relations with the life of which they form a part. It were mere humanity to relieve them of their loneliness. After they had been schooled in this work, which believe me, someone must do, and that right promptly, our advanced students of history and of historical method would be ready to go on, if it were only after graduation, after the fateful doctor's degree, to the further task of making new collections of fact, which they would then instinctively view in their connection with the known circumstances of the age in which they happened. Thus, perhaps thus only, will the spirit and the practice of synthesis be bred.

If this change should be successfully brought about, there would no longer be any painful question of hierarchy among historians: the specialist would have the same spirit as the national historian, would use the same power, display the same art, and pass from the ranks of artisans to the ranks of artists, making cameos as much to be prized as great canvases or heroic statues. Until this happens history will cease to be a part of literature, and that is but another way of saying that it will lose its influence in the world, its monographs prove about as vital as the specimens in a museum. It is not only the delightful prerogative of our studies to view man as a whole, as a living, breathing spirit, it is also their certain fate that if they do not view him so, no living, breathing spirit will heed them. We have used the wrong words in speaking of our art and craft. History must be revealed, not recorded, conceived before it is written, and we must all in our several degrees be seers, not clerks. It is a high calling and should not be belittled. Statesmen are guided and formed by what we write, patriots stimulated, tyrants checked. Reform and progress, charity and freedom of belief, the dreams of artists and the fancies of poets, have at once their record and their source with us. We must not suffer ourselves to fall dull and pedantic, must not lose our visions or cease to speak the large words of inspiration and guidance. It were a shame upon us to drop from the ranks of those who walk at the van and sink into the ranks of those who only follow after, to pick up the scattered traces of the marching host as things merely to pore upon and keep. We cannot do this. We will return to our traditions and compel our fellow historians of literature to write of us as of those who were masters of a great art.

Appendix II
Two Memoranda on the Nature of Peace
by Thorstein Veblen*

1. SUGGESTIONS TOUCHING THE WORKING PROGRAM OF AN INQUIRY INTO THE PROSPECTIVE TERMS OF PEACE

I

The contemplated settlement will take one or another of two contrasted lines of approach: a peace of diplomatic compromise, to include primarily the eight greater Powers, on a footing of parity; or, a league (federation) of the pacific Peoples on a footing of national disclaimer, to include primarily the democratic peoples of the Entente. The part logically to be taken by the United States in such a coalition of peoples will be very materially different according as the one or the other of these two lines of settlement is held in prospect. In the former case—a

---

* From *Essays in Our Changing Order* by Thorstein Veblen. Copyright 1934, 1962 by The Viking Press, Inc. Reprinted by permission of The Viking Press, Inc.
First published in the *Political Science Quarterly,* Vol. XLVII, No. 2 (June 1932). In a prefatory note, Professor Joseph Dorfman of Columbia University pointed out that although Veblen, a leading economist, had just published *An Inquiry into the Nature of Peace and the Terms of Its Perpetuation,* he was not invited to become a member of the Inquiry when it was formally established in the fall of 1917. Veblen did, however, submit to the Inquiry two detailed memoranda, "Suggestions Touching the Working Program of an Inquiry into the Prospective Terms of Peace" and "Outline of a Policy for the Control of the 'Economic Penetration' of Backward Countries and of Foreign Investments." The manuscript of the latter, Professor Dorfman wrote, "is still to be found in the papers of the Inquiry, which were placed in the archives of the State Department. A copy of the former, which cannot be found in the archives, was supplied through the courtesy of a friend of Veblen."—F.L.L.

peace compact of diplomatic compromise—America's part logically becomes that of an interested outsider, since the settlement in that case
will be primarily an arrangement between the European Powers; whereas
in the latter case—a League of the pacific Peoples—America will necessarily come in as an integral factor, perhaps the central and decisive
factor in the settlement.

Evidently the range of inquiry with a view to feasible terms of peace
will differ notably according to the part which will prospectively be
taken by America. In the former case—a diplomatic settlement—America
has little interest in what may be called the internal policies of Europe,
whether international or intranational; and the range and purpose of this
Inquiry would therefore, in that case, be chiefly confined to questions of
domestic policy and of maritime trade. In the latter case—a neutral
League of Peoples—the range of this Inquiry would necessarily extend
to all countries and peoples concerned, but its scope would at the same
time be narrowed by neglect of many things which the constitution of
such a neutral league would take notice of only to disallow them, e.g.,
trade discriminations and the commercial engrossing of natural resources.
In the former case, America's chief interest should logically be the realignment of its own internal forces, with a view to keeping the peace
at home, and to provide against the assured event of its being presently
broken abroad. The stipulations of a "diplomatic peace" are of relatively
slight interest to America, since they would in any case be observed only
so far as the Powers might find it convenient to observe them in the
course of preparation for the eventually ensuing war, whereas the measures to be taken in domestic policy in this case, with a view to a solidarity of sentiment and resources under all contingencies, will be of paramount consequence and should claim the chief attention of the Inquiry.

II

To reach a tenable settlement on anything like a democratic footing
the support of popular sentiment must be had for all substantial points
that are to be agreed on or argued for. Therefore, it is urgently necessary to keep in touch with current opinion and sentiment, to inform
all men of what is under advisement as being desirable to be done or
possible to be accomplished, and to guide public attention so far as
may be in respect of the purposes that are aimed at, and the ways and
means and adjustments necessary to their accomplishment. Therefore
it becomes incumbent on the Inquiry not only to turn unreservedly to
that method of "open diplomacy" that has latterly been made much of,
but also deliberately to enter on a campaign of publicity designed to
cover all moot questions.

By way of parenthesis it may be suggested that this work of publicity
might advantageously take the following forms: Men associated in the

Inquiry should put into the form of written bulletins a detailed presentation of particular questions that are to be taken under advisement, to be published and circulated as bulletins of the Inquiry or of the State Department, but with a specific avowal that the views set out in these bulletins have been submitted to and are taken under advisement by the Inquiry, and inviting free discussion and suggestions. Preferably, these bulletins should carry the signatures of their writers, rather than the informal endorsement of the Inquiry, so that their publication should not commit the Inquiry in any official way to the views embodied in the bulletins.

It is hoped that the outcome of such publicity would be of appreciable use in the way of ascertainment, standardization and guidance of popular sentiment touching the ways and means of keeping the peace, as well as the adaptations of policy and administration necessary to be accepted to that end.

III

Any degree of reflection will show that deliberation or debate on these matters must result directly in a two-sided division of opinion and endeavor, in such a way that spokesmen of the vested interests and of the unqualified maintenance of the established order, on the one hand, will be found opposed to the spokesmen of resolute maintenance of the peace at the cost of any necessary revision or adjustment within this established order, on the other hand; and it should be equally evident that the Inquiry will find itself taking sides and will presently be committed to a position, either favoring the vested interests at some risk to the maintenance of peace at home and abroad, or favoring a workable realignment of the country's available resources designed to keep the peace even at the cost of some appreciable derangements to these vested interests.

What is involved in the logic of the situation is apparently a question of bias, a matter of inclination for or against the vested rights on the one hand, and the domestic and international tranquility on the other hand; and it would appear that the Inquiry, following the apparent inclination of the Administration, should presently, by force of the logical situation, find itself searching for feasible ways and means of assuring the domestic tranquility even at the cost of any contingent derangement of the established scheme of vested rights, whether private or national.

IV

Assuming that the settlement will result in a League of the pacific Peoples, drawn on a plan of neutralization and a pooling of issues, rather than a negotiated compact of diplomatic compromises between rival Powers, then it logically follows that the French and English-speaking Peoples will make up the substantial core of the League, and also that initiative and discretion will continue to vest in these Peoples primarily. But it follows likewise that in such a case, the United States will be thrown into the center, and the initiative and discretion in the formation, structure and carrying on of the League will in effect come to vest primarily in the American Administration; which so will be put on its honor, and will at the same time be enabled to give effect to its unselfish profession.

At the same time, the sooner the American Administration takes initial measures toward this end the better the chance of its effectually realising its professed ideals, and the better the chance of maturing these ideal aims and progressively embodying them in definitively tenable concrete working arrangements. It is also apparent that a League designed eventually to keep the peace had best be such a League as would now expediently be contrived for achieving an advantageous settlement, from which it follows: (a) that an enduring coalition of these chief Entente belligerents (the French and English-speaking Peoples) for the conduct of the war should be arrived at as expeditiously as may be done, and should be an organization drawn with a view to its continuation as the core of the eventual Pacific League; and (b) that this Inquiry, as being an organ of the Administration, should therefore turn its present and continued attention to discovering and presenting the lowest terms and the most neutral claims on which such a working coalition can be made sufficiently compact for this purpose and can be held together as a going concern.

2. OUTLINE OF A POLICY FOR THE CONTROL OF THE "ECONOMIC PENETRATION" OF BACKWARD COUNTRIES AND OF FOREIGN INVESTMENTS

It is assumed as a major premise that the constant and controlling purpose in any arrangements entered into in the prospective settlement will be the keeping of the peace at large; that the need of peace is paramount; that any special interest which may come up for consideration must wait on this paramount exigence of such measures as seem necessary to the state of peace and security at large.

Evidently this paramount consideration will impose a limit and enforce a bias of its own at every point where any measure looking to another purpose is proposed, and wherever the continued expediency of any given item of law or custom is brought under advisement. If the claims of peace and security are to be allowed without reservation, the immediate consequence should be the disallowance and disclaimer of all such special interests and ambitions as may give rise to estrangement or dissension among the peoples associated together for the keeping of the peace.

But the case is not so simple. By tradition and ingrained conceit, all modern nations harbor certain interests and pretensions to which they attach a high value, whether this value is real or fancied. War is commonly entered on in defense or furtherance of some such national interest, real or fancied, tangible or intangible. The current war is an instance in point. And it is even yet a safe generalisation that no modern nation would be ready now, out of hand, to disclaim or disavow all such interests and pretensions tangible and intangible, commercial and patriotic, even after the national integrity had been duly safe-guarded. Therefore it is to be presumed that the compact, league or coalition of peoples for the keeping of the peace, which is expected to be set afoot in the terms of settlement, will take the line of a mutual concessive disclaimer and disallowance of such usages, claims and pretensions as appear to be patently incompatible with the uninterrupted continuance of peace and security.

The "Pacific League" which is to come out of the prospective settlement may accordingly be anything, from a temporary treaty engagement between the pacific nations, to a close-knit and irrevocable coalition of peoples who have thrown in their fortunes together and have subordinated their national ambitions to the common good. And the contemplated "economic penetration," as well as the measures to be taken for its control, will take on a different character according to the complexion which the Pacific League will take on, and according to the degree of control which it will be in a position to exercise. Therefore it appears necessary, by way of a definition of premises, to indicate at the outset with what scope and manner of jurisdiction the League is here conceived to be invested, in so far as bears on the question in hand. Adequately to control such "economic penetration," the Pacific League will have to be vested with a relatively very large discretion; which in turn implies an extensive surrender of powers on the part of the associated peoples of the League.

Provisional outline of a projected League of the Pacific Peoples; so far as touches its control of the "Economic Penetration" of backward countries.

The abiding purpose of the projected League is to be the keeping of the peace at large; not the furtherance of commercial enterprise, nor the pursuit of national ambitions. Therefore the latter are necessarily and unreservedly to be subordinated to the former. Dissension among nations commonly arises out of conflicting commercial aims and national pretensions; therefore it will be incumbent on the associated pacific peoples, so far as may be, to divest themselves of all commercial discrimination and national ambition. Therefore the projected League can comprise only such of the modern peoples as are content to put away so much of their self-direction and national rivalry as would be incompatible with the maintenance of peace under the League's collective surveillance. And unless a sufficiently large and consequential proportion of civilised mankind can be brought into a sufficiently close coalition, on such terms, the League will prove nugatory. Therefore it is here assumed that the avowedly pacific peoples will be found in such a tolerant frame of mind as will answer the purposes for which the Pacific League is to be formed. Otherwise the argument fails.

In the phrase of President Wilson, the end to be sought in the prospective settlement is to make the world safe for democracy. And within the meaning of the term as employed by the American Administration in its occasional pronouncements, Democracy may be described as that frame of mind by virtue of which a people chooses to be collectively fortunate rather than nationally formidable. The modern peoples partake of this animus in varying degrees; and the question of any given people's inclusion as a constituent factor in the projected League therefore becomes substantially a question of the degree in which they are imbued with this requisite frame of mind.

In the past, indeed in the recent past—in that recently past time when statesmen still placed their dependence on the Balance of Power—in this past out of which it is hopefully believed that the modern peoples are now emerging, it was an accepted principle underlying all effectual statecraft that no people could hope to be collectively fortunate except at the cost of being nationally formidable. But it is now proposed deliberately to shift the ground of policy from that ancient principle of worldly wisdom to a new principle of what may be called standardised forbearance, whereby it shall cease to be expedient for any nation to be formidable. Under this prospective regime any formidable nation would become a menace to itself and its neighbors alike, inasmuch as it would be a menace to that peace at large within which alone its people can hope to be collectively fortunate. Therefore, incidentally, it becomes the duty of the Pacific League to eliminate all formidable nations.

In varying degrees the modern nations meet these requirements; or it could perhaps rather be said that they are in varying degrees approaching such a frame of mind under the discipline of their war experience; and it may be added that they are due to make a closer approach to this required frame of mind in the further course of the like experience. The chief belligerents on the side of the Entente are already coming to the persuasion that no national aggrandisement and no profits of commercial enterprise are worth the hazard of a return to the *status quo ante*.

It is these chief belligerents, or rather it is such of these chief belligerents as are now in a way to achieve this required spirit of forbearance, that will by force of circumstance be elected to take the
initiative, shape its policy, and continue to constitute the core of the
Pacific League. There is, at any rate, no prospect that beginning can
be made without them. And there is at the same time also no reason
to put off this beginning until the close of hostilities. Indeed, the main
lines of organisation and administration should best be designed,
materialised, and tried out in actual work while the pressure of an
urgent present common emergency can still be counted on to keep
mutual jealousies and cupidity in abeyance; so that the League would
then both serve as a means of conducting the war to a successful issue,
and also be ready to enter on the settlement and further conduct of
affairs as a going concern.

These chief belligerents that so may hopefully be looked to as the
prime movers and the chief support of the projected coalition would be
the French and the English-speaking peoples, together with the Chinese
and a more or less considerable group of like-minded accessories in
Latin America and western Europe. Necessarily included in the League's
jurisdiction would also be two further categories: the backward peoples
of what are now the colonial possessions of these belligerents and of
what have been the colonial possessions of their opponents in the war;
and the undemocratic peoples at present comprised in the warlike coalition of the Centrals.

In outline, the forms of organisation, the fashion in which the several
constituent peoples are to be articulated into a going concern, and the
distribution of responsibilities and obligations among them—in all this
it should seem the part of wisdom to draw on the experience of the
United States and the British, who have been the chief successful
pioneers in the extension of democratic institutions hitherto. Neither
has reason to boast of work well done in this respect; the short-comings
of both are sufficiently grave and notorious; but the best after all, is
always better than something else, and between them these two are
after all the most signal experiment in democratic pioneering, or rather
the nearest approach to a democratic conduct of affairs on a modern
scale and over a widely diversified range of peoples and countries. And
it should be added that the defects and mistakes which have come to
light in the course of these democratic experiments should prove no
less instructive for the purposes now in hand.

For the immediate purpose—for an inquiry into the line of policy
by which "economic penetration" and investment in foreign parts is
best to be controlled—the features which the British and American
experiments in democracy have in common are more to the point
than their differences; although it may well be that the differences
would be no less instructive in another connection. The two are more
alike in the working parts of their structure than appears on the surface;

the difference being, in good part, that the articulation of the working parts is more sharply defined and more visible in the American case. Loosely, and with a margin of disparities, the working organisation through which coordination is effected falls into a three-fold gradation of units in either case, but more obvious in the American case; chiefly a gradation in the scope of such self-direction as they are endowed with. There is in either case a substantial core of constituent communities, in which is finally vested the over-ruling initiative, discretion and responsibility—the seat of sovereignty, as it would be called in political theory; in the American case this central body is the States of the Union. Then there are the Territories; held under surveillance and concessively vested with a degree of self-government; beyond which come the backward communities of the outlying possessions; who are wards of the Union, held in tutelage and administered under discretionary control. The parallel facts will be visible in the British case to any attentive observer, but they need scarcely be traced out here.

To follow the analogy, in the projected League the substantial core would be constituted, at the outset, by the chief democratic belligerents already spoken of; admission being free to any others possessed of the necessary qualifications. What these requisite qualifications are to be, need not detain the argument here, since it does not greatly concern the topic of the memorandum. The second class or group of peoples under the League's jurisdiction—those who would answer to the Territories in the American scheme—would be made up, in the main, of nationalities which are now under German, Austrian, Bulgarian or Turkish rule; to be held under surveillance, on probation, with so much of self-direction in their administrative affairs as the circumstances would admit, and with a view to their presently coming into standing as qualified members of the democratic federation of peoples. The third and outlying group, the wards of the League, would comprise those characteristically backward peoples that inhabit Colonial Possessions. By grace of fortune, the greater proportion of these pronouncedly backward peoples have now come under the hands of those nations who will presumably exercise the discretion in laying down the lines of the Pacific League's economic policy.

Drawn on these lines, then, the scheme contemplates a very appreciable number and variety of outstanding independent nations; standing outside of the League's jurisdiction by their own choice or because they do not fill the necessary qualifications for admission as democratic commonwealths; and ranging, in point of cultural status, all the way from barbarian Abyssinia to the pseudo-constitutional monarchy of civilised Spain.

Within the confines of the League, it is evident, a sane policy looking to the perpetuation of the peace at large, should consistently incline to discard, or at least to disregard, distinctions of nationality, so far as the sentimental preconceptions of its constituent peoples will allow. The most fortunate outcome at this point would be the total obsolescence or obliteration of national demarkations; but the best that can be anticipated, in view of the present state of sentiment, would be a very dubious modicum of approach toward that end.

Abolition of national frontiers would go far to dispose of many questions of economic policy, particularly questions of penetration and trade. Any degree of coalition or federation among these pacific peoples will submerge national distinctions in some degree; and measures are doubtless due to be taken looking to the submergence of national divisions and national integrity wherever their maintenance visibly jeopardises the peace at large. Some appreciable disallowance of national discretion in commercial matters is reasonably to be expected; and an untempered insistence on the removal of whatever is likely to engender jealousy, distrust and dissension would logically result in the discontinuance of all national establishments, as such. Their place and functions as political or civil units would then be supplied by a neutral scheme of administrative divisions, drawn without regard to present political frontiers and with an eye single to administrative convenience, as determined by the natural—topographical, climatic, or linguistic—parcelment of the countries to be taken care of.

The nationalities so drawn into the scheme of redistricting need not be disturbed in any other respect than that of their civil and political powers. They would cease to have any civil status, but their integrity or solidarity in the cultural and sentimental respect would be left undisturbed and, indeed, legally unnoticed; very much as is now formally the case with various minor nationalities in some parts of the Balkans and the Russian dominions; or, again, the Armenian nation; or the Jews in the English-speaking countries.

Failing that—and there need be no doubt of its failure—any degree of approach to such a measure of neutralisation would be a measure of relief from perplexity in all that concerns international trade relations.

Now, in view of the many-sided uncertainty of the prospective situation, which is still taking shape in ways that had not been foreseen, it is here proposed to argue the questions of "economic penetration" and foreign investments on the broad assumption that the prospective league will be free and competent to deal with all these matters on a footing of neutrality and plenary discretion. From the positions so arrived at it should be practicable to pursue the argument further, as shifting circumstances may dictate, by way of adaptation, reservations and curtailment of these provisional positions at points where the plan of settlement eventually to be adopted may fall short of full discretionary power.

So also in case the settlement should unexpectedly take the form of a negotiated peace, with treaty agreements covering international trade and investment, the formulations arrived at on the assumption here made could still stand over as a formulation of desiderata to be aimed at by those negotiators with whom the keeping of the peace at large remains the paramount end of endeavor. It will serve as a point of departure for any expedient concession that may have to be made under pressure of stubborn nationalist preconceptions.

As touches the case, then, of such outlying backward peoples as will by force of circumstance come into the status of wards, and so will come under the guardianship of the Pacific League—or in the measure in which any given people comes into this relation—the league will of necessity arrogate to itself a plenary jurisdiction—somewhat after the fashion of that authority over the North American Indians which the United States government has arrogated to itself. In these cases, and they are large, many and diverse, there is nothing for it but that the League must take over the administration of affairs quite unreservedly; and by the same token it becomes incumbent on the League, in its character as guardian, deliberately and consistently to conserve the natural resources of these countries—mineral, forest, grazing and agricultural—with a view to the least practicable infraction or exhaustion of the resources that so are taken over in trust.

What will be the practicable minimum of infraction and usufruct in any given case can of course not be described in a general proposition. The circumstances vary widely. But some degree of admininstrative surveillance and direction will be unavoidable in nearly every case. Some measure of police surveillance becomes incumbent on the League by virtue of its responsibility as guardian; and in some measure these outlying resources will have to be turned to present account as a source of raw materials indispensable in modern industry—as, e.g., certain cabinet woods, fibers, rubber, and various materials used as drugs, pigments, oils and varnishes, not otherwise obtainable—and the like holds true for certain fruits and foodstuffs.

On this head there is something due to be said by way of explaining and correcting certain uncritical preconceptions commonly met with; and the same considerations will also apply to "economic penetration" of undeveloped countries more at large, apart from the special case of those outlying virgin resources of the savage world. Popular discussion, in the press and elsewhere, commonly assumes as a matter of course that the speediest and most comprehensive "development" of all hitherto idle resources is altogether desirable and expedient, both for the present inhabitants of these outlying countries and for the nations at the hands of whose citizens the contemplated development is to be effected. On the other hand it is an easy generalisation out of the past history of colonisation that the rate of industrial penetration and conversion to use of any new country may readily be too swift for the continued well-being of the native population; and in taking over the direction of affairs the League will perforce become the guardian of these outlying peoples, and therefore the responsible keeper of their fortunes. At the same time, a Pacific League, whose paramount aim it is in peace and security to hold fast that which is good in democracy, can not carry on an exploitation of its help-less wards and dependent neighbors, as a wide line in its policy of peace and good-will. Considered simply as a matter of moral profit and loss, dishonesty is not the best policy.

On these grounds of equity and of self-preservation from moral dry-rot, it should fairly be a matter of course that the line to be followed in any effectual industrial penetration of these outlying countries should be a policy of retardation and continence, rather than the reverse. A well-advised and tenacious policy of moderation would appear to be the only salutary course, all the more since—contrary to the prevalent mis-conceptions—these outlying natural resources are not needed for present use of the civilised nations, apart from a certain special range of raw materials not conveniently to be had elsewhere.

As a general proposition, the natural resources already in hand among the modern nations are fully adequate to their current and their calculable future needs; the reservations under this broad rule being, that the strategy of competitive investment at present somewhat hampers the use of resources otherwise available, and that a relatively slight supply of indispensable materials will necessarily have to be drawn from these out-lying countries beyond the pale. Within the range of those raw materials which are afforded by the temperate latitudes there is no shortage, present or prospective, among the civilised countries, taken in the aggregate and in time of peace. The sole notable exception under this broad statement is the timber supply; which, it happens, is also the particular one among the outlying natural resources that may be largely laid under contribution without danger of exhaustion and without unavoidable risk of cultural disaster to these outlying peoples of the lower civilisation.

There is, of course, an urgent and unremitting pressure for the head-long "Development," that is to say for commercial exploitation, of all these outlying natural resources; but this is a clamor for private gain, not for public use. The promoters and financiers are seeking profitable con-cessions and investment, and they are actuated uniformly by the business-like motive of special advantages to themselves, not by considerations of material advantage to anyone else or to the community at large; nor is it at all apparent that any net gain commonly accrues to anyone else from enterprises of this kind. More frequently than not, the aim is a com-petitive advantage as against rival business concerns, or the monopolisa-tion of materials with a view to the control of the market.

In those countries where this pursuit of private gain at the cost of the country's resources has been allowed freely to run its enthusiastic career, as, e.g., in America, the consequences have been a wasteful exhaustion of certain natural resources (e.g., the destruction of forests by the lumber interests); together with a hurried appropriation of the tillable land, followed up with a slovenly cultivation and impoverishment of the soil, resulting in low yields and high aggregate cost per unit of goods delivered; so also the speculative holding of natural resources out of present use with a view to a prospective unearned gain (as in American land speculation, rural and urban, and the monopolisations of transportation franchises, water-power, or mineral deposits); and, as will commonly, though it may be less patently, happen in the like case, the gravest mischief has been a pervasive deterioration of industrial enterprise into a collusive chicanery and a speculative traffic in unearned gains.

To such pressure for private gain under the shield of the League's countenance the League can on no account afford to yield; inasmuch as, among other things, all traffic of this kind is a fertile source of commercial jealousies and intrigue, and these habitually give rise to international difficulties and eventual grievances to be redressed. All of which would appear to dictate that these natural resources started among the outlying peoples who so come under surveillance should in no case be alienated, that they should at the farthest concession be worked under lease, for a short term only, and under such control and power of revision and revocation as would lower the inducements offered to private enterprise to the practicable minimum. It follows also that permanent improvements and plant incident and necessary to the usufruct of these resources, as, e.g., docks, harbor works, roads, means of storage and transport, should be taken over by the common authority and held in common usufruct under surveillance. And in general terms, no encouragement should be extended to private enterprise to enter this field, no discrimination is to be countenanced, and no vested interest must be allowed to take effect in these premises.

Larger and more complex and delicate questions of "economic penetration" will arise in connection with those backward peoples who are nominally independent nations and who are outside the jurisdiction of the Pacific League. This class of outstanding nations comprises such countries as, e.g., Abyssinia, Mesopotamia, Persia and Afghanistan. The traffic between the federated peoples of the League and these outstanding nations will unavoidably be large, continued, highly diversified, and ever increasing with the passage of time and the growth of industry. In this intercourse the League will be dealing with these nations as outside parties; so that the question resolves itself into a matter of what regulations can be put into effect within the limits of tolerance drawn by the consent and good-will of these outstanding nations. There are also vested interests which have already found lodgment in the countries in question, in the way of investments, concessions, and an established clientele; and there are further enterprising persons who are due incontinently to seek similar privileges and opportunities for commercial gain in these countries so soon as settled conditions return.

It should be recalled that the paramount aim of the League is to keep

the peace on a footing of good-will at large; and that the pacific peoples
federated under the terms of the League, therefore, stand to claim no
special or exceptional advantages of trade or investment, for themselves
or their citizens. With this proviso in mind the logical course to be
pursued should not be particularly obscure, in outline; although it may
prove perplexing enough to follow out the simple logic of the case in the
face of obstinate preconceptions and a partisan bias standing over out
of the past. Insistence on national rights and obligations is as incompatible with a safe economic policy at this point as the primary aim of
the Pacific League is incompatible with that *status quo ante* against a
relapse into which the League is designed to provide.

The aim here must plainly be to avoid those conflicts of claim and
jurisdiction out of which disputes arise. To this end, it is plain, all international discriminations among the associated peoples of the League are
to be disallowed. It is with a view to avoiding jealousy and friction of
this kind, that it has been proposed in an earlier passage to submerge all
national distinctions within the League and reapportion the several
countries of the League into administrative and electoral districts without
regard to previously existing national boundaries. At the same time, the
details of usage and civil law vary greatly from one country to another,
both among the peoples to be comprised in the Pacific League and
among the outstanding nations, and there is little chance of doing away
with such differences of use and wont and law within any moderate
period of time.

Therefore, the expedient course in dealing with international relations
of trade and investments should apparently be to disclaim and disallow all
extra-territorial jurisdiction and all extra-territorial enforcement of
pecuniary claims, both among the several peoples of the League and as
between these peoples and the outstanding nations; in short, all pecuniary
claims and obligations should be neutralised, with the effect of throwing
their adjudication unreservedly under the local jurisdiction in whose
territory they come up.

Commercial traffic and investment would under this rule be accounted
a private venture, in pursuit of which the merchant or investor is acting
on his own initiative, for his own ends, at his own risk; in which his
compatriots share neither profit nor loss, and for the successful issue of
which they assume no collective responsibility. What it comes to is that
the community will no longer collectively promote or safe-guard any
private enterprise in pursuit of private gain beyond its own territorial
bounds.

That such a plan of neutralisation and mutual disavowal of overlapping
jurisdictions should govern trade and investment among the peoples of
the League should be plain without argument, and so far it will probably
commend itself on slight reflection to most of those concerned. That
much would presumably be accepted as a corollary following immediately

from the League's primary aim—to keep the peace at large on a footing
of good-will. That the same plan is good and reasonable also for the same
kind of relations between the peoples of the League and the outstanding
nations may at first sight seem more doubtful. The application of the
principle may be more difficult in the latter case, where mutual consent
may not readily be had, in the face of national jealousy and national
self-interest. But this difficulty appears less formidable on a closer view
of the circumstances of the case. The outstanding nations are small and
commercially dependent, as compared with the League, and by so much
they will be driven to accept any reasonable conditions offered. The
League will be in a position to disallow interference from outside in the
case of any alien trader, traveler or investor who has a grievance to
present; as well as to disclaim all special rights and immunities of its own
citizens in a like case. It may fairly be doubted if public sentiment in any
of the pacific countries can be brought to countenance so radical a departure from the established order of national rights and obligations; but
it should plainly be the wiser policy to move as far as practicable in this
direction, and then to leave an avowed presumption in favor of non-
interference in every case of doubt.

To this plan of neutralisation and disclaimer it will be objected that
the country's trade and investment interests would suffer irreparably
under such a policy, being left at the mercy of these habitually greedy
alien nations. It is doubtless true that many an enterprise in the way of
investments and concessions in foreign parts would find itself at a disadvantage in its pursuit of gain if it so lost the backing of its home government; but it is equally true that the cost to its home government of
keeping such a business concern secure in its pursuit of gain in foreign
parts will at an average exceed the advantage which such an enterprise
will bring to the rest of the community, who have no share in the gains
that may accrue to such an enterprising business concern.

Reduced to elementary terms, the economic effects and bearings of
such foreign investments may be described as follows. Investment is made
in the foreign country to get a higher rate of profits than at home; which
draws a part of the available means of industry out of the country;
which advances the rate of profits in the country, or keeps up the rate
on home investments, by keeping the productiveness of the country's
industry down; which enhances or keeps up prices, and the cost of living;
which conduces to activity in industry so long as prices are advancing—
in case there is such an advance, which is not always the case. So far the
net result is a loss to the home community, though there may be a gain
to the interested business concern, except for the (doubtful) gain that may
come of enhanced activity—in case such an effect is had. Further, the
gains which accrue to the investor from these foreign investments are
presumed to be received in cash or its equivalent, by the investor, who is
commonly well-to-do; this will then be spent chiefly for consumption, by

the recipient or on his account, and largely on superfluities; which acts
to advance prices at the same time that it diverts so much of the country's
industry to the production of goods suitable for such consumption; which
limits the production of goods to meet the ordinary needs of the community by that much; which acts to advance, or to keep up, the cost of
necessary consumable goods and thereby to increase or keep up the cost
of living. Certain remoter consequences, chiefly having to do with the
availability of funds for warlike politics, have no interest in this immediate connection.

Analysis will readily show that the community has nothing substantial
to gain in such a case; but it is not overlooked that all modern nations
are possessed of a very grave sentimental conviction to the contrary. It
is an article of patriotic faith and is accepted as a matter of course and
of common sense. Even the most judicially pacific among them will have
great difficulty in persuading themselves to disclaim these presumed national advantages, however illusory they may be in fact. In favor of such
a policy of renunciation it will probably be more to the point to urge
that the policy can be put into effect at no prohibitive cost, and that something appreciable along this line is urgently needful as a means to the
paramount end of keeping the peace at large.

Doubtless, one and another of the outstanding nations may be counted
on to watch their chance and take advantage of such forbearance on the
part of the League, and to abuse it so far as their short-sighted worldly
wisdom will carry them—for they will remain outstanding nations only
because and so long as they continue to be dominated by the old-fashioned
principles of statecraft according to which a foreign people is always a
potential enemy. But it is to be recalled that the Pacific League is designed to comprise the greater part of civilised mankind—at any rate the
greater proportion as counted in terms of trade and industry—and that
the greater part of the world's outlying resources are also to be held under
the surveillance and administered at the discretion of this same coalition
of pacific peoples; whereas the outstanding nations, whose mischievous
national ambitions bar them out, are a relatively feeble and scattered lot
of industrially immature peoples, each pursuing its own archaic illusions
and exposed to the vicissitudes of their mutual political intrigue and commercial chicanery. There will, presumptively, be some two or three nations of some appreciable consequence among these outstanding ones—
what would be called second-rate Powers, both politically and industrially;
but when all allowance has been made, it remains a secure generalisation
that the good-will of the League will be indispensable to the continued
prosperity of any one, or of any group, among these outstanding nations.
And it follows no less unavoidably from the broad facts that the active
good-will of the peoples of the League will accrue to those among the
outstanding nations who conduct their affairs most nearly in the same
spirit that moves the peoples of the League.

Still, the limits of human presumption are not easy to define, and it may always come to pass that one and another among the outstanding nations will overpass the limits of tolerance, and so call for remedial attention at the hands of the Pacific League. In such a case, still following the line of neutrality and disallowance, the remedy logically to be sought would appear to be an interruption or curtailment of intercourse with the mischief-making nation. Most conveniently and effectually this would take the form of an export duty on goods destined for the country in question, or in case of urgency, an embargo on traffic with nations who are found to be working at cross purposes with the policy of the League.

Such a Pacific League would, in effect, hold the balance of prosperity and of success between the outstanding nations. From which it follows that the League should be able effectually to govern traffic beyond its confines on much the same lines and by much the same methods as may be found wise and expeditious for the control of affairs among the peoples who are immediately amenable to its jurisdiction. The difficulties to be apprehended are difficulties in the way of its adoption rather than in the way of the successful administration of such a policy, once it has been adopted. What is proposed is little else than an unreserved extension of the principles of free trade, but with the inclusion of foreign investments as well as commercial traffic in the scope of this free-trade policy. The proposed scheme, therefore, has the merits and the defects that attach to any free-trade proposal.

It would be quite bootless to go into an argument here on the merits of a free-trade policy. The objections to such a policy are almost wholly a matter of interest, sentiment and preconception, and are not amenable to reason. Although the novelty of such a proposal to apply to foreign investments, as contrasted with foreign commerce, may conceivably give it a slightly better chance of reasonable consideration.

What is expedient in the way of a collective policy among the pacific peoples, for the control of economic penetration, foreign commerce, and foreign investments, accordingly appears to be exceedingly simple in principle—so simple as to leave its advocates embarrassed for want of debatable ground. It comes, in principle, to nothing much more than a collusive disallowance of privileges and preference, with safe-guarding of the weak and destitute and without respect of persons. How nearly such a single-minded policy could be approximated in any prospective settlement it is presumably not worth while to hazard a guess; but the nearer it comes to being realised, the more promising appears to be the chance of a lasting peace.

Under such a policy private enterprise is not to be supported or countenanced in making use of backward peoples or their resources; foreign investors will take their chances where they find them, without capitalising the support of their home government; justiciable questions will be decided under the law of the place where they arise, without prejudice by the litigants' domicile.

Appendix III
International Political Parties in a Durable League of Nations*
by Frederick Jackson Turner

November 1918

The following is an *abstract* of suggestions (derived from the study of the history of American sectionalism and the geography of American political parties) upon the bearing of American experience on the problems of a League of Nations. The conclusion is reached that in such a League there should be a Legislative body, with substantial, but at first limited, functions, as well as a Court, or Council of Nations, and particularly that the *operation of international political parties in connection with such a Legislature* would promote the permanence of the League. Whether the difficulties and social dangers inherent in the suggestion overbalance the other considerations is left undetermined.

The weakness inherent in a League of Nations is that it is exposed to intrigues by one or more of its component nations among the others most amenable to such influences to produce a situation requiring the application of League force, economic or military and naval, as the alternative to submission to intolerable results. But such application of force may well prove to amount to another World War. The danger lies partly in the European habit of diplomacy, the traditions and the training of her statesmen, and the analogy of a Congress of Nations to the historic Congresses of diplomats, and partly in the economic interests and ambitions of the nations under old-time leaders.

On the other hand, American ideals as so nobly set forth by the President, have found a quicker response among the European laboring classes

* First published in the *American Historical Review*, Vol. XLVII, No. 3 (April 1942). Reprinted by permission of the Henry E. Huntington Library.

than elsewhere, and in the passion for democratic peace among the masses lies the hope of the peace of the World internationally. What light does American experience cast upon the possibility of so using the masses as to promote international unity?

1. The area of the United States is about that of Europe; its geographic provinces or sections are comparable in area and in resources to Nations of Europe; in some respects these sections have cultural features clearly distinguishing each. Nevertheless, the history of the United States offers a sharp contrast to that of Europe in that *these sections have not become rival nations.*

2. Although in *form the federal aspect* of the United States is that of a union of *States,* in fact such States have acted in *sectional groups,* or have acted with the knowledge that they were backed by a common sectional sympathy. *Actually the federation has been between sections.* concealing their operation for the most part under the form of state action, or under the form of votes in Congress, in National political conventions, or in the distribution of votes in Presidential elections. A rather careful study of such material has shown that such votes are much more often evidences of sectional rather than mere party action than is usually realized. Even when a State has included in its borders parts of two sections, the state's representatives have shown a tendency to divide on sectional lines. In the notable case of Virginia there was division into two states, and the attitude of the counties adjacent to the Alleghany mountains in the South during the Civil War is a familiar illustration of how far this phenomenon may go.

3. In short, *the section is the imperfect image of a nation in the European sense, deprived of those attributes of a European nation which have been most productive of war.* Except for the tragedy of the Civil War, there has been a *Pax Americana between these sections stretched across a continent* for a period of over a century and a quarter. This has not been because there was an absence of grounds for sectional antagonisms, or of those antagonisms themselves. Current newspaper discussion in criticism of the alleged domination in Congress by this or the other section made by those out of power, shows often a real bitterness. The history of the construction of tariff schedules, transportation problems, the currency, the public lands, etc., is the history of sectional political contests. It is possible to translate American political history into European terms and thereby to make clearer the resemblances between European history and these partly concealed aspects of American history.

Sectional rivalries and combinations in dealing with the growing power of the new Western states, as the nation expanded, are analogous to European contests for "spheres of influence"; rival sections viewed the West as a reservoir for re-adjustment of sectional "balance of power"; their leaders in Congress consciously and avowedly negotiated sectional alliances and *ententes;* sectional contests over the termini of extensive railroad lines, first into the Mississippi Valley from the coast of the Atlantic and later from the Mississippi to the Pacific, were fundamentally like the "Bagdad Railway" contest. We have actually recognized and organized the sectional element in our laws, such as the act for the regional system of reserve banks. Of these facts there is abundant evidence in the utterances of statesmen throughout American history, as well as in the distribution of votes.

4. Granting the powerful influence of economic consolidation, as in business and transportation, the binding force of a common tongue, and institutions, and various other elements which distinguish the American from the European conditions, it is significant that there is so much of likeness between the mild American section and its stronger sister, the European state. So real was the sectional factor that if sectional governments had replaced state governments with sectional customs houses (as Calhoun in his *Exposition* suggested), it may well be doubted whether the influences of interstate commerce and transportation would not have been quite as much occasions for contention between sections as binding forces. Even the provision of the federal constitution for action upon individuals rather than upon states in the matters assigned to the central government might have been too weak for the divisive forces of sectional controversy.

Had the Union been merely a League of Nations or States, with provisions even as advanced as those of the Articles of Confederation, it may well be doubted if the nation could have been held together. This doubt grows when we remember that at various crises it was to the interest of European nations to foster this division in the interest of their own policy, and that connection with some European state was always reckoned with by a remonstrating section. In fact Civil War between sections did finally occur. It would have come earlier in case of a League.

5. Divergent as are the conditions and the development of Europe and America, the very freedom of this country from some of the complexities of Europe, the large lines in which her simpler story has run, may be helpful, not only as a warning, but as a constructive contribution to the new order. That Europe is in a receptive mood appears in the attention which it has given to American ideals of the worth of the common man, of the hope and faith in democracy and fair play, and the advantage of self-sacrifice and disinterestedness, which the President has so nobly set forth.

We have given evidence that immigrants from all nations of the world can live together peacefully under a single government that does justice. *In our political institutions also are elements worthy of consideration.*

Notice has already been taken of the utility of the provision of the Constitution which assigns to the federal government a direct relation to the individual in important assigned spheres of jurisdiction. This may not be at first practicable in a League of Nations. But it is important to call attention to the *significance of the American national political parties, operating upon the whole Union, not confined to a section. The last tie that snapped before the Civil War, was the party tie.* This has, perhaps, in its working, been *the most effective single political institution for the prevention of sectional disunion.*

In a region as diversified in some respects as Europe itself, and as large, the *national political parties ran across all sections, evoked intersectional or nonsectional party loyalty,* checked the *exclusive* claim of the section to a vote in the interest of the section, furnished the dissenting minority within the section *an organic connection with party associates in other sections, at the same time that this connection was dependent upon just recognition of the special section* in which the minority lived. It was an *elastic bond, but one that was strong. It ran horizontal cross-sections of party ties across the vertical lines of sectional division.* It *enabled the voter to act continentally,* and it compelled the statesman to act on lines of policy that transcended his section, if he would secure a continental following strong enough to bring success.

6. There is a distinct advantage in utilizing this party system in a League of Nations, if it does not carry with it countervailing disadvantages grave enough to lead to its rejection. In essence it means the utilization of that body of internationalism already in evidence not only in such organizations as radical political parties, such as the International, the I.W.W., Socialists generally, etc., but also the opposite tendencies seen in international business combinations, scientific and educational international organizations, and conservative forces generally. The class struggle, so called, is in fact not a national but an international struggle. If party organization of the radical element alone exists, and if this organization is also dominated and shaped by some one or two nations, as Germany or Russia, it will be extended, as it has been, to other countries in the form of secret, or intriguing societies, proceeding by revolutionary methods, with little or no regard for the separate interests of the nation into which it is introduced as an alien, and with its helmsman operating from the outside, and steering a course which almost necessarily involves adhesion to the primary interest of the country in which such a party is recognized as a powerful element in the determination of the policy.

Is it better to try to exclude these international political forces from the organization of the new order, or to utilize their internationalizing tendencies by enabling them to operate upon an international legislative body, responsive to play of parties? Is it worth while to use the fact of class consciousness to diminish the violence of national consciousness?

There can be little doubt that the common people, whether of the extreme radical wing of socialists, or of the conservative party groups, were reluctant to enter the war, and are now in Germany and Austria-Hungary the severest critics of the autocratic group which deceived them and misled them. The labor groups have been more reponsive to the policy of internationalism than, as yet, the other groups. At critical junctures their support, in England and France, has been important to the policy of President Wilson. They have a measure of international self-consciousness, partly because they have international organizations. There is no reason why similar organization on an international basis might not be given to conservative parties.

7. One recoils from any suggestion of adding a party loyalty international in its appeal to the loyalty to the individual nation. But the very idea of a League of Nations involves some diminution of the national feeling, some cultivation of international loyalty. If one could keep the Bolsheviki serpent out of the American Eden, he would hesitate to admit any international party organization which permitted such organization.

But in the reconstruction and the ferment which will follow the return of peace, there will be doubt about the existence of Edens anywhere, and the Bolsheviki serpent will creep in under whatever fence be attempted. May it not be safer to give him a job of international legislation rather than to leave him to strike from dark corners, and with no sense of responsibility?

On these questions, I am not sure. Consideration might be given to the probable actual vote possible, considering the estimated strength of political parties in the component nations of such a League, before assigning legislative functions in detail. We should have at least a rough estimate of the probable power and probable policies of the various groups. This I have not. So far as the special interests of the United States, however, operate on the decision, she has less to lose by an improvement in the conditions of labor and wages in Europe or Asia than she has to gain. If such a central legislative body, therefore, should gain even the power to standardize labor conditions, it must standardize them upward to avoid revolution, and this result, desirable in itself, does not diminish but rather increases the power of the United States to develop international commerce, etc., and makes plain our relatively higher standards.

8. For the operation of international parties as a check upon nationalism, there is requisite a Legislative body in the League, with limited but real powers. The evils of combining class struggles with national feeling would be apparent in a mere judicial or executive tribunal with international coercion as its sanction. The League should take to itself a field of legislation.

At first this might be merely certain fiscal subjects, funds for supporting the League activities. Its action might be required precedent to the use of force either by a component state, or by the League as a sanction to its decisions. The kind of economic pressure to be placed upon a delinquent state might be there determined. Principles to apply to the internationally controlled areas might be determined. International tariff legislation might be assigned to it. Legislation upon labor questions as advocated by some of the international labor congresses might even be finally confided to such an organization. Possibly at first its power in such matters might be recommendatory, the formulation of bills or policies to be urged upon national legislatures.

There is an abundant field from which to select. The choice should be made with two ideas prominent: first that progress should be made carefully, without hazarding the system by too sudden a construction, liable to fail by its newness and radical nature; and second that unless some real powers are conferred upon such a legislature, it will fail to call out international parties to affect its action, these parties will be under the domination of special states where their influence will be greatest, and the unifying influence of non-national party organization will not be secured.

I have no doubt that all things considered the international party would tend toward unity in such a league as the intersectional parties did in the United States. But the price to be paid in the loss of national control over important interests of its own, and the danger to the orderly states may be too great. It must also be admitted that the differences between section and nation are many and deep, and that there are some points in which international jealousy and controversy might be promoted rather than restrained by internationally organized parties operating on a legislature. It might conceivably be used by [an] ultraconservative majority to restrain reform in a particular nation. But similar difficulties will exist in the charges of special combinations within a League equipped only with judicial tribunals or consultative congresses, or with administrative organizations. There will be sectional jealousy and suspicion in any League, with whatever form of political organization. It is inherent in its nature. The problem is the introduction of checks and antidotes to this tendency.

Index